HOW THE BIBLE WOF

COGNITIVE SCIENCE OF RELIGION SERIES

Series Editors: Harvey Whitehouse
and Luther H. Martin

The Cognitive Science of Religion Series publishes research into the cognitive foundations of religious thinking and behavior, and their consequences for social morphology. The emphasis of the series is on scientific approaches to the study of religion within the framework of the cognitive sciences, including experimental, clinical, or laboratory studies, but works drawing upon ethnographic, linguistic, archaeological, or historical research are welcome, as are critical appraisals of research in these areas. In addition to providing a forum for presenting new empirical evidence and major theoretical innovations, the series publishes concise overviews of issues in the field suitable for students and general readers. The series is published in cooperation with the Institute for Cognition and Culture at Queen's University, Belfast.

TITLES IN THE SERIES:

FORTHCOMING TITLES:

HOW THE BIBLE WORKS

An Anthropological Study
of Evangelical Biblicism

BRIAN MALLEY

ALTAMIRA PRESS
A Division of Rowman & Littlefield Publishers, Inc.
Walnut Creek • Lanham • New York • Toronto • Oxford

AltaMira Press
A division of Rowman & Littlefield Publishers, Inc.
1630 North Main Street, #367
Walnut Creek, CA 94596
www.altamirapress.com

Rowman & Littlefield Publishers, Inc.
A wholly owned subsidary of The Rowman & Littlefield Publishing Group, Inc.
4501 Forbes Boulevard, Suite 200
Lanham, MD 20706

PO Box 317
Oxford
OX2 9RU, UK

British Library Cataloguing in Publication Information Available

Library of Congress Cataloging-in-Publication Data

Malley, Brian, 1969–
    How the Bible works : an anthropological study of evangelical
    biblicism / Brian Malley.
       p. cm.
    Includes bibliographical references and index.
    ISBN 0-7591-0664-9 (alk. paper) — ISBN 0-7591-0665-7 (pbk. : alk.
    paper)
    1. Bible—Evidences, authority, etc. 2. Evangelicalism—United
    States—Psychology. I. Title.

    BS480.M226 2004
    220.1—dc22   2003025596

Printed in the United States of America

∞™ The paper used in this publication meets the minimum requirements of American
National Standard for Information Sciences—Permanence of Paper for Printed Library
Materials, ANSI/NISO Z39.48-1992.

To my dearest Judy

CONTENTS

Acknowledgments

A LTHOUGH MANY PEOPLE CONTRIBUTED to this book in one way or another, the efforts of several individuals require special acknowledgment. Larry Hirschfeld, Webb Keane, Bruce Mannheim, and Dick Nisbett provided many excellent and insightful suggestions on the thesis version of this work. Tom Lawson, Luther Martin, Barbara Sarnecka, and Harvey Whitehouse read the entire manuscript and prodded it toward greater clarity and precision. Nicola Knight and Paulo Sousa both read and commented on specific chapters. Jim Lepkowski provided invaluable help in survey design and analysis, and Traianos Gagos provided assistance in matters papyrological. Judy Malley, Barbara Sarnecka, Nicola Knight, Paulo Sousa, Tom Lawson, Pascal Boyer, Bob McCauley, Scott Atran, and Dan Sperber provided much needed encouragement at many points in this project. Financial support for this project was provided by the Culture and Cognition Program and the Michigan Society of Fellows. And, of course, this project would not have been possible except for the support of the people of Creekside Baptist Church. Finally, I would like to thank my editors—Erik Hanson, Melissa McNitt, and Brigitte Scott—for shepherding this manuscript through the publishing process and improving it at innumerable points along the way.

Introduction

For the word of God is living and active. Sharper than any double-edged sword, it penetrates even to dividing soul and spirit, joints and marrow; it judges the thoughts and attitudes of the heart.

—EPISTLE TO THE HEBREWS 4:12 (NIV)

SOME TEXTS DEFY HISTORY. Rather than being relegated to the official archive or the historian's files, these texts seem to achieve a certain timelessness, a kind of superhistorical status, such that they continue to be read, recited, and expounded as part of ongoing social life. Such texts are "living and active," but how? This book explores the processes by which one ancient textual tradition—"the Bible"—holds and shapes a modern audience—American evangelical Christians. My purpose is to outline the cognitive and social processes that cause evangelical Christians to feel that the Bible is "living and active" in their lives today.

American evangelicals number in the millions, and although this is a somewhat amorphous group, one of the defining evangelical beliefs is that the Bible is a divinely inspired book—the word of God. As they see it, the Bible is God's message of salvation and guidance to a suffering and confused humanity, and a special conduit by which God convicts, encourages, and illuminates them in their pursuit of him. American evangelicals regard the Bible as one certain truth—a book, many say, completely without error—in a world preoccupied with things of merely temporal value. Thus evangelicals return to their Bibles frequently, seeking to lead "biblical" lives. The Bible holds a special place in their communal activities, being constantly quoted, displayed, referenced, expounded—and even occasionally thumped. The expectation is communicated that they will also read their Bibles privately, and indeed many do—several times a week, daily, or even more frequently. How are we to understand the clearly special relation between these people and this text?

The present study is anthropological in two senses of the term. First, it is anthropological in the sense of being about people rather than being about God. When a troubled husband climbs into bed and, reading a few pages from his well-worn Bible, finds that a passage convicts him of imperfectly loving his wife, evangelicals say that the man's experience is the result of God speaking through his word, the Bible. I do not disagree: when the husband reads his Bible, perhaps angels smile and God does indeed speak to him. Perhaps. But evangelicals' experiences, beliefs, and practices may also be regarded as earthly, human phenomena. It is certain that a troubled man, possessed of all the normal human cognitive faculties, has opened a book that he regards as special and to which he brings special expectations. It is this human side that is the focus of my analysis.

As a human phenomenon, evangelical Biblicism may be approached in a second anthropological sense, with resources drawn from the fields of cognitive psychology and cultural anthropology. My agenda is to explore evangelical Biblicism as a site of interaction between culture and cognition. I take culture to be socially transmitted patterns of thought and behavior, and cognition to be the organization of the mind's information processing, the structure of mental activities (Chomsky 1957; von Neumann 1958; Bateson 1972). Evangelical Biblicism is cultural inasmuch as it is a pattern of beliefs and practices inherited by individuals as part of their membership in evangelical communities.

Inheriting the Biblicist tradition involves much more than acquiring a theology—a set of beliefs about God, humanity, and the Bible. It is more too than a set of practices or behavioral habits ingrained since childhood for many evangelicals. Acquiring the Biblicist tradition involves developing a set of skills—primarily cognitive skills—and the retasking of existing cognitive proclivities. The cultural transmission of the evangelical Biblicist tradition involves transformations of cognition in the individual, a point further refined by comparing two recent frameworks for the study of cultural transmission.

Evolutionary biologist Richard Dawkins (1976, 1997) has proposed that cultural phenomena, like genes, are instances of Darwinian evolution in that their ability to produce copies of themselves in other minds is homologous, in terms of evolutionary theory, to the ability of genes to produce copies of themselves in new bodies. Dawkins calls the particles of cultural transmission *memes*, because they reproduce themselves in memory through imitation (*mimesis*).

Dawkins offers no well-developed analyses of highly fit memes—his examples are of an illustrative nature only—but his Darwinian framework suggests that, in some sense, the replicability of an idea in a population is a part of the *explanation* for that idea or behavior. Just as Darwinian evolution constitutes a kind of general theory of biological evolution, but requires the reconstruction of specific environments for the explanation of any particular population's phylogenetic history, so Dawkins's memetics constitutes only a very general explanation for an idea's distribution, and must of course be wedded to particular historical reconstructions to provide a genuine account. But the core notion is that the particular patterns of thought and behavior in any given community are a function of those memes' reproductive advantages in that environment. The key explanatory concept is reproductive advantage in a given environment.

Dawkins and others have been very keen to identify religions as examples—often paradigmatic examples—of memes. Dawkins's classification of religion as a "virus of the mind" (Dawkins 1993; Dawkins and Krasny 1997; Dawkins 1997) sums up both his theoretical construal of and his opprobrium for religion. Dawkins (1993, 37–40), adopting the voice of a medical manual, describes religion as follows:

1. The patient typically finds himself impelled by some deep, inner conviction that something is true, or right, or virtuous: a conviction that doesn't seem to owe anything to evidence or reason, but which, nevertheless, he feels as totally compelling and convincing. We doctors refer to such a belief as "faith."

2. Patients typically make a positive virtue of faith's being strong and unshakeable, in spite of not being based upon evidence. Indeed, they may feel that the less evidence there is, the more virtuous the belief. . . .

3. A related symptom, which a faith-sufferer may also present, is the conviction that "mystery," *per se*, is a good thing. It is not a virtue to solve mysteries. Rather we should enjoy them, even revel in their insolubility. . . .

4. The sufferer may find himself behaving intolerantly toward vectors of rival faiths, in extreme cases even killing them or advocating their deaths. He may be similarly violent in his disposition toward apostates (people who once held the faith but have renounced it); or toward heretics (people who espouse different—often, perhaps significantly, only very slightly different—versions of the faith). He may also feel hostile toward other modes of thought that are potentially inimical to his faith, such as the methods of scientific reason that may function rather like a piece of antiviral software. . . .

5. The patient may notice that the particular convictions that he holds, while having nothing to do with evidence, do seem to owe a great deal to epidemiology. Why, he may wonder, do I hold this set of convictions rather than that set? Is it because I surveyed all the world's faiths and chose the one whose claims seemed most convincing? Almost certainly not. If you have faith, it is statistically overwhelmingly likely that it is the same faith as your parents and grandparents had. . . . By far the most important variable determining your religion is the accident of birth. The convictions that you so passionately believe would

have been a completely different, and largely contradictory, set of convictions, if only you had happened to be born in a different place. Epidemiology, not evidence.

6. If the patient is one of the rare exceptions who follows a different religion from his parents, the explanation may still be epidemiological. To be sure, it is *possible* that he dispassionately surveyed the world's faiths and chose the most convincing one. But it is statistically more probable that he has been exposed to a particularly potent infective agent—a John Wesley, a Jim Jones, or a St. Paul. Here we are talking about horizontal transmission, as in measles. Before, the epidemiology was that of vertical transmission, as in Huntington's Chorea.

7. The internal sensations of the patient may be startlingly reminiscent of those more ordinarily associated with sexual love.

Dawkins's analysis of religion need not be taken seriously, as he is clearly unaware of the large empirical literature on religion. But his explanation does illustrate the central explanatory strategy of memetics: ideas (such as "faith," point one) are widespread because they are good at preserving (points two through four, seven) and spreading (points five and six) themselves.

Dawkins's model leaves very little room for human cognition beyond a tendency to imitate, remember, and communicate. As Susan Blackmore, an advocate of Dawkins's memetic framework, writes (2000, 66): "Thinking memetically [i.e., from a meme theory perspective] gives rise to a new vision of the world, one that, when you 'get' it, transforms everything. From the meme's-eye view, every human is a machine for making more memes—a vehicle for propagation, an opportunity for replication, and a resource to compete for."

To be fair, Dawkins and Blackmore do not claim that humans are *nothing more* than meme machines—they allow that we may have subjective experience, biologically based behaviors like eating and coughing, and a general capacity for learning associations—but nearly everything cultural is considered a meme.

Dawkins's view is curiously similar to many cultural anthropologists' views of cultural transmission, what Claudia Strauss and Naomi Quinn have called the "fax model" of communication, whereby "publicly accessible symbols straightforwardly determine people's understandings" (Strauss and Quinn 1997, 23). Following Clifford Geertz (1973), anthropologists often take culture to be purely external to the individual, with no appreciable or significant role played by individual minds.

I will argue that crucial elements of evangelical Biblicism make use of cognitive abilities located in the individual. A more active role for human cognition is envisioned in a second framework for understanding cultural transmission, Dan Sperber's "epidemiology of representations" model (Sperber 1985, 1996). Like the memeticists, Sperber would have an account of an idea's transmissibility in a social and cognitive environment be a necessary part of any explanation of that idea as a cultural phenomenon. But his epidemiology-of-representations framework is broader than the memetic one in that he regards (1) specific cognitive predispositions and (2) the activities of institutions as important factors affecting the spread of ideas. In an epidemiology-of-representations framework, the spread of god concepts, myths, and mathematics are all affected by the ease with which the human cognitive architecture can form the necessary mental representations, and by the prevalence, intensity, and authority of institutional activities devoted to spreading them. Studies of memory show that god concepts are rather easily acquired, and require only minimal institutional support to spread across a population (Barrett 2004). Algebra or calculus, on the other hand, can be acquired only with conscious effort, and tend to spread only with intensive institutional support. There is thus room in this framework for both specific cognitive constraints on learned materials and the activities of institutions in promoting or persecuting specific representations.

This study adopts an epidemiology-of-representations framework for understanding evangelical Biblicism. If cultural phenomena are going to be the subject of empirical study then difficult questions about their causes must be faced squarely. An epidemiology of representations foregrounds some critical questions: not only how a cultural phenomenon gets communicated and how it is understood by different people, but also what people actually learn when they acquire it, and under what conditions it becomes plausible and relevant to them. It seems to me that answers to these questions would take us a long way toward understanding cultural phenomena in general, and evangelical Biblicism in particular.

Studies in the epidemiology-of-representations framework have usually emphasized cognitive constraints favoring the spread of certain ideas over others. Lawrence Hirschfeld (1996), for instance, has argued that the concept of race—specifically the division of people into racial groupings—results not from observation of human differences (which are much greater within racial groupings than across them), but from talk about race activating children's innate proclivity to search for social categories. Because children are evolutionarily prepared to search the environment for social categories, simplistic race categories spread more easily than the biological view of human variation as complex and multidimensional. The simplistic categories are acquired early in life, even without much explicit institutional support; the biological view is acquired only with many years of schooling. (Of course, extensive schooling is no guarantee that the biological view will be adopted.)

A similar approach is adopted by Pascal Boyer (1994, 2001) and Scott Atran (2002) in their treatments of religious phenomena: both of them explain much of the structure of religious phenomena in terms of evolved cognitive predispositions. They argue not that humans evolved to be religious, but that religious representations spread easily, and take the forms they do, because they activate cognitive predispositions that were initially designed for other purposes related to survival in Pleistocene environments.

Boyer (2001, chapter 7), for example, argues that the widespread emphasis on precise performance of rituals (complete with associated tales of sudden catastrophe for those who violate the prescribed form) arises from an evolved intuition that some things must be done very, very carefully. This intuition is the product of a contagion-avoidance mechanism that originally evolved through selection against those who did not avoid contaminated substances, such as decaying bodies or fecal matter. This cognitive mechanism causes us to search our environments for clues to what might be contaminated, and to take special precautions in handling such substances. Boyer suggests that in many cases, ritual behavior activates the contagion-avoidance mechanism, thus giving ritual participants the strong sense that the slightest mistake might have life-or-death consequences.

These accounts, I think, have much to offer, but they are lopsided: surely not all religious phenomena are the result of evolutionary preparedness. Surely the religious beliefs in a given community are to a significant degree the result of that community's history. Boyer's and Atran's accounts are designed to explain the cross-cultural recurrence of religious representations, and so the influence of local factors is quite irrelevant to their overall proposals, save as confounding variables. Their accounts therefore sometimes give the impression that all the real work has been done by evolution—that culture is merely a filling in of evolutionarily specified blanks. But of course enculturation involves much more than this: the complexity of cultural phenomena results from the interaction of specific evolutionarily prepared cognitive dispositions, our general cognitive architecture, material constraints, social organization, and the history of ideas in a community. For an understanding of a *particular* cultural tradition, the omission of any of these factors results in caricature rather than explanation.

While this study is cast in an epidemiology-of-representations framework, it focuses on recurrence *within* a tradition. Evangelical Biblicism does indeed take advantage of innate cognitive abilities, and it is possible that these specific abilities were selected for in the course of human evolution. But many of the important factors in evangelical Biblicism—including all of those that make it scripturalist and evangelical—are historical, and I would tell a poor story indeed if I did not say what role these play.

Text and Culture

Since an obviously historical element of Biblicism is its use of a text, it is worth spelling out how this study relates to the intellectual traditions that have dealt with texts. Literacy, from an anthropological standpoint, entails more than knowing one's letters (Collins 1995). The various elements of this technology have tended to cluster along social–structural lines, demarcating social differences often related to power: in many societies the ability to compose, read, write, retain, or own texts has served as a primary distinctive of a social elite. This social context is often reflected in a text's perspective. Also reflected in texts are various other assumptions about what is permissible, appropriate, or necessary to write, what is relevant to say and what goes without saying. Then too, though often less obviously, texts reflect a set of assumptions about what language is, and what it means to fix something in writing. Literacy is a heavily social, heavily cognitive technology. Consequently, texts enter social life only when the door is opened by a host of background assumptions and understandings.

Michael Silverstein, Greg Urban, and other linguistic anthropologists (Silverstein and Urban 1996a) have explored the processes of "entextualization," processes by which moments of ongoing discourse are segmented off from their social surround, atomized, and reified. Subsequent reperformance of these discursive bits—texts—carries with it reference to the interaction in which the text originated. For example, Americans today cannot echo Richard Nixon's "I am not a crook" without a touch of irony, irony that originates in the speaker's and listener's shared knowledge that Nixon knew himself to have engaged in criminal activities.

In their essay "Natural History of Discourse," Silverstein and Urban (1996b) suggest that the use of texts as units of meaning independent of the communication events in which they originate is a means of constructing "culture." By recognizing certain bits of speech (e.g., "I am not a crook") as *texts* with particular sorts of *con*textual implications (e.g., reference to Nixon's intentional duplicity), interlocutors draw on and reproduce part of their shared cultural background. *Text* is thus a metadiscursive notion, a way of referring to those segmented, atomized, and reified bits of discourse.

Although Silverstein and Urban have oral texts primarily in mind, parallel issues arise in the study of written texts. Text artifacts too are separated from the social surround in which they originated, and it is often unclear what that surround was, what elements of that surround are reflected in the texts (and by what elements in the text), or what the intended relation was between the text and its surround.

And like oral texts, written texts are often assumed to "bear" or "have" "content" or "meaning." The importance of this assumption was impressed on me when I spent about ten hours a week over a three-month period working with a partner to decipher a twenty-two-line papyrus (P. Mich. 4017). The papyrus had been recovered as part of an archeological dig at Karanis, a site in Upper Egypt, and proved to be from the fourth century. At first, despite our knowledge of Greek, we were able to make out only a few words. With perseverance we were able to make out more, and with help from parallel texts and the skills of our expert instructors, we were finally able to transcribe most of the text. In many cases, we were able to "read" our papyrus only after we had some idea what it was likely to say. And such, it seems, is the experience of most papyrologists (cf. Youtie 1973). What carries the activity forward is the confidence—though it is really an assumption—that the papyrus really does say *something*, though at first one is not sure *what*. In a sense, the meaning arises only because it is presumed.

The presumption of textual meaning, it seems to me, is a specific case of the general principle proposed by Dan Sperber and Deirdre Wilson (1995), that although humans generally transmit only partial and ambiguous representations of the messages they intend to communicate, listeners' presumption of an intended message's relevance enables them to select, from among the possible interpretations, the one intended by the speaker. On Sperber and Wilson's view, all communicative signals are partial and ambiguous representations of their intended messages. The recipients of signals are therefore confronted with the task of sorting out which of the possible interpretations is intended by the speaker. They are aided in this task by the speaker's implicit promise that the signal is as appropriate as possible for the intended message (Grice 1989). Sperber and Wilson give a cognitive explication of this promise: the speaker, in attracting the listener's attention and offering an utterance, implicitly guarantees that the informational value of the intended message is greater than the energetic cost of cognitively processing it. The listener recognizes this implicit guarantee, and selects the first interpretation that meets this standard of relevance. It may be that further interpretations could be explored with more cognitive effort, but once the promise of relevance is satisfied, interpretation stops. (Of course, the guarantee of relevance may not be given in good faith, or a speaker may misjudge the conditions of relevance for the listener, or a number of other things might go wrong, but in general, the principle of relevance guides the listener to the speaker's intended meaning.) In ordinary conversations, then, interpretation is both initiated and guided by the expectation of relevant meaning.

The interpretation of texts, it seems to me, constitutes a special case of this general principle of relevance: texts are inherently partial and ambiguous with respect to their intended messages; texts too carry with them the implicit promise that they are worth interpreting. This interpretive impulse is so deeply ingrained that it is sometimes difficult to look at a text and to see it *only* as a jumble of points and lines. Thus one is drawn into an interpretive relation with a text, and begins the process of sorting through its possible messages. The text comes to "have" "content" or "meaning." And like oral texts, written texts can, by virtue of their presumed meaning, serve as part of a society's discursive background, and create the impression of shared culture.

Perhaps the broadest classification of written texts is the papyrologist's distinction between *documentary* and *literary* texts. Documentary texts include receipts, contracts, deeds, promissory notes, court rulings, and other such records. The value of such texts is primarily mnemonic (or evidential), even for the participants in the transaction, and the few copies that are made are almost always explicitly dated. Literary texts, in contrast, include novels, histories, plays, speeches, and other such texts whose value is felt to be less context-specific. Literary texts are often widely published, and, until modern times, were usually not dated. Indeed, if anything was dated, it was likely to be the text's reproduction rather than its original publication; in contrast, even copies of documentary texts carry the date of the original (Nielsen 2000).

The distinction between documentary and literary texts is far from perfect. Not only are there intermediate cases, such as amulets and personal letters, but the types *literary* and *documentary* are aggregates of characteristics, having to do variously with the texts themselves (material, dates, quality of hand(s), use of templates), with their content, and with their purpose. Papyrologists do not take these categories too seriously, and neither shall I. But these categories do point up a general distinction, it seems to me, relevant to texts' longevity: literary texts seem to have a much broader, much less occasion-bound appeal to readers, whereas documentary texts rarely have any aesthetic appeal at all, and tend to be narrowly functional within the institutional system that constitutes their general raison d'etre.

It is the literary texts that are generally taken to constitute part of a society's discursive background, both by members of that society and by scholars of it. This is not to say that any two members of the society recognize precisely the same set of texts, but that the texts that form the discursive background are generally of the literary type.

It should be clear by now that the use of texts is part of the general problem of culture and requires for its solution much the same sort of analysis required by other cultural phenomena. The approach here is thus the converse of a long-standing heuristic in anthropological research. For thirty years now, cultural phenomena have been treated as texts (following Ricoeur 1971 and Geertz 1973), an approach that brought hermeneutic and literary theory to bear on cultural phenomena. What is attempted here is to bring anthropological theory to bear on a textual phenomenon, to investigate the social, psychological, and material processes by which a text holds a place in the discursive ground of a community.

Where texts have reasonably regular psychological and social effects, literary approaches tend to seek the source of these effects in the texts themselves. Hence, texts are deconstructed to illuminate the various ways in which they selectively reflect and reinforce particular psychosocial ideologies. Such approaches are necessary, for some texts—especially those recognized as "literature"—are of immense complexity and subtle effect.

Reader response theory and reception theory maintain that the meaning of a text lies with the reader, and is not a feature of the text itself. I adopt this assumption solely for *methodological* reasons. If, with literary formalists, one assumes that texts have intrinsic meanings, then the next question seems often to be how those meanings are best recovered or recognized; if, with reader response theorists, one assumes that texts do not have intrinsic meanings, then the next question is why people think they do and what processes lead to the ascription of meaning. The latter questions fit more closely the purpose of this study, and so the assumption I make is that texts do not have intrinsic meanings. Supposing that the text has no intrinsic meaning, how far can a theory go in accounting for the meanings attributed to it, or the ways in which meaning is attributed to it?

I assume, as a further methodological point, that the authority and relevance of the Bible today are less a function of properties specific to the Bible than a consequence of the ways in which Bible believers encounter this ancient text. I do not deny either that the Bible has special properties or that these may in some measure account for its durability, but in this book I attempt to understand the longevity of the Bible as a function of the social and psychological elements of Bible-users' traditions.

In this perspective, the meaning constructed by Bible readers invites explanation in terms of their history, psychology, and social location. It is a truism that what a reader makes of a text turns heavily on the context the reader assigns to the text and to the sorts of hermeneutic assumptions the reader brings to bear on the text, and that these in turn bear the imprint of the social and historical context of the reader. But too often the crucial link here, from the reader's context to the reader's meaning, is glossed over vaguely as "interpretation." The present analysis develops a social and psychological account of how this link is established in evangelical Bible reading.

Several considerations make the Bible particularly appropriate for social and psychological treatment. First, the Bible has a long and relatively well-documented history. Papyrus and parchment, the materials on which biblical texts were first written, are relatively durable materials, especially in the dry sands of Upper Egypt. (In contrast, the paper on which Chinese classics were recorded, and even more so the palm leaves on which the Hindu Vedic literature was written, are much less durable materials in their climates.) These manuscripts, and later, printed Bibles, permit glimpses into the various forms of the Bible over much of its history.

Second, the Bible continues to be heavily used today. The processes underlying the Bible's contemporary importance may be observed firsthand, and interpretations of this use are subject to further study and new data. Of course, there is no guarantee—perhaps even little likelihood—that these processes are the same as those that have sustained the Bible in earlier historical periods. Nonetheless, studies of contemporary use may provide new theoretical proposals for historical inquiry.

Third, the Bible is one of the most widely distributed texts—possibly *the* most widely distributed text—in the history of the world. Especially over the last three centuries, Christians of various stripes have taken it upon themselves to make the Bible available in as many places, among as many peoples, and in as many languages as possible. By 1978, the Bible was available in over 1500 languages ("Bible Societies" in Douglas, 1978). It is therefore possible to compare use of this text in a variety of social, psychological, and material settings. Such variations may be very helpful in disentangling properties of the text per se from the cultural assumptions of its users.

Scripturalism

A focus on the Bible invites comparison with similarly sacred texts in other communities. Though this comparison is not the object of this book, the analysis here is inspired by comparative studies of scriptures. A program of scriptural comparison goes back to Max Müller, the influential Sanskritist often credited with founding the comparative study of religion. Müller edited *Sacred Books of the East* (Palmer and Müller 1879), a massive translation project designed to make available in English some Eastern counterparts to the Bible, Torah, and Qur'an in the West. Since that time, there have been a number of smaller anthologies and comparative studies of the different "scriptures" and "sacred" or "holy" "books" or "texts" found in different communities.

The purposes of these anthologies have been various, but one of the more common aims has been to introduce the reader to the various religious communities. Lewis Browne (1946, xiv) described the purpose of his anthology thus:

> And [the sacred literature of the entire world] needs to be read. Not all of it, of course, for that would take too long, and prove too tedious. (One English translation of the *Sacred Books of the East* alone fills forty-nine volumes!) But the crucial portions, the truly basic scriptures, these certainly should be read, for without a knowledge of their contents there can be no understanding our fellowmen.
>
> Therefore this anthology.

More recently, Chung Hwan Kwak, president of the International Religious Foundation, opens his preface to *World Scripture: A Comparative Anthology of Sacred Texts* (Wilson 1991, xiii) with the following words:

> All the great religions of the world revere sacred scriptures. Such texts include the Dhammapada and Lotus Sutra of Buddhism, the New Testament of Christianity, the Qur'an of Islam, the Vedas and the Bhagavad Gita of Hinduism, the Torah of Judaism, the Confucian Analects, and the Adi Granth of Sikhism. These sacred scriptures contain essential truths. And they have immeasurably great historical significance, for they have influenced the minds, hearts and practices of billions of people in the past. They continue to exert tremendous impact in the present, and we have every reason to believe that such influence will continue into the future. The words of truth in sacred scriptures form the core beliefs of religion and thus, of civilization.

James Fieser and John Powers are particularly explicit about the relationship between text and community in the preface to their recent collection (Fieser and Powers 1998, xix):

> The present text introduces the world's religions through selections from their scriptures. There are special benefits to this avenue of exploration. In most cases the sacred texts are the oldest written documents in the tradition, and one gains a sense of immediate connection by studying the same documents that followers have been reading for millennia. The texts are also foundational to a religion's most important doctrines, rituals, and social and ethical positions. Thus, they explain the authoritative basis of traditions that might otherwise seem incomprehensible, or even groundless. Finally, the texts have become the most sacred symbols of these traditions, implying that one is on holy ground each time a sentence is read.

One need not look far in other collections to find similar statements, although some studies focus on more specific questions (Bruce and Rupp 1968; Graham 1987; Coward 1988; Smith 1993). A common assumption—not an unwarranted one—underlying such anthologies and studies is that by reading the sacred texts of a community, one gets some insight into that community's beliefs and practices. To put it another way, the assumption is that communities stand in an *interpretive* or *hermeneutic* relationship with their sacred texts (cf. Ricoeur 1979).

But this is not all that such texts are often assumed to have in common. Miriam Levering, paraphrasing the definition of scripture used by Ninian Smart and Richard Hecht (1982), has characterized the commonsense notion of scripture underlying many of these comparative studies as follows (Levering 1989, 8–9):

- There are often beliefs that the text is of divine origin, or the product of special insight.

- Whatever their origin, they are regarded and treated as sacred, that is, powerful and inviolable, to be treated with respect.
- They are regarded and consulted as normative, authoritative for a community in various aspects of its religious life: for worship, doctrine, and behavior.
- The texts, whether written or oral, are regarded as closed and fixed, not to be added to or subtracted from. In other words, they are treated as a canon.
- When the sacred text is in the form of a book, it is regarded as complete. It contains everything of importance, and can be applied to all aspects of human life.
- The texts are used by members of the community in religious and ritual contexts.
- Sacred texts testify to that which is ultimate.

Such is the commonsense notion of scripture, at least among relatively educated persons. These features are especially important because they are often taken to *explain*, in some sense, the centrality of scriptures to communities' discursive backgrounds. But whether these features constitute an anthropologically useful category may be doubted, and has been.

Comparative studies of scripture—at least the scholarly ones—inevitably call attention to deficiencies of these assumptions when folded into the analysis of non-Western religious traditions. As Levering (1989, 9) comments:

> These are intuitively appealing generalizations, yet they are curiously misleading. I suspect that these characterizations are so intuitively appealing because all but one of them belong to the widely shared common sense characterization of the Bible. But a fully formed comparative study casts considerable doubt on the universal applicability and fruitfulness of these characterizations. Characterizations that are strongly true and significant about the Bible or the Qur'an at certain historical moments turn out to be only weakly true, and far less significant (or significant in a different sense), as statements about other scriptural texts.

The cross-cultural study of scripture, then, has encountered difficulties because the commonsense notion of scripture incorporates too many of the assumptions about the role of scriptures in the Jewish, (Protestant) Christian, and Islamic traditions.

But the problem is not merely West-centrism. As Levering notes (1989, 3), "it is clear that our implicit notion of 'scripture' is not derived from a careful consideration of the whole of Jewish and Christian experience and reflection, but only from very small parts of it." Most of its elements, in fact, are traditional Christian doctrines (inspiration, canon, sufficiency) combined and generalized with notions drawn from liberal theology (sacredness, ultimacy). It tends also to be biased toward the scholarly elements of Christianity, toward the written, the reflective, and the systematic. This emphasis is not misguided—there is much here worthy of study—but it tends to be metonymically taken as a characterization of Christian practice generally.

Whether "scripture" will ultimately prove to be an interesting and productive category for cross-cultural comparison I do not know. But a possibility worth considering is that the failure of Western assumptions about scripture to generalize very well to other traditions is related to their nonsystematic character as descriptions of Western traditions. The problem with the current notion of scripture might be not that it is *Western*—for if one has to begin a theory with a particular region, the West, with its confluence of multiple scriptural traditions, should be a rather apt starting point—but that it does not systematically describe *even* the West. Rather than starting with Christian doctrine, one might take the results of comparative studies as a new starting point for developing a more systematic model of scripturalism in the West. As Wilfred Cantwell Smith writes (1993, 63): "The West has long tended to derive its concept of scripture from the Bible; it is not amiss to suggest that we are now in a position where our understanding of the Bible . . . may begin to be derived from a larger concept of scripture." Such is the aim of the present study: to examine evangelical Biblicism empirically, in light of the questions raised by comparative studies of scriptures.

This book is thus a step toward a distinctly *anthropological* theory of scriptural traditions. An anthropological theory of scripturalism would be quite different from the theological, literary, phenomenological, and historical studies available at present. Those studies have taken particular texts as their point of orientation and have articulated scripturalism in terms of those texts. An anthropological theory would focus instead on *scripturalists*, the people behind the texts who make the texts special by their beliefs and practices. The difference is sometimes subtle—saying "Evangelicals regard the Bible as authoritative" rather than "The Bible is authoritative for evangelicals"—but it can be methodologically and theoretically significant. To say "Evangelicals regard the Bible as authoritative" invites questions about when, where, and why that are less obvious from the second formulation. But more importantly, the second formulation presupposes that evangelicals regard authority as an attribute of the Bible whereas the first formulation leaves open the question of whether authority is naturalized or recognized as a convention.

Whether an anthropological account of scripture is ultimately possible remains an open question. I have Bible-believing friends who think that the activity of the Holy Spirit puts the role of the Bible in believers' lives beyond the realm of any earthly account. Presumably there are people in other traditions who would say similar things about their scriptures. Even if scripturalism is a completely earthly phenomenon, it might prove to be beyond the explanatory reach of current social and psychological theory. In any case, it is clear that scripturalism has at least a human side, and the present book is an exploration of what current anthropological and psychological theory can offer toward a theory of scripturalist beliefs and behaviors.

Plan of the Book

This ethnographic study empirically examines key components of evangelical Biblicism—the category *Bible*, biblical interpretation, and biblical authority—with an eye to establishing an improved model of evangelical scripturalism.

Chapter 1 shows how the Protestant Reformation and American religious history fomented a vigorous form of Biblicism, and how the Bible emerged as a major doctrinal issue in the twentieth century. It then describes the study's field site, Creekside Baptist Church, and shows how Bible quotation and exposition permeate a Sunday morning service.

Chapter 2 explores what, given the multiplicity of Bible versions, American evangelicals mean by "the Bible." After a brief summary of some of the factors that give rise to versional differences in English Bibles, this chapter systematically explores eight different hypotheses for how evangelicals define "the Bible." Each hypothesis is assessed against behavioral evidence, and a richer understanding of evangelicals' Bible concept emerges throughout, leading up to the conclusion that the concept has four structural elements.

Beginning with the analysis of a Sunday school interpretation where the interpretive conclusion directly contradicted the very wording of a Biblical text, chapter 3 develops a model of how evangelicals relate their ideas to the Bible. Detailed examples of interpretation and interviews about Bible-reading habits illuminate the implications of evangelicals' interpretive tradition for their engagement with the Bible. The conclusion of this chapter shows how the Bible's indefinite interpretability arises as a by-product of the presumption of relevance, the double framing of Bible reading, and practical constraints on pastors' time.

Chapter 4 examines the shape of biblical authority as it is reflected in surveys, in doctrinal statements, in citation of the Bible, and in the maintenance of a sharp distinction between the Bible and all other texts. The Bible's authority is often justified by evangelicals on the ground that it is divinely inspired, but the doctrine of biblical inspiration is less clear to evangelicals than its putative consequence, suggesting that the doctrine of inspiration is in fact made relevant for evangelicals by their otherwise anomalous practice of biblical authority. I then show how a modification of proposals by Emile Durkheim (1995 [1912]) and Roy Rappaport (1999) can account for the structure of biblical authority.

The conclusion synthesizes the new model of Biblicism that emerges from the previous chapters and shows how the model makes different predictions and invites different comparisons than do current assumptions about sacred texts. It concludes with an outline of some primary psychological and historical factors necessary to an epidemiological account of American evangelical Biblicism. The picture that emerges is, I think, strikingly different from common assumptions about evangelical practice shared, to a large degree, by evangelicals and nonevangelicals alike.

Creekside Baptist Church   I

The Bible at Issue

THE AMERICAN RELIGIOUS SCENE, over the last hundred years, has offered a nearly unparalleled opportunity for the study of scripture as an anthropological phenomenon. Although most scriptures have some following in the United States, a confluence of crises surrounding the Bible has highlighted the scripturalism centered on that text. Indeed, a core issue of Biblicism—the question of how precisely the Bible ought to be regarded—has hung heavily in the air, a palpable presence in its own right, but also a diffuse tension in debates among Christians. Several evangelical theologians have commented on the current crises of Biblicism. John Warwick Montgomery writes (1985, 59–60):

> What great doctrinal issue does the modern Church face? . . . The doctrinal problem that above all others demands resolution in the modern Church is that of the authority of Holy Scripture. All other issues of belief today pale before this issue, and indeed root in it. For example, ecumenical discussions, if they are doctrinal in nature, eventually and inevitably reach the question of religious authority. What is the final determinant of doctrinal truth, and how fully can the Bible be relied upon to establish truth in theological dialog? As the patristic age faced a Christological watershed, as the medieval and Reformation Churches confronted soteriological crises, so the contemporary Church finds itself grappling with the great epistemological question in Christian dogmatics.

Harold Lindsell, too, in the preface to his book *The Battle for the Bible* (1976), called the issue of biblical inerrancy "the most important theological topic of this age." Debates over the status of the Bible have pushed the phenomenon of scripture—or parts of it, at any rate—explicitly into public discourse.[1]

Two crises in particular have contributed to modern American Biblicism. The first was the Protestant Reformation, in which, under the credo of *Scriptura sola*— scripture alone—Protestants rejected the authority of the papacy. *Scriptura sola* cut against church tradition, too, but whereas papal authority was entirely rejected, church tradition was, in most cases, merely demoted. The Bible emerged, in Protestantism, as the ultimate—and hence unique—authority for matters of faith and practice. Protestantism is thus much more bibliocentric than Roman Catholic, Eastern Orthodox, or Ethiopian traditions. American Protestantism preserved and amplified this bibliocentrism. The historian George Marsden notes (1980, 224):

> In America, for the first two centuries Protestantism dominated overwhelmingly, and the Bible had played a role in shaping the culture for which there was no European parallel. Lacking a strong institutional church and denying the relevance of much of Christian tradition, American Protestants were united behind the principle of *Scriptura sola*. Indeed, the Bible played a major role in America's self-understanding. This Biblicism, strong among the Puritans, gained new significance in the early nineteenth century. In the wake of the Revolution, Americans saw themselves as inaugurators of a new order for the ages. The new order was conceived as a return to a pristine human condition. For Protestants this ideal was readily translated into Biblical primitivism. The true church should set aside all intervening tradition, and return to the purity of New Testament practice. The Bible alone should be one's guide.
>
> Biblicism was closely related to religious individualism, also encouraged by revivalism. The individual stood alone before God; his choices were decisive. The church, while important as a supportive community, was made up of free individuals. The Bible, moreover, was a great equalizer. With Bible in hand, the common man or woman could challenge the highest temporal authority.

The peculiar religious history of American Protestantism combined with elements of the more general American ethos to bring the Bible per se into sharp focus.

This peculiarly American emphasis on the Bible shaped the symbolism of the second crisis, the fundamentalist–modernist controversy (Marsden 1980). In the closing years of the nineteenth century, leaders of various Protestant denominations increasingly began to subscribe to a substantial reinterpretation of traditional Christian beliefs. The rise of historical consciousness, advances in hermeneutic theory, the application of literary critical techniques to the Bible, and the development of the sciences combined to motivate a reconsideration among intelligent, devout scholars of the nature of Christianity's claims. Particularly affected was Christology: stories of Jesus's virgin birth, miracles, and resurrection were no longer regarded as straightforward factual reports about the acts of a historic figure, but merely a way of expressing, in ancient Jewish and Hellenistic parlance, his followers' perception of him. Quite different theological, historical, and sometimes ethical commitments followed from the new perspective. These new views had proliferated quietly from the ivory towers of American Protestantism, and, until the second and especially third decades of the twentieth century, a majority of church constituencies were unaware of them. Fundamentalist leaders were thus able quickly to attract a large following by "exposing" mainline leaders' theological liberalism and touting their own theological conservatism. The late 1920s and early 1930s saw a series of institutional rifts develop as fundamentalists became more extreme and separated to form their own churches, colleges, seminaries, and mission organizations.

The fundamentalist–modernist debate was widely perceived as being about the status of the Bible. Was it the very word of God, perfectly and eternally true? Or was it an ancient religious document—a good book, to be sure, but not authoritative in any very direct sense? The potent symbolism of the Bible became clear in what must be regarded as the most bizarre twist in the already bizarre 1925 Scopes "Monkey" Trial: the cross-examination of the lead prosecutor, William Jennings Bryan, by the lead defense lawyer, Clarence Darrow. Although the legal issue was whether John Scopes, a high school science teacher, had broken the Butler law by teaching evolutionary theory in the classroom, the confrontation between Darrow and Bryan focused on whether the Bible gave a plausible and self-consistent historical account—not just of creation, but of the Tower of Babel and Jonah and the whale and other stories. Clearly this was a debate about issues far broader than John Scopes and the Butler law.

Following the 1925 Scopes trial came a period of what Susan Harding (2000) has called "fundamentalist exile." Fundamentalists withdrew from engagement with larger American culture, forming a subculture that, despite the number of people participating in it, did not have or really attempt to have much political voice (Noll 2001). Fundamentalists accepted exile partly because many of them had millenarian views that led them to expect the world to become increasingly corrupt and hostile to them. Their job was not to reform the world but to guard diligently their own orthodoxy and devotion. Their focus was thus largely inward.

A new movement—neo-evangelicalism—originated in the 1950s as a response to both the increasing liberalism of mainline churches on the one hand, and fundamentalist exile from mainline churches on the other (Noll 2001). In contrast to the mainline churches, evangelicals affirmed a conservative, orthodox theology. In contrast to fundamentalist churches, evangelicals advocated an open engagement with modern scholarship and the larger American culture. There appears to have been a considerable mass of people who were not satisfied with either fundamentalist or mainline options, as evangelicalism grew quickly, attracting constituencies from both camps.

Evangelicalism shed much of the defensiveness that had characterized fundamentalism. Like fundamentalists, evangelicals saw themselves as defenders of orthodox Christianity. Many felt that modern scholarship had still not provided much reason to reject orthodox Biblicism (see, for example, the essays in Youngblood 1984). Unlike fundamentalists, they tried to engage the larger American culture from an orthodox point of view.

In the late 1970s, fundamentalists and evangelicals together became actively involved in national politics on a large scale. Up to that point many had not even been registered voters, but, under the leadership of Jerry Falwell, James Dobson, and others, conservative Christians began to express their voice on the national political scene (Smith and Emerson 1998). Observers were surprised by the "fundamentalist resurgence." It is significant that a number of studies of fundamentalism began in direct response to this new presence in American politics. Since that time American fundamentalism and evangelicalism have come under increasingly sophisticated study.

Although some scholars distinguish between fundamentalists and evangelicals (Marsden 1991; Smith and Emerson 1998), the majority lump them together under one or another definition of "fundamentalist" (Barr 1978; Boone 1989; Riesebrodt 1993; Carpenter 1999; Crapanzano 2000; Harding 2000). The extension of "fundamentalist" to those who not only eschew the term but also define themselves against it is symptomatic of the hostility—often open—with which some scholars have regarded politically active Christian conservatives. In most discussions, the term "fundamentalist" has little meaning apart from strongly negative overtones (Nagata 2001). The term ought to be used with caution, although it does have an entirely appropriate use for those who self-consciously identify as "fundamentalists"—typically the direct institutional descendents of the original fundamentalists of the 1920s.

In just such an environment I was raised, in a fundamentalist church that had been formed in 1929, at the beginning of the fundamentalist exile. Growing up in such a context, I learned a great deal about the Bible and gained an intuitive familiarity with conservative Christian ideas and practices. When it came time for me to choose a field site, I wanted to select a church that was evangelical rather than fundamentalist, but which typified the forms of Biblicism I had encountered in various fundamentalist and evangelical churches. I wanted to study an evangelical church because survey data shows that evangelicalism is a rapidly expanding form of Christianity, because previous studies have tended to emphasize the fundamentalist end of the evangelical–fundamentalist spectrum, and because I felt it would be easier for me to let go of my presuppositions and embrace the discipline of empirical study if I knew that the church could not simply be identified with the environment in which I was raised. At the same time, it was important that the church manifest the sorts of general Biblicist beliefs and practices that I had observed in other churches, which had originally called my attention to Biblicism as an anthropological phenomenon. I found such a site in Creekside Baptist Church.[2]

Creekside Baptist Church

The fieldwork—participant observation, about forty interviews, and a Sunday morning survey—that forms the basis for this analysis was carried out at Creekside Baptist Church from 1997 to 2001. Creekside Baptist is a predominantly white church, with 350 to 400 attendees on an average fall or winter Sunday. Although it is nominally a Baptist church and baptism is postinfancy and by immersion, Creekside Baptist's doctrine, liturgy, ethics, and ethos are not distinctively Baptist. It is affiliated with a loose federation of churches, but, like most Baptist churches, makes decisions in-house.

Creekside Baptist Church traces its origin to January 9, 1964, when two couples started meeting on Thursday evenings for Bible study and prayer. They were soon joined by others, and by the end of the year the group had organized with a steering committee, a treasurer, and a clerk, and was calling itself "Creekside Baptist Church." The first ordinance observed by the church was communion, in the evening service of November 22, 1964. In May 1965, fifty-two people signed a charter membership, a constitution was approved, and deacons were elected. In March of 1966, the first permanent pastor was called, and in the same year, they purchased some wooded land for a church. By 1968, two hundred people were attending Sunday services each week.

Today, Creekside Baptist is still located on its original property in what has become a relatively wealthy neighborhood in a fairly wealthy town. The road on which the church is located was, until a few years ago, kept unpaved so as to limit traffic in this residential area. The location of the church on a steep hill made the ride in a jarring experience, especially when the spring thaws left the dirt road pocked and gullied. When the church recently succeeded in getting the road paved, the ride to church became much more pleasant, though still a bit scary during icy conditions owing to the steep grade.

The dark brick exterior of the building, the double sets of wooden doors, and the forested surroundings combine to give the overall impression of a quiet, meditative, solemn place. The parking lot wraps around the church, descending from the first floor in front to the lower level in back. Families with young children typically park in back, by the lower level, where most of the children's programs are held.

An Evangelical Church

In its brochures, Creekside Baptist identifies itself as an evangelical congregation. To get some sense of how the people of the church understood their religious identity, I began interviews with a standard set of four questions:

1. Do you consider yourself a *Christian*?
2. Do you consider yourself an *evangelical* Christian?
3. Do you consider yourself a *fundamentalist* Christian?
4. Do you consider yourself a *Baptist*?

After each response, I asked people what they meant by the term—that is, if a person said "yes" in response to question two, I asked them to define the term *evangelical*. In this way I was able to elicit information about religious identity without stipulating definitions of these key terms.

The following conversation with a middle-aged woman who had attended the church for some years is fairly representative of the interviews I conducted:

BRIAN: Do you consider yourself a Christian?

SANDRA: Yes.

BRIAN: And what do you mean by that?

SANDRA: By that I mean what's commonly referred to as a born again Christian in that I have a personal relationship with Jesus Christ.

BRIAN: Do you consider yourself an evangelical Christian?

SANDRA: Yes.

BRIAN: And what do you mean by that?

SANDRA: Again, the born again thing enters into it. The literal belief in the Bible. Those are the two basic components of what I deem to be evangelical.

BRIAN: Do you consider yourself a fundamentalist Christian?

SANDRA: That word has gotten such a bad rap, but yes. Not in the sense that you hear in the news. Basically I view those words as being interchangeable— evangelical and fundamentalist.

BRIAN: Do you consider yourself a Baptist?

SANDRA: Yes.

BRIAN: And what do you mean by that?

SANDRA: People that believe in baptism by immersion and have a whole string of other doctrines. Fairly well defined, at least.

BRIAN: Do you have some ideas about what those are?

SANDRA: Yes and no. Yeah, I do, but I'm not so sure I can articulate them. I mean like the Apostles' Creed and again belief in the Bible as the literal word of God. . .

Sandra's answers reflect some themes that emerged from interviews. All interviewees identified themselves as Christians. The follow-up question, "And what do you mean by *Christian*?" received fairly consistent responses, often using stock phrases like "born again" and "personal relationship with Christ" or "accept Christ as your personal savior," phrases that reflect the core gospel message as that message is understood in the American evangelical tradition. One young man explicated it this way:

> A Christian is a person, I suppose the formal answer is, a Christian is a person who's accepted Jesus Christ as their personal savior, literally someone who has accepted that they are a sinner by nature, that there is nothing they can do before God to be right on their own, and they need Jesus's death to make it, and they've accepted that in a way in their lives, not just, you know, intellectually saying "that's cool."

This message of salvation, the gospel ("good news"), is taken to be a universal offer, available to everyone everywhere, and the people of Creekside Baptist recognize that there are fellow believers in many places, including in other churches. They do not regard Creekside Baptist as the sole community of the saved.

The starkness of this gospel, according to which only those who trust in Jesus's death go to heaven, is a fixation much more for outsiders than insiders. Inside the church, the doctrine of hell is not elaborated, nor have I often heard it even mentioned at Creekside Baptist. ("The word [hell] is not used in children's Sunday school classes at all," the director of Christian education told me.) Outsiders' perception that evangelicals are claiming to be part of an exclusive club is quite alien to evangelicals' perception of it. They see themselves as profoundly grateful recipients of a gift available to anyone who will have it. The notion that some are predestined for hell (double predestination) is not an explicit part of this Baptist church's doctrine, though there are members who hold it. At Creekside Baptist, they don't even talk much about heaven, emphasizing instead the relationship with God they are experiencing here on earth. To judge by how they talk, salvation is less a matter of streets of gold in the afterlife than it is about entering into communion with God right now.

Almost all of the people I interviewed were willing to identify themselves as "evangelical." Sandra defined *evangelical* in such a way that it added only a "literal belief in the Bible" to her definition of *Christian*. The young man quoted above answered somewhat differently: "I think of an evangelical as someone who believes that each individual has to make the decision for Jesus on their own, they can't be born into it, and also considers it to be a responsibility to get the word to unbelievers and to make sure people you encounter in your life have the opportunity to make that decision."

His emphasis was on the proselytization (usually called *evangelism* among conservative Christians) facet of being an evangelical. The same emphasis came through in an interview with a middle-aged man:

> You know that's a good question in the sense that that [the term *evangelical*], you know, in the last five or six years has taken on a different attitude, a more negative attitude, that evangelical is identified with certain causes and beliefs, you know, like pro-life or antigay. There's all kinds of—I think in our culture anyway—negative descriptions of evangelical. But in the sense of personally, I think I am evangelical, but I am not a talking evangelical as much as a living evangelical, a person. What I see my role in our culture is that I live my faith and make that as attractive to people who may or may not have faith in [such a way] that they would want to know about it. And that's when I feel absolutely open to talk about it; but I'm not one to lead off with it. I'm not looking to—some of my friends are—[find an] opportunity every moment to share the gospel. I don't do that in the sense of taking advantage of people in different situations. I would compare it to me becoming your friend because I want you to join the Amway club. But if the person is seriously, you know, questioning, that's really up to God, not up to me, as to where they are in their faith walk or need for faith. So in that sense I'm an evangelical but I'm not a Bible-thumping, down-on-the-street-corner-yelling-at-people person.

Here again the emphasis was on sharing his faith, albeit in a low-key, indirect way. Both emphases—on belief in the Bible and sharing one's faith—are core components of the cluster of meanings that evangelicalism has had historically in the United States.

Only a minority of informants identified themselves as *fundamentalist* Christians. Like Sandra, some people identified fundamentalist with *evangelical*, or defined *fundamentalist* in a very general way. The young man previously quoted defined fundamentalism by its doctrine of the Bible: "I am a fundamentalist. I believe the Bible is the word of God, I believe it's inerrant, although I am willing to accept that there may have been either translation or copyist mistakes."

The middle-aged man, however, defined it more stereotypically:

> That even has a more negative connotation to me. I think of it as a person. "Fundamentalist" to me today means more of a judging person that has a whole series of rules that they follow and I don't think that's right. I'm not on the other end of the spectrum either, a wild liberal person either. I guess I don't live primarily by rules but by principles. The principles come from the Bible. But I don't see myself as what I hear people describing fundamentalist as today.

Another young man, Stan, rejected the term for himself because of its stereotyping:

STAN: I don't like the term because of the connotations that it has.

BRIAN: Which ones specifically?

STAN: Connotations being I think that if you said that in this country, a fundamentalist would be considered kind of a far-right-wing wacko, and is way extreme almost to the point of being non-Christian, something other than Christian. Probably in its true identity, the definition of the word is you believe the fundamentals of Christianity, the basics of Christianity, that term would apply. But that definition doesn't apply anymore in this country.

A young man named Todd made similar distinctions, drawing out what he thought was useful from fundamentalism:

TODD: Again, "fundamentalist" is another term which I fear has been misunderstood and caricatured and stereotyped widely across modern American culture. I'm not really familiar with what I consider properly called "fundamentalist culture." I know a bit of fundamentalist theology, but . . . I think properly understood, especially if you look at historical roots of fundamentalism, it gets down to what are the fundamentals of the faith, and I think most fundamentalists and I agree what the fundamentals of the faith are, if you boil it down. I think in fundamentalist culture there has been a lot of emphasis upon certain types of behavior that are either encouraged or prohibited, and in some circles I think that has maybe become too codified, or maybe those have been treated as absolute truths when maybe in reality they might be very good suggestions, or ideas, or guidelines, but were overemphasized. I guess I should pause and say that I think human nature is to do that in all manner of things, is to take something that's good or proper or useful and to exalt it to become, you know, the leading dictate, the leading code of behavior. It happens not only among people who are considered conservative but also among people who are considered liberal. Maybe I think that one of the things that's happening in some of the strands of fundamentalist culture in the [United States], and, like I said, those things that aren't really at the center of the faith, but have become prominent—preeminent—in fundamentalist traditions. I agree with the root concern or cause or direction, but I think it's the degree to which that has been emphasized or codified or enforced in some cases, I feel is out of step with God's guidelines for our lives.

BRIAN: I hear a distinction between fundamentalist theology and fundamentalist culture.

TODD: Yes. Fundamentalist theology I resonate with quite a bit, I think. I guess I don't consider myself an expert on fundamentalist theology. But fundamentalist culture, again I agree with the motivation, but in some cases, in some circles, it's gone too far in a way. Maybe run roughshod over what should be central principles of the Christian faith, the Christian life.

BRIAN: Do you have particular issues in mind where you think that about fundamentalist culture?

TODD: I do, I suppose. I hesitate to list them because it makes me sound like I'm an apologist for those things or think they're wonderful behaviors. Things like modern dancing. Things like the use of alcohol. Things like certain cultural entertainment arts events, whether it's theaters or movies or centuries-ago novels. I was briefly part of a church that had a handbook, a guidebook, that even as late as the 1980s still prohibited watching TV, going to movies, dancing, things like that. And I'm not an apologist for those things, but I think all those areas of life can be used properly and responsibly and can be redeemed by God for his purposes. Sometimes it's harder than others. Some areas are harder than others. That's the other thing about fundamentalist culture. Again, I may be subject to some of the stereotypes and caricatures, but I think sometimes there's not a willingness to be open to some of the ways God uses things, some of the ways God can redeem some things. And I always want to be open to see the redeeming power of God and what he can do, sometimes through us, sometimes in spite of us, for his good purposes.

Todd's articulation is significant because, although only a few interviewees were willing to identify themselves as fundamentalists, most interviewees largely agreed with the core assumptions of fundamentalist theology.

Answers to the question "Are you a Baptist?" were predominantly negative, and even when they were positive they had a different character than answers to the first three questions. Greg, the young man quoted earlier, gave an answer that seemed to sum up the sentiments of many informants:

BRIAN: Do you consider yourself a Baptist?

GREG: Yes, although I don't answer that, I mean not in the same sense I said "yes" to the previous questions. I consider myself a Baptist, because, of the four churches I've been seriously involved with over my lifetime, three of them were Baptist, and that would be the last three in a row, too. The Baptist churches I've been familiar with happen to have been good churches, so to some extent I could say I consider myself a Baptist. But the church before was, my first church as a Christian, was independent. There were some variations in their doctrine [laughs] that I don't find offensive. One of the ones was that they did not perform infant baptism, but if you came to the church, with that as your baptism and felt you'd been brought up as a Christian, they would accept that as adequate for church membership. I think a true Baptist would have a coronary over that issue. I never felt it was that big a deal.

BRIAN: So it sounds almost like you're saying, "Well I'm as much a Baptist as anything."

GREG: I'm a Christian. To your previous questions, yes I'm a fundamentalist. I'm an evangelical. Baptist?—by association.

Probably the most common answer was, "Well, I attend a Baptist church, right now. . . ." Identity as a Baptist seemed to be reckoned corporately, by virtue of an individual's participation in a Baptist community, rather than individualistically, as were identities as Christian, evangelical, and fundamentalist. By the same token, most informants were only very weakly committed to being Baptist. In response to my question "Are you a Baptist?" Stan said:

I guess I am because I'm a member of Creekside Baptist Church. I guess I am, but . . . I wouldn't say exclusively. Technically, I grew up in a Presbyterian church, and technically I'm still a member of my home church. So I guess I am. I would have to consider myself a Baptist, but not solely a Baptist. You know if I moved to a different town, or something, I could just as easily take up with a Presbyterian church—Christian, evangelical—or some other denomination. I'm not wedded to the denomination. And I just told to you this story where in pastoral counseling the pastor said, when I first started going to [Creekside] Baptist Church . . . his comment to put me at ease was, "Well you'll find we're not *too* Baptist here," because he knew I was coming from a Presbyterian church.

Although the church is called Creekside *Baptist*, many people in the church come from other denominations, and many interviewees expressed the view that, were they to relocate, they might well attend a church of another denomination.

People come to Creekside Baptist from a variety of different backgrounds: Episcopalian and charismatic, Reformed and Southern Baptist, Catholic and fundamentalist. In its worship style, organization, and even doctrine, Creekside Baptist generally adopts a kind of middle path, meeting people of a variety of differing views halfway.

Creekside Baptist has an unusually highly educated congregation. The majority of attendees are professionals: teachers, engineers, computer programmers, nurses, and small business owners. Of those adults old enough to have completed postgraduate work, the majority—64 percent—had done so. Further, a handful of attendees were either current or former faculty members at the University of Michigan.

What unites people from such different backgrounds is, precisely, their evangelicalism. Historically, both fundamentalism and evangelicalism have always cut across denominational divides, though they have usually been stronger in some denominations than in others, and they have sometimes had significant effects on denominations.

Table 1.1.   Basic Gospel Beliefs

Survey Statement	Yes	No	Undecided	Number of Respondents
All people are sinners	100.0%			83
Jesus Christ died and rose from the dead to provide a way of salvation	96.3%	2.5%	1.3%	80
People are saved only by faith in Jesus Christ	96.3%		3.7%	81

As evangelicals, the people of Creekside Baptist are largely agreed about the basic gospel message. My survey included three items designed to examine these core beliefs. The survey was administered on May 21, 2000, to all high school and adult Sunday school attendees. I received a total of eighty-three responses, forty of whom identified themselves as members, thirty-seven as regular attendees, two as occasional attendees, and four as visitors. Responses to items about basic gospel beliefs are summarized in table 1.1. Each survey statement elicited wide agreement, and when church members alone were considered, all three statements received 100 percent affirmation.

As evangelicals, the members of Creekside Baptist are also agreed about the inspiration and authority of the Bible. They take the Bible to be the inspired and inerrant word of God, given as a gift to all humanity. When asked to agree or disagree with the statement "The Bible is inspired by God," 100 percent of survey respondents (n = 83) said that it was. The majority (69.5 percent, n = 82) also affirmed that the Bible is inerrant even in matters of science and history.

The special status of the Bible was not the subject of much explicit discourse. People seemed to assume the Bible was special, and to assume that others agreed, and so it was little discussed. But it was ubiquitous. The importance of the Bible was particularly evident in the structure of church activities.

A Sunday Morning Service

The church's central function is the Sunday morning service, taking place at 9:30 and 11:00 in the sanctuary. The sanctuary, constructed as an addition on the original building and completed in 1985, is relatively plain in comparison with those of many other churches, but not austere. It is essentially a very large room, approximately pentagonal in shape, with a high, vaulting ceiling. The evangelical deemphasis on liturgy extends to the architecture, which resembles an auditorium more than a cathedral. Instead of pews, there are lines of sturdy wooden chairs with brown padding, each with a shelf underneath on which is stored a Bible and a hymnal for those in the row behind. There are enough chairs to seat about three hundred. The chairs are, like the fixed seating in movie theaters, always set a bit too close for American comfort: sometimes people shift them over to create a bit of breathing room for themselves and their neighbors, and one often sees chairs used to hold a Bible. But in general people snug themselves into place, especially when the sanctuary is full. At the front of the sanctuary, flanked on the left by the piano, on the right by the organ, is the pulpit. In front of the pulpit is a table bearing a flower arrangement or an open Bible, save for the monthly celebration of the Lord's Supper, when it displays the elements. Over the pulpit, on the front wall of the sanctuary, is a cross. The sanctuary windows look out onto the serene, wooded portion of the church's property.

Services begin promptly on time and end after approximately an hour. The service of January 11, 1998, will serve as my example, as it was, in all relevant respects, typical for Creekside Baptist Church. As people file into the sanctuary, ushers stationed at the doors distribute bulletins and assist with seating when necessary. The cover of the bulletin reads "Come, follow me, and I will make you fishers of men," and indicates the source of the text as Mark 1:17. This week, as most, the bulletin cover bears a scriptural text, on which people can meditate as they are seated in the sanctuary.

The first part of the service is titled, in the bulletin, "We Honor the Lord." Dr. Ted Williams, the lead pastor, approaches the pulpit. Williams wears no liturgical robes, only a suit and tie. Many people in the congregation too are dressed nicely—men in jackets and ties, women in dresses—but there are also always rumpled khakis, jeans, and t-shirts in evidence. The air is serious but not solemn, structured but not quite formal.

Williams invites the congregation to "Please stand with me as we worship our Lord together today." The ensuing dialogue is printed in the bulletin so that everyone knows what to say—the particular exchange is a one-off event.

WILLIAMS: God's mighty acts among us are well known.

CONGREGATION: We are a people of history.

WILLIAMS: God's redemptive acts were epitomized in Christ Jesus.

CONGREGATION: We are a people of faith.

WILLIAMS: God's salvation gives us hope and courage to affect history.

CONGREGATION: We are a people of history.

ALL: May our lives magnify the Lord in what we have been given, what we are, and what by God's grace we may become.

The congregation remains standing as they sing a praise medley, the words for which are provided in the bulletin, followed by two hymns from their hymnals. Williams then returns to the podium for the invocation: "Lord we come this morning in that wonderful name [Jesus] to offer our praise and our honor to you. Grant that everything we do today will bring glory to you as you are at work in us. We ask through that wonderful name of Jesus, Amen." The congregation now sits as the choir sings. The words are given in the bulletin, though the congregation does not sing along.

The next part of the service is titled in the bulletin "We Celebrate Life Together." It begins with announcements about the new Sunday school classes beginning that week, an upcoming conference, and opportunities to help out with the Interfaith Hospitality Network, an organization that uses churches as shelters for homeless families on a rotating basis. Visitors are welcomed, and a couple comes forward to report on their counseling ministry activities at the church. The pastor prays and an offertory plays while offering plates are passed down the rows for those who want to contribute. When the offering is completed, the congregation stands for a hymn.

The balance of the service is titled "We Listen and Respond to What God Is Saying." It begins with a scripture lesson, read by Williams.

> You may be seated. Our scripture lesson today comes from Mark's Gospel, and we'll be reading from chapter one, verses fourteen through thirty-four. We're just getting started now in the ministry of Jesus in this account. Mark chapter one, beginning at verse fourteen. [Pause.]
>
> Listen now to the word of the Lord:
>
> "After John was put in prison, Jesus went into Galilee, proclaiming the good news of God. 'The time has come,' he said. 'The kingdom of God is near. Repent and believe the good news!' As Jesus walked beside the Sea of Galilee, he saw Simon and his brother Andrew casting a net into the lake, for they were fishermen. 'Come, follow me,' Jesus said, 'and I will make you fishers of men.' At once they left their nets and followed him. When he had gone a little farther, he saw James son of Zebedee and his brother John in a boat, preparing their nets. Without delay he called them, and they left their father Zebedee in the boat with the hired men and followed him. They went to Capernaum, and when the Sabbath came, Jesus went into the synagogue and began to teach. The people were amazed at his teaching, because he taught them as one who had authority, not as the teachers of the law. Just then a man in their synagogue who was possessed by an evil spirit cried out, 'What do you want with us, Jesus of Nazareth? Have you come to destroy us? I know who you are—the Holy One of God!' 'Be quiet!' said Jesus sternly. 'Come out of him!' The evil spirit shook the man violently and came out of him with a shriek. The people were all so amazed that they asked each other, 'What is this? A new teaching—and with authority! He even gives orders to evil spirits and they obey him.' News about him spread quickly over the whole region of Galilee. As soon as they left the synagogue, they went with James and John to the home of Simon and Andrew. Simon's mother-in-law was in bed with a fever,

and they told Jesus about her. So he went to her, took her hand and helped her up. The fever left her and she began to wait on them. That evening after sunset the people brought to Jesus all the sick and demon-possessed. The whole town gathered at the door, and Jesus healed many who had various diseases. He also drove out many demons, but he would not let the demons speak because they knew who he was."

[Pause.] Let's turn in our hymnals now to number 390 as we prepare to hear God's word proclaimed. Shall we stand.

The congregation stands for what the bulletin calls a "Hymn of Preparation," after which Williams resumes the pulpit to speak.

Sermons at Creekside Baptist are supposed to be "biblical" and "expository"—that is, reflections that, whatever their topic, take the Bible as their point of departure and their ground of authority. Williams begins his sermon by asking (rhetorically) who would be a good role model:

It seems that one of the marks of our time is both a longing for and, at the same time, a confusion about heroes. Who are the people we should be emulating? Who should we be following? Are there in fact people worth following? I think that confusion or ambivalence was demonstrated particularly during recent months when Princess Diana and Mother Theresa both died so close together. And to watch the world, and the clamor that went after the first half of that glorious duo and how we ignored, at least relatively speaking, the one who in my estimation was the true hero in that setting.

But we don't know who to follow: politicians, entertainers, sports figures? You know with sort of a disgusting regularity they all manage to disappoint us. Something comes up where they mess up and the people we think we might follow don't really seem to deserve to be followed. So we're left with people who tend to appeal to our lowest instincts: greed and power and lust and independence from restraint. They become the ones that we end up becoming attracted to, unfortunately.

Having posed this question, he segues back to the scripture just read: "It makes me wonder what would have happened if Jesus had appeared in our time rather than 2000 years ago. Would he have been a hero? Or would he have been rejected even as he was then? It may even be that after today's study we'll start to come up with our own answer to that question."

From here he moves to the scripture passage and begins by explicating Jesus's message—"The time has come. The kingdom of God is near. Repent and believe the good news!"—as given in Mark 1:15:

[It] says that after John was put in prison, Jesus went into Galilee and he proclaimed the good news of God. Interesting phrase—"Good news of God"—that is just as ambivalent in English as it is in the original. What does that mean? It could mean "Good news originating in God," "of God" in that way, or it could mean "Good news about God"—"Good news of God." And, in the Greek, it can be either way too. And I choose to think that perhaps here it is both. It is good news that originates in God from God and it's about God as well. What does he say about that good news? He simply says "The time has come. The kingdom of God is near. Repent and believe the good news." I am suspicious that that is a compression of more that was said. That's pretty powerful stuff. "The time has come." The moment, in God's plan, is here. And then he puts it in kingdom talk, "The Kingdom of God is near." And as his followers are going to find out, all through his lifetime, his definition of kingdom always starts inside us. It's where God is in charge, supposed to be in charge of us, ultimately he will be in charge of the world. But kingdom talk always begins internally. And as if to seal that he then says "Repent and believe." Powerful words. "Repent"—that's the 180-degree turn. A whole new focus in life. A change in how we look at everything. Turn, and believe. Don't simply submit to some sort of intellectual assent about some facts, but have a life change, turn your life around and do it by believing, by placing your trust in the one who is the head of the kingdom. And this, he says, is good news. You know one only has to look around at how we mess up our lives and our world to understand that perhaps letting God be in charge would be good news. You could go through the paper this morning, and I'm, without having looked at it yet, I'm convinced that if you leaf through enough pages you could find story after story where you could say "Boy, if those people had let God be in charge, what difference might it have made." "If those nations, those communities, those places in the world, would have let God be in charge, how might it change the story? That could be good news. Somehow our society has twisted that around to be calling it bad news. To give up your rights? To no longer be in charge yourself? To no longer be self-reliant? Why that's not good, is it? Well, it depends who's in charge. It depends to whom you give that right to be in charge. If you give it to the one who made us, it really is good news.

He then follows the text through the call of Simon, Andrew, James, and John, the curing of the demon-possessed man, to the healing of Peter's mother-in-law and others in the unnamed village. He suggests that the miracles showed the disciples that their decision to follow Jesus had been a good one, but that they only perceived the full import of it because they had already responded to Jesus in faith.

Williams then draws together the themes he has developed in an application to his audience:

Well, there's good news in a passage like this, let's review it. It's good news, that when we turn around, when there is a change in focus in our lives, when we believe and place our trust in Christ and follow him, that when we do that, the exchange is that we get as our life manager the one who made us. And that's *good*, not bad. That's *good news*. To have God as the manager of life is good news. To follow his prescriptions for life makes life work the way it's supposed to. That's good news! It's good news to know that God is still at work.

And if I will open my eyes I can recognize where he is at work. And it will confirm my decision to follow him as a good one. I mean, if you have trouble seeing God at work, look at yourself, first of all, if you really have turned to him in faith. Do you realize the magnitude of what it means to be a forgiven righteous person? Declared righteous when you have no claim to it whatsoever? Or have we got so used to feeling like we're pretty good people that that doesn't impress us anymore? Have we lost sight of how hopeless we are without him? If there is nothing else to show his power, it ought to be what he's done for us as a demonstration of it. That's God at work! But my contention would be that beyond, beyond that, if you just will open your eyes, you'll see God at work! Where have you seen him this week, have you watched, have you looked? Have we gotten our arrogant little hands off of life enough to recognize that it isn't us doing everything? God is at work. Can we see it? And when we do, can it help to confirm that to follow him is a good position?

And then finally, we need to be encouraged by the fact that the disciples didn't turn perfect at this point. [Laughs.] They went through their periods of doubt and failure—we're going to see that as we go through this book. But *all* through that time, once they had made this decision to follow, even in those periods of doubt and failure, his offer to lead them never was withdrawn. I can't help but think of dear ol' Peter, ya know, at the end of Jesus's time here on Earth—it's recorded for you in the twenty-first chapter of John, you remember the story, many of you do—where the disciples met Jesus by the side of the lake after the resurrection. And Jesus sort of pinpointed Peter, 'cause Peter, ya know, had not particularly meant very well during the whole period of Jesus's trial and crucifixion. But he pinpointed Peter and he said "Do you love me?"

"Yes."

"Feed my sheep. Do you love me?"

"Yes. . . ." You know, he went through that three times. The same number of times Peter denied Jesus. And at the end of that, these words come, *same* words that we find here at the beginning of this whole business. You read John 21 after that whole incident then Jesus says, "Follow me." It's still there—the offer is still there! Even through the doubt and the disappointment, the offer is still there: *Follow me, let me be in charge.*

Well here're some questions for you to take with you today. Have you, number one, turned, believed, and followed, so as to make your life a part of his kingdom? Have you come to that point in your life, where you have opened yourself to him and invited him to be your leader and your Lord? Another question: are you recognizing his work in you and around you as confirmation as his right to call you? Finally: are you one, who maybe like Peter, even now needs to renew your decision to follow, even as you hear him lovingly continue to invite you to do it?

Jesus doesn't call us blindly; he gives us every reason to follow him. He confirms it. What will you do about that? Amen.

The sermon closes with the invitation to stand for a "Hymn of Response," printed in the bulletin. This is followed by a brief benediction: "And now as you go may God's love embrace you, his wisdom guide you, his spirit empower you and his mercy keep you, so that you may live to one day hear those wonderful words, 'Well done, good and faithful servant.' Amen."

Williams's benediction is formulaic, but varies seasonally. The quotation at the end is from Matthew 25:21. Following the benediction Williams walks down the main aisle to the back of the church, where he stands at the door and greets people as they file out. A large wooden banner over the back of the sanctuary reads "Blessed Are Those Who Hear the Word of God and Obey It."

People are in no hurry to leave, and the sanctuary stays dotted with clusters of friends catching up until it is nearly time for the next service to begin. Outside the sanctuary the lobby is similarly crowded as some people catch up while others try to wiggle their way to the coffee machine, or make their way downstairs to the Sunday school classes.

Following a thirty-minute time for socializing, the second service and set of Sunday school classes begin. The second service is basically the same as the first except for minor changes in personnel. The church also has Wednesday night club activities and a nursery school, both of which involve Bible-related curricula, though the connection here is less emphatic than in the Sunday morning functions.

The Sunday morning service is structured around the focal event of the scripture reading and exposition, and, from the bulletin to the benediction, seeded with biblical quotations and allusions. The Bible is central to the life of this community. The goal of the next few chapters is to explicate the nature and structure of this Biblicism.

Methodological Reflections

In conducting this study, my own background in fundamentalist Christianity was of tremendous help. I was an insider, recognized as a fellow conservative Christian. After all, I had the same knowledge of the Bible that they did. In fact, in some ways, I had more: not only did I have a fair ability to recall parallel passages and to note relevant theological and exegetical controversies, but my knowledge of ancient Greek even gave me some expertise in the Bible. I also had the skills required to participate in Bible study conversations, knowing how to tie the Bible to the conditions of modern life. Whereas other investigators have had to work around the perception of them as outsiders—most evident in the incessant witnessing they report, but more subtly evident also in the other conversations they describe—I could relate to evangelicals with a co-believer footing.

This footing was occasionally disadvantageous. In gathering data about practices, I often had to ask individuals very basic questions covering information that is normally left tacit. My informants seemed sometimes perplexed that I, a fellow Christian, would need to ask such questions. How could I not know the answer already? In many cases, I did know the answer already, but I asked anyway, and on a few occasions I was genuinely surprised by the answers I was given. A related disadvantage as an insider was that informants found it difficult to understand that I was interested in simple description rather than evaluation. When I asked about Bible reading, for instance, people would begin by saying that they didn't read the Bible as much as they should, or that, for one reason or another, their reading had recently fallen off. I don't think that anyone was intentionally deceptive, but I do think that people tended to describe their reading experiences in terms of what were, from their point of view, the "best" instances. But, overall, I think the distorting effect of normative expectations was probably less for an insider, who is to some degree a confidante, than for outsiders, who are to be drawn into the fold.

My background also enabled me to understand, on an intuitive level, much of what I witnessed. I was able fairly quickly to close in on an interpretive understanding—their own account—of their actions. After all, their accounts were quite similar to those I had at one time known as my own.

The task of setting aside Christian categories and interpreting Christian belief and behavior from an anthropological perspective proved easier than I had expected. This should probably not have been surprising: it was precisely my dissatisfaction with the Christian categories that first interested me in scripturalism as an anthropological phenomenon. If I had been satisfied with the Christian accounts, I would not have seen the need for research. This dissatisfaction also benefited me in that I went into the study prepared to exoticize, to ponder, reflect on, and marvel at practices similar to those I had grown up with. I devoted the majority of my energy trying to peer behind the veil of familiarity, to perceive the underlying assumptions and processes, and to check them empirically lest I slip too easily into an inadequate interpretation.

It is often said that the anthropologist requires some professional distance in order to do a proper analysis, and whether I have achieved the appropriate distance from my informants is an open question. My analysis certainly bears little resemblance to any doctrine of scripture, and I have taken seriously pervasive practices, such as Bible dipping, that evangelicals themselves usually repudiate or ignore in their discussions of scripture. This is not the account they would give of themselves.

Nor, on the other hand, is this analysis any account of my own departure from fundamentalism. Doubtless, much of my personal interest in scripturalism is a product of my own struggles over it. Yet the questions and problems that ultimately drove me from fundamentalism receive scant treatment here. I encountered a few other people wrestling with the same issues I did, but this analysis is about the majority of my informants, for whom scripture is rather less problematic.

When I shared with evangelical friends my skepticism about traditional interpretations of Bible use, they would often ask, with a genuine openness, what I thought was going on. What follows, then, is an attempt at a satisfactory answer.

Notes

1. It has also created the possibility of research on scripturalism. In other historical moments or in other places, the possibility and relevance of examining scripturalism has been foreclosed. The historical formation of the Christian canon was hardly studied in the Middle Ages: inquiry into the process of canonization must be regarded as a modern phenomenon (Metzger 1987). And indeed at present one need only consider the state of textual criticism of the Qur'an to see that even this most banal sort of study is not always permitted.

2. The name of the church and the names of all informants are pseudonyms.

What Is "the Bible"? **2**

A STUDY OF EVANGELICAL BIBLICISM is a study of how the implications of one bit of text—the Bible—are organized in the minds of evangelicals. What sets Biblicists apart from non-Biblicists is their notion of how the Bible is related to other texts, talk, and behavior. But at the core of this is an enigmatic concept: the Bible. It sounds like the name of a book, but in fact there are many different Bibles. So a primary question is this: given a number of different texts that count as Bibles, what do evangelicals mean by "the Bible"?

For the study of text concepts, the case of the English Bible is particularly instructive because its complex textual history has given rise to a number of coexisting "versions" used by a large number of people who know that they differ but regard them as nonetheless alike. As a prelude to the conceptual analysis, the following section briefly reviews the causes and dimensions of variation in modern printed Bibles so as to acquaint the reader with the environment in which those who use English Bibles find themselves. (The reader already familiar with the history of the Bible and the complexities of Bible translation may wish to skip ahead.)

Versions and Variants

The plethora of English Bibles available today can overwhelm the novice. About twenty major English Bible translations are on the shelves of local bookstores, and many more are available in libraries and over the Internet. Although Bibles appear to be simple representations—"translations"—of ancient texts, they are not. A brief excursus into the kinds of complexities underlying the array of modern English Bibles will set the stage for consideration of the Bible concept as it appears among American evangelicals.

Most English Bibles are translations of texts in classical Hebrew, Aramaic, and Koine Greek. A first, obvious source of complication is translation: English Bibles are produced by committees with quite disparate translation philosophies. The King James Version (1611), also known as the Authorized Version (AV) and its revisions were all intended to be "literal" translations, to stay as close to word-for-word correspondence between the source and target languages as possible. The resulting texts are usually a bit stilted in English. But most recent translations— notably the New International Version (1984)—attempt rather to render into English the meaning and flavor of the source text without necessarily preserving any of its grammatical structures. The result of this "dynamic equivalence" philosophy is that the English text is highly readable—ideally, does not read like a translation at all—but often takes greater liberties with the text than do more literal translations. Still less literal than dynamic equivalence translations are retellings, or paraphrases. The different translation philosophies underlying some modern English versions are summarized in figure 2.1. Bibles, therefore, may sound quite stilted or natural, formal or informal, literary or plain, depending on the philosophy of the translation committee and its target audience.

A second complication comes in establishing the translation's source text. Some translations take as the basis for their New Testament the *textus receptus*. The *textus receptus* is a variant of the Greek New Testament text standardized by the eighth-century AD. It is represented in the vast majority of medieval Greek manuscripts, and is usually referred to simply as the Majority text.[1] Because late manuscripts were used as models, a variant of the Majority text served, with slight modifications, as the most widely used Greek New Testament from Desiderius Erasmus's first printed edition of 1516 until the meticulous research of Brooke Fost Westcott and Fenton John Anthony Hort (1881) introduced modern textual criticism.[2] Since the Revised Version of 1881, most major translations of the New Testament have taken as their source text an eclectic New Testament text, usually based on one of the published critical editions.

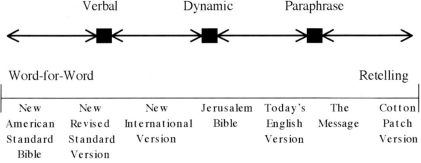

Figure 2.1.   A Spectrum of Approaches to Translation

Critical editions are syntheses of the best (i.e., most likely to be original) readings found in various manuscripts. The manuscripts themselves are very similar, but not identical. The critical editions pick and choose the readings most likely to be original from among the various manuscripts to come up with an eclectic text. The resultant text is not identical to that of *any* extant manuscript.[3] Bible versions are thus based on slightly different texts depending on the manuscript evidence available to translators.

An example will illustrate this sort of textual variation. The rejection of the *comma Johannem* (1 John 5:7) as the result of textual criticism is clear in the comparison of the King James Version with the Revised Standard Version (1952):

King James Version:
[6]This is he that came by water and blood, even Jesus Christ; not by water only, but by water and blood. And it is the Spirit that beareth witness, because the Spirit is truth. [7]For there are three that bear record in heaven, the Father, the Word, and the Holy Ghost: and these three are one. [8]And there are three that bear witness in earth, the Spirit, and the water, and the blood: and these three agree in one.

Revised Standard Version:
[6]This is he who came by water and blood, Jesus Christ, not with the water only but with the water and the blood. [7]And the Spirit is the witness, because the Spirit is the truth. [8]There are three witnesses, the Spirit, the water, and the blood; and these three agree.

This passage is markedly shorter in the Revised Standard Version (and most modern translations, including the American Standard Version [ASV], New American Standard Version [NAS], New International Version [NIV], New Revised Standard Version [NRSV], Contemporary English Version [CEV], and New Living Translation [NLT]) because verse seven of the King James Version has been eliminated on text-critical grounds. The longer variant appears only in late manuscripts, and its nonoriginality is accepted by nearly all textual critics. The versification has been maintained by dividing verse six. While the NAS, NIV, NRSV, and NLT give the extended reading in the margin, the alternate reading is not even noted in the ASV, RSV, and CEV.

Different committees also sometimes weigh evidence differently: whereas the Septuagint (roughly, the ancient Greek translation of the Hebrew scriptures) was once considered unreliable, evidence from the Dead Sea Scrolls has suggested that it may in some cases be the best witness to the Hebrew scriptures at the time of Christ (Jobes and Silva 2000), and so recent committees have weighed the Septuagint more heavily when making text-critical judgments.

A third complication—though one on which the various translations largely agree—arises because the manuscripts themselves are often editions, in the sense that, at some point in their textual history, they added to the texts information

Table 2.1.   Various Subscriptions to the Epistle to the Hebrews

Subscription	Manuscript
To the Hebrews	04
To the Hebrews, he wrote from Rome	02
To the Hebrews, he wrote from Italy through Timothy	018
The epistle of the apostle Paul to the Hebrews, he wrote from Italy through Timothy	404

about the author, date, and place of the original text's composition. Table 2.1 illustrates manuscripts of the Epistle to the Hebrews to which a variety of subscriptions are added.

Many times, as here, the subscriptions themselves are copied and occasionally modified from earlier manuscripts. In this case, there is little question that the original subscription was simply "To the Hebrews" and that later church traditions added information about its Pauline and Roman origin. But the earliest subscription was not part of the original text, probably being added when the letter was included in a collection of Pauline epistles circulating by the end of the first Christian century. All of these epistles were given simple titles referring to their destinations but not specifying the author—To the Romans, To the Corinthians, To the Galatians, To the Hebrews, etc.—and are grouped together in most manuscripts (Trobisch 2000). The subscription has a different textual history than the epistle itself.

Most English Bibles are translations of a critical text rather than any particular manuscript, but include in this critical text book titles and authorship information that—even if accurate—were not original. The criterion of originality used for the text is replaced by criteria of accuracy and convenience for the titles. This makes sense, given that the book titles mainly serve as points of orientation, but it means that Bibles are really more than simple *translations*.

Finally, English Bibles vary in their canons. The early Christians adopted as their Scripture one of the then-current Jewish scriptures, the Septuagint. The Septuagint differed from the Hebrew scriptures in that it included not only more books, but longer versions of some books that existed in the Hebrew collection. The church adopted the Septuagint as its "Old Testament." During the Reformation, under the influence of Renaissance sensibilities, Protestants rejected all elements of the Septuagint that were not part of the Hebrew scriptures. The Roman Catholic Church, however, maintained these "apocryphal" books because they were part of its authorized version of the Bible, the Latin Vulgate. English Bibles, as a result, differ in the set of books they include depending on whether they are Catholic or Protestant in orientation. (The canon of the Ethiopian Church is not represented in any English version of which I am aware.)

Those who would read, believe, and trust "the Bible," then, find themselves in an environment where multiple versions of "the Bible" are available. The question I consider here is what, given a bunch of texts described as "translations" or "versions" and a name ("the Bible"), evangelicals think "the Bible" is. What sort of concept is "the Bible"? How is it organized?

Name

Consider first the obvious hypothesis that, for the people of Creekside Baptist, "the Bible" is a name, serving as the conventional way of referring to a particular text. On this hypothesis, they would regard "the Bible" as a proper noun, referring uniquely to some book.

As stated, this hypothesis is susceptible to two interpretations, owing to the ambiguity of the English word "book":

1. "The Bible" is the name of a particular text artifact, the physical artifact that is a particular instantiation of a text. This exemplar would then define the category "Bible": "Bibles" would then be "copies of" the Bible by virtue of some regular relation to this exemplar.
2. "The Bible" is the name of an abstract text, but not any particular copy of that text. The text of the Bible would then define the category "Bible": "Bibles" would be those text-artifacts that stand in some regular relation to it.

I will consider these hypotheses in turn.

"The Bible" as Text-Artifact

Let me start with facts before moving to evangelical beliefs. Is there in fact some text-artifact to which all Bibles are related? There are several candidate answers worth considering here:

1. The autographs. All biblical texts must have had some first copy, and all Bibles may therefore be said to be *genealogically related* to these originals. The genealogical relation, for texts, is not especially regular, but almost all of the Bibles in use at Creekside Baptist are closely related to the originals, as they are based on scholarly attempts to reconstruct those originals.
2. Important manuscript witnesses. P^{46}, housed partly in the University of Michigan's papyrus collection, is the earliest copy of the Pauline letters, dating to c. 200 AD. All attempts to reconstruct the autographs must at least reckon with this papyrus, and so they may be said to stand in some relation to it.

English Bibles do in fact stand in some relation to the autographs and to important textual witnesses like P[46], and it is a possibility worth considering that people use these as exemplars to define the category "Bible." But this problem admits of another kind of answer as well.

3. My first Bible. Another possibility is that at the core of every individual's Bible concept is the memory of the first Bible that individual encountered. For each individual, that first Bible is "the Bible," and serves as the measure of all subsequent "Bibles." Even though people would be basing their Bible concepts on different exemplars, the resemblance among these exemplars may suffice to generate similarity in their uses of the term "Bible."

I will consider the first two hypotheses together, inasmuch as the same kind of evidence is relevant to both, before turning to the third.

MANUSCRIPTS. One of the pastors of Creekside Baptist suggested to me in an interview that laypersons sometimes assume that behind Bible translations lies an actual *manuscript*:

> We did a Sunday school class . . . about a year ago on what the Bible is and so . . . we just talked about that, I talked about the transmission of the biblical text. And the main reason I did that is because I just think that Christians should know, so that they can know how reliable it is, but they should also know that the New Testament in particular is a set of best readings. It's not like there's a manuscript out there that exists that *exactly* mirrors what the New Testament is. I find that that's more of a surprise to people. They've always thought it's a translation but they've never thought that it's a translation that's pieced together. . . . I just think there's a vast ignorance on the transmission of the [Bible].

This comment piqued my curiosity, and I began asking people, in interviews, *of what* did they think Bibles were translations? What did translators work with? The following is from an interview with Sidney, a forty-year-old business owner who was heavily involved in church life.

> BRIAN: If you think about a Bible, like this one right here [pointing to a Bible sitting on an end table in the living room], what is this Bible a translation of? When a committee goes to make this translation, what do they have in front of them?
>
> SIDNEY: Well, at some point they had original manuscripts. Whether for this particular Bible they actually looked through original manuscripts or something that was taken from the original manuscripts, but the original documents would have been, original manuscripts. In the original languages.

BRIAN: But you think of them as looking at the manuscripts when they prepare this?

SIDNEY: That's a New International Version. Did they do that for the New International Version? Did they actually look at the papyrus, or did they look at, I'm sure some of them are very frail now and they probably don't have access to them, are they looking at the actual papyrus? I don't know. Were they taking what someone else had done who had looked at the original papyrus? I don't know.

BRIAN: Can you tell me what you know about this original papyrus?

SIDNEY: There are a lot of different sources, and there are thousands of different manuscripts, most of which corroborate one another in great detail. Some are copies, and then there are copies made of the originals and so forth. There's the Q document in the New Testament and so forth . . . believed to have been used to. . . . Is that what it is? Q?

BRIAN: In the Synoptic Gospels, yes.

SIDNEY: And, you know, they believe it is the basis of the Synoptic Gospels, but not John, type of thing, so. . . .[his voice trails off]

BRIAN: What I'm trying to find out, is whether people think there is a particular manuscript lying behind translations? Whether somewhere there is an actual Hebrew and Greek manuscript that translations are made from?

SIDNEY: I don't think there's a *single* one. But there are hundreds and hundreds of early manuscripts that corroborate one another, that make up the whole New Testament. You know, there's bits and pieces here and there. At one point, did they all exist in one location? I don't know—I'd have to say probably not. Probably not in the original writings, they were by so many different people. I don't think they were ever put together until it was assembled in the sixty-six books that [the Bible] is.

BRIAN: Do you know when that happened?

SIDNEY: The Middle Ages, wasn't it? That's pretty broad. [Laughter.] I was reading *The Case for Christ*, and it has a lot of that detail and it's, which I can't whip off the top of my head. [Laughter.] It's in the book. [Laughter.]

Sidney clearly had only vague ideas about what might lie behind modern translations like the NIV, and stated repeatedly that he did not know. Similar uncertainty was evident in an interview with a young woman who had attended the church for eight years.

BRIAN: What is the Bible a translation of? If I was to give you a regular English Bible and ask you what it is a translation of, could you tell me what you think it is a translation of?

JULIE: It's a translation of the collection of works by the disciples of Jesus Christ, and some apostles, and prophets, I guess, of God, in the Old Testament.

BRIAN: Do you know what languages these are in?

JULIE: Um, Greek, and I think there's some Latin?

BRIAN: Is there a Bible manuscript that underlies our Bible? What do the translators look at, when they sit down to do their translating, what do you think they're looking at?

JULIE: Um, Dead Sea Scrolls?

BRIAN: Do you think they are sitting down with, just for an example, pictures of the Dead Sea Scrolls? When you envision it, what comes to mind?

JULIE: Well since they're still assembling the Dead Sea Scrolls and fixing them, they must be looking at pictures of them because I assume there are pictures of them. Of course, it's already been done in English translations. And there are supposedly thousands of letters and. . . .[her voice drifts off]

Julie had some idea of what manuscripts and processes lay behind English Bibles, but she knew few specifics. In her last answer, she resorts to inference rather than recall ("since . . . they must be . . . I assume. . . ."), encounters a contradiction (they are still assembling the Dead Sea Scrolls, but English translations are already completed), before referring vaguely to "thousands of letters" without saying whose letters these are or whether these are many copies of the same letter or copies of many more letters than appear in the Bible.

Other interviewees gave similar responses. All recognized that English Bibles are translations, and most recognized that there are various manuscripts of the Bible, but none seemed to have more than vague ideas about how Bible versions are produced. The pastor's surmise, that people thought an actual manuscript lay behind English versions, was not particularly supported by the responses I received, not because people had some other well-defined view but because they had few ideas about it at all.

This is not to say that the relationship between modern Bibles and the autographs is unimportant to evangelicals. In evangelical doctrine, the authority of modern Bibles is derived from their status as the word of God revealed to ancient prophets and apostles, and so the authority of a Bible version is often linked to its accuracy. This evangelical doctrine contrasts with traditional Catholic doctrine from at least the Councils of Trent (1545–1547, 1551–1552, 1562–1563 AD) to Vatican II (1952–1965 AD), according to which the official text of the church—the Vulgate ("the old Latin vulgate edition," Waterworth 1848, 17)—defined the Bible even over earlier Hebrew and Greek manuscripts. This is connected with the longer-standing Roman Catholic doctrine that the authority of the scripture is derived from the authority of the church. Protestants, in elevating the authority of scripture over that of the church, linked the authority of the Bible to its status as God's word—that is, the word of God revealed in a series of historical events. The reliability of modern Bibles as representations of the *texts* given in those events is therefore very important to evangelicals, and so modern English translations have eagerly taken advantage of advancements in textual criticism and philology (for an overview see Comfort 1990); the most widely used critical edition of the Greek New Testament is a product of the International Bible Society, designed to make the state of the art in New Testament textual scholarship available to translators (Aland et al. 1993). But their concern in these endeavors is to establish the text of the Bible, and not particularly to reconstruct the autographs as artifacts: they are not concerned particularly with the reconstruction of the autographs' number of columns and lines per column, size, hand, etc. (It might be objected that this information has been hopelessly lost to history, a point that must be conceded. Yet the fact that the text rather than all of these other features were copied suggests that the early copyists saw only the text of the autographs, rather than their other artifactual properties, as important.) I will consider the role of the autographs in establishing the biblical *text* below.

Overall, then, it is clear that the category "Bible" as used by the majority of people at Creekside Baptist is not anchored by reference to either autographs or important manuscript witnesses. Most of the people who use the term "Bible" do so without having any clear ideas about textual history or the translational processes.

MY FIRST BIBLE. The third version of the name-of-an-artifact hypothesis is that the concept Bible is defined by reference to the first copy of the Bible an individual uses.

There is evidence that the children of Creekside Baptist are intentionally exposed, early on, to most common artifactual features of Bibles. As part of the Sunday school curriculum, two-year-olds sing the *Pat the Bible* song. The children sit in a circle on carpet squares. The class size, during the time I observed, ranged from three to seven children, so the circles were always small. The lead teacher at the time was a male in his forties. Sitting on a carpet square himself, he pulls out a plastic bin full of Gideon New Testaments. Gideon New Testaments are small, imitation-leather Bibles with gold lettering on the cover, a two-color picture of the American flag inside, and the King James Version text. Save for the ribbon marker, they fit the Bible stereotype exactly. They are nothing like the Bibles designed for children. The children come up and take a Bible each back to their carpet squares. The teacher says, just before the *Pat the Bible* song: "God made my eyes to read his words. God made my hands to pat the Bible. Let's pat the Bible. We love the Bible."[4] The teacher and the students then sing a song together, all the while holding the little Bibles and patting their imitation leather covers. Four songs are used, each at a different time of the year:

> *Oh I Like to Pat the Bible* (to the tune of *Did You Ever See a Lassie?*)
> Oh I like to pat the Bible, the Bible, the Bible
> Oh I like to pat the Bible with hands God gave me.
> I'll pat-pat and pat-pat, I'll pat-pat and pat-pat,
> Oh I like to pat the Bible with hands God gave me.

> *Pat the Bible* (to the tune of *The Wheels on the Bus*)
> The children in our class can pat pat pat
> Pat pat pat, pat pat pat
> The children in our class can pat pat pat
> Pat the Holy Bible

> *Pat the Bible* (to the tune of *Here We Go 'Round the Mulberry Bush*)
> Oh it's fun to read the Bible
> The Bible, the Bible
> Oh it's fun to read the Bible
> The Bible today
> We read it, we learn it
> We pat it, we love it
> Oh it's fun to read the Bible
> It is God's way.

> *Pat the Bible* (to the tune of *This Is the Way*)
> This is the way we pat the Bible
> Pat the Bible, pat the Bible
> This is the way we pat the Bible
> With our little hands

Sometimes the children hold onto the Bibles through story time, other times they return the Bibles to the plastic bin after the song. Once they have done this, the teacher prays, "Oh, Thank You God, for our hands to pat the Bible." *Pat the Bible* is a fun activity for two-year-olds, and those who are playing along do so (as is the way of two-year-olds) with relish.

The purpose of the *Pat the Bible* song is not necessarily to acquaint children with the stereotypical look and feel of Bibles. I interviewed the director of Christian education about the goals of the two-year-olds' curriculum.

BRIAN: What are some key things you try to teach kids about the Bible?

MARY: Well, let's see, for the very youngest child it's just to love that book, treat it very, very specially, up to the children who can go right to a particular book of the Bible, finding it. In other words, well if you can't use the book, what good is it? So there is that gamut of just the physical book itself, and then understanding how the books are divided into certain sections, and then knowing that there are different interpretations, and there's just all kinds of things, and I could probably go from the two's on up to fifth graders let's say, and each class would have some different goals, and of course carry along the other goals that they learned before. Do you want more specifics?

BRIAN: Sure, let's start with the two's. What are the goals for teaching the two's?

MARY: Well, like I say, respecting that book. And how do you respect it as a two-year-old? Well, they pat the Bible. You may remember that [from helping out in the class]: they pat the Bible. And that is showing love and respect and care for something. Otherwise what do you do with a book? Well, you throw it on the floor or you scribble in the pages. At two, that's the kind of thing that can be done. But no, you don't do that with this particular book. And of course we do that with small ones. We use actually New Testaments because they are small and the young child can hold them easily.

BRIAN: Do you select them at all because they look a lot like an adult Bible? Was that a factor in your selection of them?

MARY: Actually I don't, all the New Testaments that I know are going to look about the same. The New Testaments that I know all look pretty much the same, whether it's the Gideons or some other publisher. So, it's selected because of its size. . . . Think about that little two-year-old hand. They really need something that they can hold and cradle in their hand. And that is on purpose in the curriculum.

Clearly, the diminutive size of the Gideon New Testaments is paramount in their selection for the *Pat the Bible* song. (The fact that they were probably free would not hurt either.) Yet the object of the lesson—to teach children to love and respect the Bible in particular, differently from other books—depends on the identifiability of Bibles. Whether or not this activity is designed to acquaint two-year-olds with the stereotypical characteristics of Bibles, it has this effect. Long before they can read the Bible, and well before they will have their own (very different) Bibles, these children were learning what adult Bibles look—and feel—like.

This sort of artifactual knowledge is instilled by early contacts with Bibles, and one might imagine that "the Bible" is taken by these children to be the name of the particular artifact held in hand, and that all other Bibles are identified as such by virtue of their resemblance to this one.

But if the stereotypical appearance of Bibles makes a lasting impression on these children, it does not amount to a *definition*. One of the curriculum goals for three-year-olds is to have them bring their own Bibles. Not all of them do, but, in the three months I observed this class, *not a single child* brought a Gideon New

Testament or any Bible that looked like one to the three-year-olds' Sunday school class. In fact, most of them brought children's Bibles, books that bear only a very abstract similarity either to the Gideon New Testament or to any other adult Bible. (They didn't even have the flag, the feature most studied by two-year-olds in the Gideon Bibles.) Moreover, when children enter first grade, they are given a NIV Adventure Bible, which is hardbound with a purple and gold cover. I found, in short, no evidence that children categorize Bibles by their similarity to Bibles encountered early on. While I do think that the stereotypical appearance of Bibles leaves a lasting impression on these children, it does not amount to a definition.

"The Bible" therefore does not seem to be the name of an artifact, whether autograph or manuscript or first Bible. The people of Creekside Baptist do not know enough about textual history or translation to identify Bibles on this basis, and they admit too many exemplars into the Bible category to be defining that category in terms of the first Bible they encounter. I turn now to the second interpretation of the Bible-as-name hypothesis, the claim that "the Bible" is the name not of a physical book but of a text.

"The Bible" as Text

The name-of-a-text hypothesis is subtly different from the name-of-an-artifact hypothesis. On the name-of-an-artifact hypothesis, "the Bible" is the name of an exemplar, a particular physical book, and the category Bible (as in "a Bible" and "Bibles") is defined by some regular relation to that exemplar. The category Bible, on this view, is organized around an exemplar, and other books' inclusion in the category "Bible" is derivative. The name-of-a-text hypothesis, in contrast, is an abstract category definition. A book is a Bible if it meets the criterion of having a particular text, and all copies of that text have the same sort of claim to category membership—no one copy defines the category. Thus the objection that there is no particular physical exemplar at the core of the Bible category—the stumbling block of the name-of-an-artifact hypothesis—is avoided by this view.

The notion of "text" used here is nicely captured by the Oxford English Dictionary's primary definition of the word: "The wording of anything written or printed; the structure formed by the words in their order; the very words, phrases, and sentences as written." This definition is biased toward highly literate societies in two ways. The first—the explicit restriction of the notion of text to written works—is normally recognized as a bias. But a second, more subtle, bias is not always identified: the very possibility of two text artifacts, equivalent in their wording, arises only with the advent of advanced print technology. (I say the possibility arises not because the exact replication of a lengthy text from one artifact to another is *absolutely* impossible in the absence of print, but because, even despite scrupulous precautions, it is *nearly* impossible, and does not describe the normal state of affairs except partially in one or two remarkable cases.) If, in the face of actual variation, text artifacts (e.g., manuscripts of the *Iliad*) are regarded as tokens of a type (e.g., the *Iliad*), people are doing something more than simply describing the environment.

Nonetheless, like the name-of-an-artifact hypothesis, the notion that "the Bible" is the name of a text must be examined with respect to several different texts.

1. The text of the autographs. On this view, "the Bible" is the name of the original text, and this text then functions to define the category Bible.
2. The text of one or another English version. On this view, "the Bible" is a particular translation, all copies of which are "Bibles."

I will consider each of these in turn.

TEXT OF THE AUTOGRAPHS. In the earlier consideration of the name-of-autographs hypothesis, I noted that evangelicals relate the authority of the Bible to ancient revelation-events, and that it is very important to them that English Bibles be faithful representations of the texts then revealed. The argument against the name-of-autographs hypothesis was that the people of Creekside Baptist have only vague and uncertain ideas about the autographs, and that these ideas are not rich enough to define the category "Bible" in relation to this exemplar.

Yet it is still possible that evangelicals define Bibles as copies of the autographs' text. Such a definition is compatible with very vague and uncertain ideas about the events of revelation, the autographs, the history of the Bible, or the process of translation. It would require no more than the definition of a text, perhaps only assumed to be the text of the autographs. (Indeed, given that the autographs are lost, it could only be an assumption that a particular text is the autographic text.)

I did find some evidence that the people of Creekside Baptist imagine that a particular original-language text lies behind English translations. During a 9:30 a.m. Sunday school class with thirty-five to forty attendees, volunteers had just finished taking turns reading the text aloud for the class. A woman read John 1:19–27; a man, 1:29–34; and another man, 1:35–51. The discussion began with the Sunday school teacher noting that the woman had read "Bethabara" in 1:28, whereas the NIV has "Bethany." The name of the translation the woman was using was never mentioned, but I could see she was using the MacArthur Study Bible

(MacArthur 1997), which is available in the New King James Version, and the NKJV does indeed read "Bethabara" there. The Sunday school teacher said, "This is a translation issue." I thought this odd, given that names are not usually translated, and quickly consulted the critical apparatus of my *Novum Testamentum Graece* (Nestle et al. 1985), which showed that Bethabara was an old and well-attested reading. I spoke up, "The manuscripts vary here." The teacher then said to the class, "That's why it's good to have Brian in class—he has the original! So it's a translation issue. . . ," and he proceeded to discuss the location of Bethany.

The difference between the NKJV text read aloud and the NIV text on which the teacher had based his preparation had surprised him, and he dismissed the difference as a "translation issue." When I suggested it was due to variation in the textual tradition, he seemed to take my comment as an *elaboration* of what he said rather than as an *alternative* explanation of the difference. This is suggested also by his reference to my Greek New Testament as "the original"—as if there was a single underlying text of which "Bethany" and "Bethabara" were alternate *translations*.

If churchgoers have gotten the impression that a particular text lies behind the different Bible versions, it is probably partly due to the way in which preachers refer to the underlying Hebrew and Greek. The following is drawn from the sermon preached on January 11, 1998, at Creekside Baptist:

> [Mark 1:14–15] says that "after John was put in prison, Jesus went into Galilee and he proclaimed the good news of God."[5] Interesting phrase—"Good news of God"—that is just as ambivalent in English as it is in the original. What does that mean? It, it could mean "Good news originating in God"—"of God" in that way—or it could mean "Good news about God"—"Good news of God." And, in the Greek, it can be either way too. And I choose to think that perhaps here it is both. It is good news that originates in God from God and it's about God as well.

The foregoing comment implies two things of relevance to the hypothesis under consideration. First, reference to "the Greek" is a bit misleading. There are in fact two well-attested Greek texts of the ending of Mark 1:14:

- τὸ εὐαγγέλιον τοῦ θεοῦ ("the good news of God")
- τὸ εὐαγγέλιον τῆς βασιλείας τοῦ θεοῦ ("the good news **of the kingdom** of God")[6]

By "the Greek," the preacher had in mind the text of his United Bible Society (UBS) Greek New Testament, which he recognized as an eclectic text, but which his audience would probably understand as the text of the autographs, as they understood my *Novum Testamentum Graece*. The preacher's passing reference was not quite deceptive, but between his understanding of "the Greek" and his audience lay the entire history of manuscript variation and scholarly reconstruction.

Second, the preacher, when confronted with ambiguity in the English translation (NIV), implied that "the Greek" might resolve the ambiguity. Although in this case it did not, the reasoning in his comment suggests that it might have. "The Greek" was thus assigned a kind of primacy in determining the text's meaning. This was not purely a result of the English text's ambiguity: in other instances the same preacher appealed to "the Greek" over the English translation, as in the following discussion on Romans 12:1–2, from October 18, 1998:

> And Paul [the author of Romans] even says that's "your logical response." There are some translations which say in that verse that it's "your spiritual worship," but really the basic underlying meaning there is it's your logical response to what God's done for you. And then, Paul, and here we get a little Greek lesson which I keep reminding you about, but this is in a tense which speaks about a once-for-all decisive sort of decision, an action. "I beg you, present—once and for all." "Get it settled, do it, present your bodies as living sacrifices."

Here the preacher, faced with slightly different semantics of the Greek and English, assigned to the original language texts a kind of primacy in relation to English language Bibles. (This of course seems quite reasonable when dealing with translations, but only from within a certain epistemology of texts, which should not be taken for granted.)

It appears, therefore, that the people of Creekside Baptist assume that there is a single original-language text underlying the Bibles they use, and that this text has a kind of primacy with respect to English Bibles. The next question is whether this underlying text functions cognitively to define the category "Bible."

I informally tested this with five informants. I held an English Bible in one hand and some other book—my notebook or any other book that was handy—in the other hand and asked if one of these two books was "the Bible." My informants (1) looked at me as if I were a raving lunatic, and (2) pointed to the Bible. I then took an English Bible in each hand and asked whether one of these two books was "the Bible," to which informants invariably replied that they were both Bibles. I said, "No, I mean *the* Bible." All five said, "They're *both* Bibles." I then held a Greek New Testament in one hand and an English Bible in the other and asked if the Greek New Testament was *the* Bible. (I asked them to imagine that the

Greek New Testament was the very one used for the translation in the English Bible.) They always replied that it was "*a* Bible," but were unwilling to call it "*the* Bible." Their responses were the same when an English and an original language text were compared as when two English versions were compared. I only carried this out a few times, in an exploratory fashion, and the results might be variously interpreted, but my impression is that while the Greek text may be preferred in matters of semantics, it is considered no more "the Bible" than the English Bibles. Moreover, they thought the whole line of questioning quite strange, and had difficulty understanding what I was asking—not what one would expect if I was accessing a concept already in place. "The Bible" does not therefore seem to be the name of the autographic text.

TEXT OF AN ENGLISH VERSION. The next hypothesis is that "the Bible" is the name of some English text. The text might be selected in a couple of ways:

- It might be stipulated on doctrinal grounds. "The Bible," on this view, is the name of a particular translation.
- It might be the first Bible text read. Perhaps "the Bible" is taken to be the name of the first text a person hears called "the Bible" and reads. Once again, convergence among individuals' Bible categories would be the result of similarity between first Bibles.

Of these two means of selection, some readers will recognize the first as the condition that seems to obtain among "KJV-only" advocates, those who believe that the King James Version of 1611 is the very word of God and reject all other English translations. I will consider these folks below. First, however, I will examine the name-of-a-version hypothesis in the context of Creekside Baptist Church.

CREEKSIDE BAPTIST CHURCH. Creekside Baptist is a community in which a number of different Bibles are in use. In my survey, I asked attendees how many Bibles they owned, which versions they owned, and which they primarily used.

The people of Creekside Baptist own a lot of Bibles. Preliminary interviews suggested that, for the determination of effective access to Bibles, the most natural unit of Bible ownership was the household rather than the individual, inasmuch as members of a household readily made use of each others' Bibles. The survey question thus asked how many Bibles people had in their household, and respondents wrote in their answers. While most people gave specific numbers, a few wrote in verbal quantifiers. "A lot" was coded as ten; "several," as four. The results were as follows:

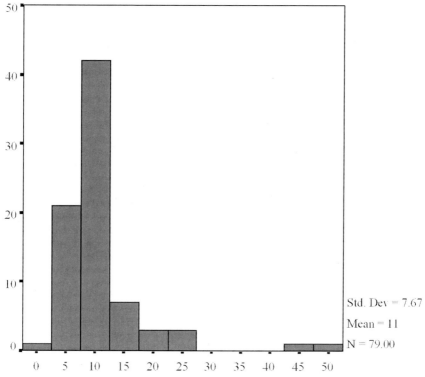

Figure 2.2. Number of Bibles per Household at Creekside Baptist

The numbers given here, while accurately representing survey answers, must be regarded as only approximate. It was difficult for people to count, from memory, the number of Bibles in their households. The number ten, either alone or as part of a range (e.g., "ten or more," "ten to twelve") figures in twenty-four responses, strongly suggesting that people were rounding off their estimates. On the other hand, it is clear that the average number of Bibles per household must be large. Those people who had between one and four Bibles in their households usually gave specific numbers, suggesting that they were counting rather than estimating. These numbers may therefore be regarded as more accurate than the larger ones. Conversely, however, there was a tendency—apparent from subsequent interviews—for people to overlook infrequently used Bibles: one man, who initially reported owning four Bibles, e-mailed me later that day saying that when he went home and counted, he had seventeen!

My initial impulse was to discard reports of forty-five and fifty Bibles, on the assumption that such answers were forms of noncooperation with the survey. Yet subsequent interviews suggested that such figures were not unreasonable for those

Table 2.2.   Bible Ownership at Creekside Baptist

Version	Number of Respondents Claiming to Own Version
The New International Version	76
The King James Version	63
The Living Bible	45
The New American Standard	43
The Revised Standard Version	29
The New King James Version	27
The New Revised Standard Version	23
The New Living Translation	15
The Amplified Bible	14
The Contemporary English Version	14
The Message	13
The Good News Bible	7
J. B. Phillips' New Testament	4
The New English Version	3
The Discovery Bible	2
The Revised English Version	2
William Barclay's New Testament	2
The 20th Century Version	1
The Geneva Bible	1
The Revised New English Bible	1
The Revised Webster's Translation	1
The Word	1
Young's Literal Translation	1

who stockpile cheap Bibles for evangelistic distribution. One man told me that he and his wife would periodically purchase cases of Bibles from the International Bible Society to have on hand for the purpose of distributing to interested friends and acquaintances. It is therefore quite possible that these figures are accurate, if rounded. The central tendency of the responses therefore remains: the people of Creekside Baptist Church have a lot of Bibles.

More importantly, for consideration of the name-of-an-English-version hypothesis, they have a lot of *different* Bibles. Seventy-nine people indicated which versions of the Bible they currently own or have owned.

Although the New International Version is far and away the most popular version at Creekside Baptist—in a separate item fully 75 percent of respondents reported that it was the primary version they used—most of the people had other versions that they occasionally read.

In interviews I inquired about how these different versions were used. Some people had different versions in different places in their home or workplace, and read indifferently from whichever was convenient. Others kept several versions together and, although primarily using one, occasionally consulted the others. They told me that they sometimes would consult several versions in order to "get a different perspective" or to "see it put another way." The following excerpt is from an interview with a man who occasionally used a variety of different versions and clearly enjoyed comparing them.

> SCOTT: I have several Bibles and I have like a bookshelf, like a little section in that room [his reading room] where I keep the Bibles I'm reading. And usually I'll read a paraphrase like *The Message*. I like *The Message* because it makes me think in a new way about things. I don't always agree with his interpretations and his paraphrase, but. . . . And then I probably use the NIV more than any [other] one, and I like the RSV too, not the new ones but the older ones. . . . I have a Jerusalem Bible, it's got kind of a Catholic slant to it, and then I bought a long time ago a quadraphonic New Testament, it's got four versions together. . . .
>
> BRIAN: A parallel Bible?
>
> SCOTT: Yes, and that's fun to kind of see . . . the Amplified, the New English, the RSV, and I think the other one's a Living Bible, all right together.

Many of the adults with whom I talked had used several different Bible versions over their life spans, such that they had memorized passages from the King James Version, read from the Revised Standard Version as young adults, and now used the New International Version.

A plurality of versions in use does not necessarily count against the name-of-a-version hypothesis, because one might imagine that while a particular version defines "the Bible," interested readers consult other versions as commentaries. On this view, the NIV, for instance, might really be "the Bible," but a person might have an NRSV to consult on difficult passages. The NRSV, in this case, would be considered a commentary, not a Bible.

Yet this sort of ranking of versions is quite alien to normal practice at Creekside Baptist. Indeed, versional differences are practically celebrated, even in the most formal of all church contexts, the Sunday morning service.

Liturgical Bible reading at Creekside Baptist is usually carried out by regular attendees rather than church officials. Readers are typically contacted a week or so in advance of the service in which they are asked to read. The pastor asks them if they would be willing to read a particular passage. The reading is performed, in the order of service, shortly before the sermon. The reader walks from a pew to the front, and often begins with an introductory formula—most commonly, "Hear the word of the Lord"—and sometimes an identification of the passage to be read. The reader then reads the Bible passage while many in the audience follow along in their own Bibles, simultaneously listening and reading. The reading often concludes with "This has been the word of the Lord" or some similar phrase.

In interviews, I asked several people who had done the liturgical scripture reading about their preparation for reading. Their preparation ranged from merely reading over the passage ahead of time to a careful comparison of different versions and different intonations in reading the text. Some selected the NIV (used by the pastor) or a similar version, so as to provide listeners with the text to be preached upon. Others, focusing more on the impact of the reading itself, chose freer translations or even paraphrases. The purpose of choosing such translations was to enable the audience to hear the familiar text "in a new way," to be jarred into seeing it "from a different perspective."

To see how significant this impulse was for the practice of the church, I examined the liturgical Bible reading during forty-nine Sunday morning services in 1998. Of the fifty-seven liturgical scripture reading events in these services, forty-two were carried out by lay readers. In one instance, the same man read twice during the same service, and inasmuch as these two instances amount to a single choice of version, I have counted them together, reducing the total to forty-one. Given that the NIV is the preferred Bible of 75 percent of the congregation, I would expect this version to be selected at least 75 percent of the time. Yet the NIV was used only 65 percent of the time, suggesting that at least some of the readers were indeed purposely selecting unusual versions.

This interpretation receives further support from several other considerations. First, some of the people who read from versions other than the NIV customarily used the NIV as their preferred version. Second, four of the readings were taken from Eugene Peterson's *The Message* (1995), a paraphrase that has become popular for its restatement of biblical ideas in modern terms—a particularly effective way of putting a passage in a new light. Third, both the NIV and other versions were sometimes introduced with formulas describing the text as "the word of the Lord" or "God's word." Finally, this conscious eclecticism is manifest also in Sunday school practices, where different translations of a difficult passage are sometimes explicitly compared. Taken together, these considerations strongly suggest that no particular English version defines the Bible at Creekside Baptist Church.

While use of multiple versions is common among American evangelicals, there are groups that use only a single English translation. In some places, this is simply a matter of preference, but in other churches the exclusive use of the KJV is actually a matter of doctrine. In institutions where the KJV is used exclusively and other versions are actively rejected, the name-of-an-English-version hypothesis might fare better than it does at Creekside Baptist, and so the KJV-only advocates merit special consideration in this regard.

KJV-ONLY. The KJV-only debate traces its origin to the publication of the Revised Version of 1881 and its adoption of the Greek New Testament of Westcott and Hort. Westcott and Hort's new critical text marked the advent of modern textual criticism, and was perceived by some as a radical departure from the traditional New Testament reflected in the KJV of 1611. Most of the differences were small, but they were enough to arouse the ire of the influential John Burgon, dean of Chichester, who wrote a number of vitriolic tirades against the "new" Bible (Burgon 1990). Burgon's central contentions were that the Majority text (the Greek text underlying the KJV New Testament) providentially preserved that of the autographs (the use of the Masoretic text for the Old Testament was then regarded as secure), and that the King James Version was the best translation available of that text.

The debate has been renewed in recent years both in the form of a defense of the Majority text (for theoretical justification see Hodges 1968 and Pickering 1981; for a critical edition see Hodges and Farstad 1985; for reviews and critiques see Fee 1978 and Wallace 1994) and as an attack on the spate of new translations and revisions that have appeared in the last few decades, most notably the NIV. Criticism of new Bibles has focused on allegedly heretical "changes to the Bible." Among the most vocal "defenders" of the KJV have been David Fuller (1975), Edward Hills (1984 [1956]), Gail Riplinger (1993; 1994) and Peter Ruckman (1964; 1983; 1988; 1990).

One of the central rhetorical devices of KJV-only advocates is to compare the text of the new Bibles with that of the KJV. The central argument of these works is to suggest that the changes are concessions to various heresies, secularism, or New Age religion. The following is taken from Gail Riplinger's *New Age Bible Versions* (1993, 56–57), one of the more influential KJV-only books: "Perhaps the most shocking discovery of my research was the admission by the New Age movement and esoteric community that there is, in fact, an occult version of the "Our Father" and it has found its way into Luke 11:2 in the new versions."

Riplinger then provides a comparison of Luke 11:2–4:

Table 2.3. Gail Riplinger's Comparison of Luke 11:2–4 in the KJV and Modern Bible Versions

KJV	NIV, NASB, et al.
Our Father **which art in heaven**	Father
Hallowed be thy name	Hallowed be your name
Thy Kingdom come	Your kingdom come
Thy will be done, as in heaven, so on earth	
Give us this day our daily bread	Give us each day our daily bread
And forgive us our sins	Forgive us our sins
For we also forgive everyone that is indebted to us	For we also forgive everyone who sins against us.
And lead us not into temptation	And lead us not into temptation
But deliver us from evil	

After which she comments:

> The bold sections on the left indicate the words and sections which have been re-
> moved from the prayer in all modern versions, such as the NIV, NASB, *Living Bible*,
> NRSV, *Good News for Modern Man*, *New Century Version*, *The New American Bible*, and
> *The New Jerusalem Bible*. They are the very words which distinguish "Our" Father "in
> heaven" who "delivers us from evil" from "your father the devil" [John 8:44], who
> is "the god of . . . this present world."[7]

The structure of her critique is clear: the differences between the KJV and the
modern versions are of a sinister sort.

Initially, this sort of argument seems to suggest that "the Bible" may be simply identified with the KJV, especially since the KJV is being used as the standard for a true Bible. Yet on closer examination, Riplinger's argument does not
support this identification. Note that she does not object to textual differences
per se, such as are evident in virtually every line of the prayer above. Her objection is to textual differences where she thinks she can discern a satanic agenda
to misdirect prayers. The problem with new versions, according to Riplinger, is
that they do not *mean* the same thing as the KJV. Even for Riplinger, "the Bible"
is not defined by the text of the KJV: she argues not against *textual* departure
from the KJV, but against (putative) differences in *meaning*—a point to which I
shall return below.

But if the Bible is not defined by a particular text, still it is thought to have
certain characteristics as a text. However much modern translations are used, the
Bible is expected to sound stately, slightly archaic, with a nice prosody and maybe
even some thee's and thou's. This stereototype is maintained despite the fact that
no modern translation since the Revised Standard Version uses thee's and thou's.
At Creekside Baptist Church, this expectation is maintained partly by recitations
of the Lord's Prayer, as found in Matthew 6.9-13, which most people have memorized. Table 2.4 gives the Lord's prayer, recited in its usual form at the end of
the pastoral prayer on October 4, 1998, in comparison to the King James Version,
the Revised Standard Version, and the version most popular at Creekside Baptist
Church, the New International Version.

The Lord's Prayer as prayed is *least* like the Bible version most people actually read, the NIV. It is closest, textually, to the Revised Standard Version, but
with the longer ending of the King James Version. The Lord's Prayer in the Revised Standard Version is itself minimally changed from the King James Version,
even the use of "thee" being retained here because God is addressed. The King
James Version, with its elegant if archaic language, continues to form the stereotype for the way the Bible sounds. Thus the stereotype of the Bible as an ar-

Table 2.4. Versions of the Lord's Prayer

Prayer	KJV	RSV	NIV
Our Father,	Our father,	Our Father	Our Father
Who art in heaven,	who art in heaven,	who art in heaven,	in heaven,
Hallowed be thy name,	Hallowed be thy name.	Hallowed be thy name.	hallowed be your name,
Thy kingdom come,	Thy kingdom come.	Thy kingdom come.	your kingdom come,
Thy will be done,	Thy will be done	Thy will be done,	your will be done
On earth as it is in heaven,	in earth, as it is in heaven.	On earth as it is in heaven.	on earth as it is in heaven.
Give us this day our daily bread,	Give us this day our daily bread.	Give us this day our daily bread;	Give us today our daily bread.
And forgive us our sins,	And forgive us our debts,	And forgive us our debts,	and forgive us our debts
As we forgive those who sin against us,[1]	as we forgive our debtors.	As we also have forgiven our debtors;	as we also have forgiven our debtors.
And lead us not into temptation,	And lead us not into temptation,	And lead us not into temptation,	And lead us not into temptation,
But deliver us from evil,	but deliver us from evil:	But deliver us from evil.	but deliver us from the evil one.
For thine is the kingdom, and the power, and the glory for ever, Amen.	For thine is the kingdom, and the power, and the glory, for ever. Amen.		

1. This variant, in which "and forgive us our sins as we forgive those who sin against us" replaces "and forgive us our sins as we forgive those who sin against us" (NIV), is customary at Creekside Baptist Church, the result of explicit direction from the pastor. A variant similar to this appears in the NLT—"and forgive us our sins, just as we have forgiven those who have sinned against us"—but the NLT is used seldom if at all at Creekside Baptist Church.

chaic text continues to be propagated despite the modernized language of most contemporary Bibles.

"The Bible" is not a name, or at least not the name *of anything*. It is worth noting that "the Bible" has all the linguistic characteristics of a generic noun: it can take the indefinite article—"a Bible"—and it can take adjectives between the definite article and the noun, as it does in the titles *The Holy Bible, The Amplified Bible,* and *The Good News Bible.* Among evangelicals, "the Bible" is not a proper noun, not a name.

But there is surely something namelike about "the Bible," and it is patent that most Bibles incorporate "the Bible" into their titles. "The Bible" seems rather like a metaname, a naming template that is normally tailored in the course of application (e.g., *The New American Standard Bible, The Amplified Bible*), but which is not obligatory (e.g., *The Word, The Message, My Book—God*). This naming template aids readers in recognizing Bibles by their titles, and helps create the intuition that there really is something called "the Bible."

Category

If "the Bible" is not a name, then a second major hypothesis is that "the Bible" is a category—that is, a group of objects that are treated, in one respect or another, as an equivalence class. If the Bible is a category, then what objects are classified together, on what basis are they so classified, and in what sense are they treated as equivalent?

The set of objects classified as Bibles is, in most instances, quite clear. A list of Bibles would be sizable: I collected advertisements for English language Bibles from 1997–1999, and came up with advertisements for almost two hundred distinct editions. (This number does not include special editions, those from some smaller publishers, those sold only in bulk, or those for institutional use.) Such a list, however, would seriously misrepresent American evangelicals' Bible concept, for they do not memorize a list of all the different books that count as Bibles. Rather, they have heuristics for determining whether a book is a Bible. Whether a book is a Bible is inferred from general principles and specific environmental cues. In an interview, I asked a man how, if I gave him a book and asked him whether it was a Bible, he would go about deciding. He shrugged and said, "Well, I would look at the title. But if it didn't say Bible, I would flip through it and look for things I recognize."

"Like what?" I asked.

"Well, like words at the top of the page . . . the names, or chapter breaks, you know, those headings that tell you what's in the passage," he said, referring to the fact that book and chapter references are placed at the top of the page in most printed Bibles, and that most Bibles also intersperse the text with section headings. (Section headings are usually more frequent than chapter divisions, but do often occur at chapter breaks.) The mere presence of headers and passage summaries would provide a clue that he was looking at a Bible, and would also give him a good idea of its contents.

"And then?" He stared at me for a moment, no doubt trying to comprehend what on earth I might be after in asking about such a bizarre situation. I added, "Suppose there was still reason to doubt it was a Bible."

"I guess if I still couldn't tell I would look up some verses I know, to see what it said. If it was close to what I expected—not exactly, you know—then I would assume it was a Bible."

"And after that, if there was still doubt?"

"I don't know."

Other informants described similar heuristics. In the contemporary United States, it is normally quite clear, on even the most cursory inspection, whether a book is a Bible. Indeed, Bibles are usually highly marked volumes. I had hoped that, once the heuristics were exhausted, informants would finally give a definition of the Bible, such that, in the scenario I posed, they would know decisively whether the book was a Bible. In a sense, they did, but it took me a while to recognize their answer.

If heuristics and publishing conventions work together to delineate the Bible category's extension, then what about its intension? How is this category conceptualized by American evangelicals?

The Bible as Text

In interviews, I inquired systematically whether a Bible might be rendered in various media. A Bible may be printed, read aloud, memorized, or recorded on CD-ROM, but it cannot be danced or shaped out of clay. Could it be a radio transmission traveling through outer space? It could. A video-recorded enactment of the Bible, however, would not be a Bible. Neither would a series of pictures, such as those found in church paintings or stained-glass windows. The Bible is a text: Bibles must be made out of words. These words may be inscribed in any medium or any encoding scheme whatsoever, but it must be *words* that are so encoded.

The specification of the Bible as a text has an important consequence for the way this category is organized. The most obvious way to specify a text is to reproduce it. The Bible might then be represented by its full text, from the first sentence to the last: "In the beginning God created . . . The grace of our Lord Jesus Christ be with you all. Amen." This way of conceptualizing the Bible is, of course, impractical: the Bible is far too lengthy to be memorized entirely, though many people have memorized particular passages and I have heard tales of people committing large sections to memory. Still, it would, in principle, be possible to use sample passages to identify a book as a Bible.

But any definition that turned on the precise wording of a Bible would exclude all but one version, and I showed above that the people of Creekside Baptist Church practically celebrate versional variation.

A paradox therefore arises: American evangelicals conceive of the Bible as a text, but also know that the different Bible texts differ. "The Bible" is a text, but no specific text.

The Bible as Meaning

Texts not only *say* things, but very often also *mean* things, and usually it is the meaning of the Bible that interests evangelicals.

("Meaning" is here understood as a concept in folk hermeneutic theory. Roughly, we use the term "meaning" to describe the set of inferences most regularly and reliably generated by a text. This set of inferences is reified and treated as a property of the text. Because this folk hermeneutic theory provides the terms in which American evangelicals think about the Bible, I will use it here. Below, where a more adequate theory is required, I will introduce some refinements.)

Textual critics are interested in the text per se. They will try to distinguish which of two semantically identical texts is more likely original. Their specialty, however, is arcane and, frankly, boring to most evangelicals. Most evangelicals can understand the need for textual criticism, but only insofar as the meaning of a text is in question. Few are interested in sorting out which of two semantically identical variants is likely to be original. Their interest in texts has to do primarily with their meaning.

It is with respect to their meaning that Bibles are considered alike. The people of Creekside Baptist take the semantic differences between versions to be minimal. The following excerpt is taken from an interview with Tom, a middle-aged business owner from the church. He distinguishes between versions and paraphrases, and while he thinks he can detect the biases in paraphrases, he feels less sure about those in versions.

BRIAN: What do you think are the major differences between Bible versions?

TOM: Well, you don't mean paraphrases do you, or do you?

BRIAN: Let's include paraphrases.

TOM: Paraphrases, I think. Well, take the Living Bible. It's a Baptist Bible, I think. It comes from a very Baptist slant. It emphasizes those things that are Baptist a little more than others. So I think that the paraphrases tend to interject . . . well, first of all they're usually done by a person, Peterson [author of *The Message*, a recent and popular paraphrase], or the guy who did the Living Bible. What's his name? I can't remember. He's a Baptist. No question about it. And Peterson has a certain slant. So I think the main differences. . . . I think they take their theology into their interpretation. All of us do, I think, unless we have . . . what I hope I have . . . is a growing . . . a word people hate anymore . . . but a *tentative* theology that keeps . . . not changing in its central premises, but shifting a little bit as time goes on. I find myself doing that. I probably am frighteningly getting more liberal as I get older. Not liberal in the sense that just throw everything out, but being more graceful and less judging, and not so quick [to] snap to judgment. And sometimes that bothers me because I know that in evangelical circles that's not, for some people, a very acceptable way to be. You should toe the line. But your question about . . . now I don't know, now knowing that the more formal translations are agonized over by many people, I can't see a whole lot of, well word selection, when you get down to a word, you know, why did they do that here in the NIV and this in the RSV, that piques my curiosity, but I couldn't say I see a slant to the RSV that I don't see in the NIV. I'm not that good a scholar to know the difference. But I know how they do it, because I've had professors who've been on the NIV [translation committee]. I mean they just do one section of one book for *years*. They're on this committee evaluating, and I guess I take their word pretty quickly, you know?

Tom does not deny that versions have biases—he thinks that if he were more of a scholar he might be able to detect them—but he feels that the biases are so minor that they do not substantially affect the meaning of the text. Given the denominational diversity of most recent translation committees (which he subsequently mentioned), his assessment is largely correct. He is much less sanguine about paraphrases, though he told me that he often finds Peterson's helpful. The differences between versions are acknowledged, but felt to be relatively inconsequential with respect to the text's meaning.

Evangelicals are quite surprised in those few cases where Bible versions have different meanings. Consider James 4:5. The Greek text underlying this verse is very obscure, and honest translators differ as to what it might mean. Here are readings from two versions represented at Creekside Baptist:

New International Version:
    Or do you think Scripture says without reason that the spirit he caused to live in us envies intensely?

New American Standard Version:
    Or do you think that the Scripture speaks to no purpose: "He jealously desires the Spirit which He has made to dwell in us"?

These versions give two plausible interpretations of the underlying UBS Greek text (ἢ δοκεῖτε ὅτι κενῶς ἡ γραφὴ λέγει, Πρὸς φθόνον ἐπιποθεῖ τὸ πνεῦμα ὃ κατῴκισεν ἐν ἡμῖν); both versions note the other possibility in the margin.

I came across this passage when I had been asked to teach a Sunday school lesson on James 4:1–12. Although I personally enjoy thinking about textual problems of this sort, most evangelical laypeople do not, and the responsible thing to do was to note the problem without drawing undue attention to it. The purpose of the class was to reflect on the meaning of scripture for people's lives, not to worry about unresolved translation problems. However, in talking informally with a friend who attends a different church, I brought it up. My friend is a fundamentalist and a very careful reader. He studied the different renditions for a moment, turned to me and exclaimed, "They contradict each other!" While I do not think he lost any sleep over it, he was surprised and momentarily disturbed. Like most evangelicals, he regards God's word as perfectly accessible through our English versions. The variance, evidence of their imperfection as translations, bothered him a bit.

Textual differences per se do not bother most evangelicals. As noted, the people of Creekside Baptist use them to open interpretive possibilities. Differences of meaning are more disturbing, because they threaten the equivalence of Bibles, the meaning with respect to which all Bibles are regarded as equal.

The category "Bible," then, has a curious structure. Ontologically, Bibles are conceived as texts. But the sense in which they are considered equivalent has to do with their meaning, not with any specific feature of the texts per se.

It might be objected that evangelicals interpret the Bible in various ways, and know that they interpret the Bible in various ways. Differences between individuals' interpretations, however, are not at issue here. In fact, it does not matter in this regard *what* they think the text means. What matters is that each individual regards different Bibles as equivalent with respect to whatever that person thinks of as their contents—that no one thinks his interpretation is an interpretation only of a particular Bible. In fact, the meaning may not be defined at all: merely the presumption of common meaning would suffice. Meaning is the property in respect of which Bibles are grouped as an equivalence class, but the requisite meaning may be nothing more than a cognitive placeholder.

The NIVI Debate

The arguments that developed, among evangelical Christians, around the proposed American edition of the New International Version: Inclusive Language Edition (NIVI) illustrate the critical role of meaning for evangelical judgments about textual equivalence. An uproar erupted in 1997 when *World Magazine* reported, in a cover article entitled "Femme Fatale" (Olasky 1997), that the International Bible Society, which produced the New International Version, and Zondervan Publishers were producing a revision of the NIV in which "man" was replaced by "people" or similar generic terms in those passages where the intent of the text in the original languages is not gender specific (see Carson 1998 for a history of the NIVI debate). The author of the article, Susan Olasky, attributed the not-yet-announced NIVI (she called it the "stealth Bible") to quiet inroads that feminism was making in conservative Christian circles by covering it together with other "feminist" developments, such as churches not only allowing female elders and pastors, but ostracizing those who held to more traditional views. By announcing the proposed NIVI before the translators and publisher and portraying itself as a decrier of moral compromise, *World Magazine* was able to excite fears far beyond what the proposed textual changes might seem to merit in themselves.

Two camps quickly developed as letters to the editor, articles, and press releases flew. In defense of the NIVI was the Committee for Bible Translation (CBT) of the International Bible Society, the group responsible for the NIV. On the attack was a group headed by Wayne Grudem, a professor of biblical and systematic theology at Trinity Evangelical Divinity School and president of the Council on Biblical Manhood and Womanhood, and James Dobson, president of Focus on the Family, an influential Christian educational and political organization. The contention of the CBT was that the proposed NIVI was in fact a superior translation to the NIV, in that it rendered more faithfully the meaning of certain passages. The contention of their critics was that these changes were not justified and that they indicated moral compromise.

The central rhetorical strategy of critics was to compare the text of the NIVI to that of the NIV and to argue that the new text had a different meaning than the old. In a 1997 *World Magazine* article, Grudem offered the following comparisons of the current NIV with the Hodder and Stoughton edition of the NIVI, which was already available in England:

TEXT: Genesis 1:26–27

CURRENT NIV: Then God said, "Let us make man in our image. . . ." So God created man in his own image . . . male and female he created them.

INCLUSIVE LANGUAGE NIV: Then God said, "Let us make human beings in our image. . . ." So God created human beings in his own image . . . male and female he created them.

CHANGE IN MEANING: "Man" is the correct translation, because the Hebrew word '-ad-am is also used to refer to man in distinction from woman (Genesis 2:22, 25). An accurate translation should use the word man, which is the name both for males and for the human race. The unity of the race as "man" is also lost, and only diversity as "human beings" is affirmed. Parallel with God's unity and diversity is also lost.

Although Grudem's critique raises interesting issues of linguistic ideology (discussed in part by Carson 1998), Grudem's contention is that the textual changes have undesirable social and theological implications. His rationale is even clearer in his discussion of John 6:44:

TEXT: John 6:44

CURRENT NIV: No one can come to me unless the Father who sent me draws him, and I will raise him up at the last day.

INCLUSIVE LANGUAGE NIV: No one can come to me unless the Father who sent me draws them, and I will raise them up at the last day.

CHANGE IN MEANING: Might easily be understood to support the neo-orthodox and Arminian view that God chooses and calls groups of people, not individuals; this is done by mistranslating two singular Greek words. Individual assurance of resurrection is also obscured.

In this comparison, the NIVI's rendering is identified with Arminianism and one of the twentieth century's theological movements that most fundamentalists and evangelicals reject: neoorthodoxy.

The NIVI debate is similar to the KJV-only debate, and the form of both debates illustrates the focus on meaning rather than text. Textual changes per se were not at issue. More than one edition of the KJV is currently available, and even if a person set out to use the KJV, he might end up with any one of several texts (White 1995). The objection of KJV-only advocates is not to *textual* differences but to differences in *meaning*. Similarly, the proposed NIVI would have incorporated other changes unrelated to gender, but these were not protested. (In fact the NIV was revised in 1984 without a similar uproar.) The protests over the NIVI focused on those cases where a textual difference could be (more or less plausibly) tied to feminism as a social trend.

But there is an objection here too: neither the KJV-only advocates nor the NIVI critics denied that the translations they were protesting were Bibles. The critics said the Bibles were corrupt, but not that they weren't Bibles at all. This seems to constitute evidence against my contention that the Bible is defined by its meaning: if these new Bibles don't mean the same thing, how can they be Bibles?

Part of the issue here turns on the limitation of the folk hermeneutic notion of meaning I have used in my argument so far. Most of the Bible critics described above argued that new Bibles are corrupt in the nuances of meaning in certain passages, and suggested that these nuances can give rise (or are indicators of) doctrinal or moral compromise. But the Bibles they are criticizing look broadly similar to accepted Bibles: they have the same books, the same reference materials, and the overall text is unmistakably similar.

If, instead of "meaning," one thinks of sets of inferences, the problem is not so acute. When a reader is confronted with a text, a series of inferences are elicited, and these inferences are regarded by the reader as variously warranted by the text (Sperber and Wilson 1995, chapter 4). Some are fairly direct redescriptions of the text; these shade into other thoughts to which the text leads but which may or may not be considered "interpretations" of it in any strong sense. The reader's responsibility for the interpretation grows as its distance from the text increases.

When Bible critics object to nuances of a translation's meaning, they are attributing responsibility to the text and ultimately to the translators. They typically treat one or another existing version, however, as the word of God, and fail to recognize that the versions they accept are also—and in the same sense—the responsibility of translators (on this point see Carson 1979; White 1995; Carson 1998): hence their comparison is between a "true" version, taken to be the word of God, and one or more new versions, taken to be the word of translators. (For this reason too they are often very interested in the biographies and potential heretical leanings or moral shortcomings of the translators whose work they criticize.)

But the similarities between versions are obvious, and, since only the differences can be attributed to translators, the overwhelming majority of the interpretive inferences generated by new versions are the same as those generated by the old. Despite differences in specific texts, the majority of the generated inferences are the same, and so both are classified as Bibles, though not necessarily on a par. "Meaning" remains the key property.

"The Bible," it seems, is a bit like "Little Red Riding Hood," which does not refer to a particular text, but to a set of texts related by story line. Intuitively one feels that there really is a story of Little Red Riding Hood, and that one can pretty much tell whether a particular story is that story, but one cannot easily *define* the story. As Dan Sperber (1996, 33–34) points out, even to *describe* the story one ends up *retelling* it. "The Bible" and "Little Red Riding Hood," then, seem to occupy a kind of middle ground between name (or title) and genre. Both can be names, though as names they are not as informative as titles normally are—they do not, by themselves, individuate a particular text. To specify a particular text, one has to say "Lisa Campbell Ernst's *Little Red Riding Hood*" or *The New International Version* of the Bible. "The Bible" and "Little Red Riding Hood" refer to groups of texts linked by shared story line or meaning.

Synopsis

The various threads of this analysis may now be tied together. American evangelicals' Bible concept seems to involve several elements:

1. A designation—"the Bible"—that can refer to various modern English Bibles. The presentation of these Bibles as "translations" and their common use of "the Bible" as a naming template suggest that they are all "versions" *of the same thing*. But the *same thing* of which they are all putative versions is little understood, in no case fully known, and may never have existed in the form evangelicals imagine.
2. An artifactual stereotype—leather bound, ribbon marker, text layout, etc.—that provides recognition criteria for Bibles. Whether a particular book is a Bible is determined largely by its artifactual properties and the context in which it is encountered. Among these recognition criteria may be counted also the use of "the Bible" in the title and the use of reference points in the text itself.
3. An assumption of textuality: the Bible is expected to be a text. This assumption is supplemented by a stereotype of the text as dignified and archaic.
4. A presumption of common meaning: the various texts called Bibles are expected to have (basically) the same contents and to say (basically) the same thing.

This conceptual structure has a number of very interesting consequences, to which I now turn.

Consequences

I have argued that the Bible concept, as it is found among American evangelicals, has four elements—a designation, an artifactual stereotype, an ontological assumption about textuality, and a presumption of common meaning among exemplars—and that these elements in combination hold the category "Bible" together and underwrite a variety of the inferences and judgments that evangelicals make about Bibles. I conclude by exploring four consequences of this conceptual structure for the way in which evangelical culture is organized. The conceptual structure of "the Bible" has consequences for (1) its role as a conceptual placeholder, (2) the Bible's translatability, (3) the "Bible" category's "leakage" through paraphrases and children's Bibles, and (4) American evangelicals' fluid inference between treatment of actual Bibles and attitude toward the Bible's message.

The Bible as Placeholder

The dual presence of recognition criteria and a definitional criterion has an interesting consequence. The Bible is a text, but which texts count as Bibles, when push comes to shove, depends on their meaning. The recognition criteria that usually suffice to *identify* Bibles do not supply the *definition* of a Bible, and can be set aside in the appropriate circumstances. Thus, although the radio transmission of a Bible has none of the artifactual properties of a Bible, my informants indicated that it was a Bible nonetheless.

But in the contemporary United States, push never comes to shove. Bibles are commercially produced and thus available in highly standardized versions, and it is usually to publishers' advantage to make their Bibles highly recognizable as such. Because of this economic relation, the recognition criteria normally suffice for the identification of Bibles, and "Bible" functions as if it were a well-defined category.

The *definition* of the Bible, then, can be curiously deferred. When my informants had exhausted their heuristics for identifying Bibles, they did not give me a definition of the Bible (as I had hoped they would) because they did not *have* a definition of the Bible. What they had was the notion that there was such a thing as the Bible, recognition criteria for identifying Bibles, and an environment that readily provided them with Bibles.

If ever a situation arose in which they needed to decide whether a text was the Bible, these evangelicals would have ideas about how to go about doing so. They would know it had to be a text. They would know it had to mean the same thing as the Bibles they already have. Given sufficient time and motivation, I think each individual would be able to make that decision to his or her own satisfaction. If it had to be a group decision, quarreling would doubtless ensue, but the quarreling would fall along predictable lines: does this new text *really* mean the same thing as our old ones? The debates would be about the meaning of the text, because, in the end, it is the meaning that counts.

The Bible concept thus functions as a cognitive placeholder. Without knowing recognition criteria mentioned—physical characteristics, a title, versification, section headings, running headers—were elements added, at various points in the Bible's history, to the biblical text proper. Bibles are thus open to a certain degree of redefinition by Bible publishers, so long as the recognition criteria are preserved, and the changes are not too obvious at any one time (or are marketed as improvements in Bible scholarship).

But the suspension of definition in terms of meaning has another consequence as well: it allows the text to serve as a perpetual source of meaning. If Bibles are (or would be, if necessary) defined by their meaning, then the meaning of the Bible would have to be fully known, and interpretation would cease. Yet ongoing interpretation is vital to Biblicism.

Translatability

Defining the Bible in terms of its meaning offers a plausible account of its translatability. Not all texts are considered translatable. The Qur'an, for instance, is officially regarded by Muslims as an untranslatable text: the Qur'an is an essentially Arabic book. One explanation for this untranslatability is that the Qur'an is defined by its text, such that any text that differs from the Arabic Qur'an is, by definition, not a Qur'an. The Bible, in contrast, has been vigorously translated, and is available in more languages than any other book. In many languages it is available in more than one translation, the limiting case no doubt being English: by one count, over 2500 English-language editions of the Bible were published between 1777 and 1957 (Reid et al. 1990). Bible translations—by reputable translators (Thuesen 1999)—are considered Bibles because they are presumed to mean the same thing as the underlying Greek and Hebrew texts. They are presumed to meet the semantic criterion for a book to be a Bible.

Leakage

Definition of the Bible in terms of its meaning may explain also the Bible category's leakage through paraphrases and children's Bibles. Paraphrases and children's Bibles constitute hazy edges of the Bible category. When evangelicals are speaking loosely (that is, normally), they consider paraphrases Bibles: a woman may refer to a paraphrase as her Bible, and paraphrases may even be read aloud in the service. Children's Bibles, too, are considered Bibles, but only for children. They *are* Bibles—when parents give *Bibles* to children, they almost always give them children's Bibles—but they are not on a par with regular Bible translations. Moreover, as Ruth Bottigheimer (1996) notes in her study of children's Bibles in European languages since the invention of the printing press, children's Bibles shade seamlessly into children's Bible storybooks and then into other genres of children's books: children's Bibles are not a distinctive category the way adult Bibles are. This leakage is possible because Bibles are defined in terms of their meaning, and both paraphrases and children's Bibles reproduce, in the main, evangelicals' understanding of the Bible's meaning.

Slippage between Artifactual and Semantic Properties

In reading about Bible use, one often finds remarkable and sometimes bizarre stories about the way some particular individual or some small community handled Bibles. But such stories are scattered and seem not to reflect any coherent tradition. They seem to be individual expressions of an otherwise tacit sense of reverence for material copies of God's word. The Bible's sacredness seems to extend beyond its semantic properties to its artifactual ones.

Modern American evangelicals live in a highly literate, advanced print society, and, in general, view Bibles merely as particular copies of a text. As Protestants, they are deeply iconoclastic, and explicitly reject any notion that a Bible should be an object of worship. There is no room in Protestant theology for fetishism. Officially, Bibles are just copies of a book, albeit an especially important one.

In this respect, evangelical Christianity seems to differ widely from other scriptural traditions, many of which have elaborate rules for the treatment of sacred texts. Indeed, the tendency to elaborate rules for scriptural handling is most developed in the two traditions genetically related to Christianity—Judaism and Islam. If such special handling really is part of a more general phenomenon of scripturalism, then at least the impulse to treat the Bible specially should be present among evangelicals.

I began investigating this in interviews. When asked, "Do you treat your Bible in a special way, different from other books?" evangelicals' answers were almost uniformly negative. The Protestant rejection of fetishism was alive and well. I then tried asking people to envision various scenarios and asked them how they would feel. The scenarios varied, being tailored to each individual. One young man, Fred, kept his Bible on the floor next to his bed, where he could read it before going to sleep. It was a new Bible, and he kept it in its box. Fred also liked to read science fiction novels in bed.

BRIAN: Would it be okay if you just set it on the floor, without putting it in its box?

FRED: Yes. I only keep it in its box because it's new. I used to put my old Bible on the floor.

BRIAN: Okay, let's imagine you're getting into bed and you accidentally step on your Bible. How would you feel about that?

FRED: Oh, I would feel really bad if that happened.

BRIAN: Would you feel guilty?

FRED: Yes, guilty, for sure.

BRIAN: Okay, now let's imagine that you're getting into bed and you accidentally step on one of your novels.

FRED: I've done that before. I don't really care about those.

A number of people expressed sentiments similar to this young man, but the results were mixed: one older man read his Bible in a very special way, always laying it flat on the table, preserving it such that his King James Version, though twenty years old and in regular use, looked nearly new. But then he reminded me that he had been a librarian, and treated all books carefully. And so it went. Some people knew someone who treated the Bible specially: one man told me his mother wouldn't set anything on top of a Bible, but he himself would . . . but not the remote control to his television. A special etiquette surrounds the treatment of books in America, at least in the highly educated community of Creekside Baptist, and even when I could find special treatment of the Bible, it varied a great deal from person to person.

In a subsequent survey in a small fundamentalist church in Texas, I added an item on the special treatment of Bibles. The item, now phrased more specifically and positively than my earlier question, read "Should a copy of the Bible be handled more carefully than other books?" and subjects could check boxes labeled "yes," "no," or "undecided." The results were overwhelming: of forty-one respondents, thirty-five said "yes." This level of agreement was obtained despite the fact that they had not been explicitly taught that Bibles should be specially handled and despite the fact that, theologically, any veneration of objects is anathema. The impulse, then, to treat Bibles specially is there, but undeveloped and highly variable from one person to another.

The analysis offered here may explain this impulse. On the model given above, the dual nature of the Bible—as object on one hand and meaning on the other—turns out to be built into text concepts, such that inference from one sort of property to the other is very fluid. Any time people think of the Bible, they are automatically primed for two kinds of inferences: meaning inferences, such as "Who is the prophet criticizing here?" and object inferences such as "The print is too small." Slippage between these kinds of inferences is fluid for American evangelicals because the concept has both kinds of elements. The physical treatment of Bibles thus tends *automatically* to be interpreted as communication about the Bible's message.

A clarification: the claim here is not that physical treatment of a Bible has a particular meaning. Book burning, for instance, is, in addition to being a mechanism of censorship, a sign of abhorrence, disagreement, and disrespect. But one might imagine that it could mean something else: one might imagine that a tradition might develop whereby old, damaged Bibles, like old U.S. flags, would be ritually burned out of respect. The treatment of a text-artifact might thus be framed in different ways. The claim here is not that the physical treatment of Bibles has a particular meaning, but that such physical treatment will be taken as a metatextual message—a message about the text—performed on the text-artifact, the text's vehicle. There is nothing necessary about this transitivity. The dual nature of the concept—as a set of material objects defined by their common meaning—makes inferences between these aspects automatic.

I suggest that this automaticity gives rise to intuitive norms for treatment of the Bible. The young man who feels guilty for having accidentally stepped on his Bible does so automatically, without having to be taught that stepping on a Bible is a bad thing. Distinctiveness in Bibles' appearance, language, and presentation are felt to reflect on the distinctiveness of the message of the Bible. When individuals treat copies of the Bible specially, it is not usually because they have been taught to do so. The widespread impulse to treat Bibles specially arises in the absence of widespread Bible-handling traditions. The intuition to treat copies of the Bible specially is an intuitive inference facilitated by the dual nature of the Bible concept. The case of Protestant Christianity, then, far from undermining the comparative hypothesis that scriptures will be handled in a special way, provides a model of this impulse in the absence of an explicit tradition of special handling.

So what is "the Bible"? I have argued that "the Bible" is a fourfold concept consisting of a name, an artifactual stereotype, an expectation of textuality, and a presumption of common "meaning." The Bible concept functions as a cognitive placeholder. Without knowing precisely what defines a Bible, people are able to use Bibles. In the next chapter, I examine the most prominent of those uses: interpretation.

Notes

1. The *textus receptus* is not quite identical with the Majority text (Wallace 1994), but is quite close and the two are sometimes equated (Hodges 1968)

2. While the dominance of the *textus receptus* from 1516 to 1881 is universally acknowledged, there were a number of attempts at critical editions of the Greek New Testament prior to Westcott and Hort. Bruce Metzger (1992, 119–121) thus traces the development of textual criticism to the work of Johann Jakob Griesbach (1745–1812), and Kurt Aland and Barbara Aland (1987, 11) attribute the program of overthrowing the *textus receptus* to the classicist Karl Lachmann (1793–1851).

3. Reliance on eclectic ("pieced together," also called "theoretical") texts is the consequence of a long history in which various other ways of deciding on a text were tried. For a readable, if dated, history of this question, see Ernest Colwell (1952) .

4. These are the words as prescribed in the lesson plan. Actual performances varied, of course, but were generally similar.

5. The passage as quoted differs slightly from the actual text, which the pastor had just read aloud: "After John was put in prison, Jesus went into Galilee proclaiming the good news of God. . . ."

6. Bruce Metzger, one of the committee members who developed the Greek text used by the preacher, comments on this passage in his *Textual Commentary on the Greek New Testament* (1994): "The insertion of τῆς βασιλείας was obviously made by copyists in order to bring the unusual Markan phrase into conformity with the much more frequently used expression "the kingdom of God" (cf. ver. 15).

7. Although this last quotation sounds biblical, I have been unable to discover its source even with the aid of computer searches.

Interpretation and Tradition   3

"I NTERPRETATION" is a notoriously problematic term. Evangelicals and their
critics agree that what evangelicals do is *interpret* the Bible, but it seems to me
that they mean rather different things by this: evangelicals mean that they derive their beliefs from the Bible, and that their understandings are rooted in the
authority of God's word; their critics mean that evangelical beliefs have only a distant, selective, or indirect relation to what the Bible says. The present chapter cannot settle this issue, but it will show how each description, in its own way, captures
important features of evangelical Biblicism.

The task of this chapter is to construct an *empirical* model of what evangelical
Christians do when they read the Bible and talk about what it "says" or "means."
This chapter argues the following theses:

1. Evangelicals are inheritors of an *interpretive* tradition, a species of belief-
   tradition in which a set of beliefs is transmitted along with the
   attribution of those beliefs to a text, the Bible. The tradition presents the
   text as an object for hermeneutic activity, but the goal of that
   hermeneutic activity is not so much to establish the meaning of the text
   as to establish transitivity between the text and beliefs. The tradition
   emphasizes the *fact* of connection more than of particular connections.
   And thus a great deal of "what the Bible says" may be transmitted quite
   apart from actual exegesis.
2. Evangelicals are not inheritors of a *hermeneutic* tradition, a socially
   transmitted set of methods for reading the Bible. Evangelicals' and
   fundamentalists' widespread avowal of literalism is not evidence of a
   hermeneutic tradition. Rather, in each generation, the interpretive
   tradition mobilizes hermeneutic imaginations anew.

3. Evangelical Bible reading is driven by a search for relevance, much the way other communication is. However, dual contextualization of the act of Bible reading, use of heuristics for moving beyond the text as given, and the influence of the belief tradition combine to make interpretations of the Bible unlike interpretations of other texts.

4. The interpretive tradition is perennially caught between the Scylla of interpretive freedom and the Charybdis of irrelevance: too much hermeneutic freedom and the tradition disintegrates, loosing its epistemological appeal; too little interpretive freedom and the Bible becomes merely an irrelevant historical artifact, rather than the ever-living word of God.

This model is intended to displace the understanding of evangelical interpretation that follows from folk hermeneutic theory, the assumption that biblical texts have meanings and that people read the texts to get at those meanings. This model is not exactly wrong—it does capture part of what evangelicals do with the Bible—but it is both incomplete and distorted, in ways this chapter will make clear.

A terminological note: the term *hermeneutics* is used sometimes to refer to the *theory* of interpretation, in contrast to the interpretive *process* (sometimes called *exegesis* [Ramm 1970]); and sometimes to refer to the interpretive process itself (Ricoeur 1991 [1971]; Gadamer 1999 [1975]). In the balance of this chapter I will use the term *hermeneutic* to refer to the process of interpretation, theories of which I call *hermeneutic theories*. I will use the term *interpretation* strictly to refer to ideas about what a text says, whether those ideas result from a direct encounter with that text, with some other text, or with some person.

I begin by examining the context in which evangelical interpretations take place.

Interpretive Tradition

It was a fine spring morning when the 9:30 a.m. Sunday school class, with twelve people present, began its discussion. The previous Sunday the class had watched a video about God's power by the evangelical theologian R. C. Sproul, and this day had in hand an outline of the main points made during the video. The class leader, John, after opening the class with prayer, had described a time when he was caught in an earthquake, and how powerless he had felt as it was going on. Others had then shared similar stories about being just passed over by a tornado, or being at sea during a storm, and how powerless they had felt. Now John was introducing the topic of God's power:

> JOHN: Well, we're going to think about God and *his* power, and we had the example several weeks ago, or in one of the earlier lessons, where Jesus stood up in

a boat, well, the disciples woke him up from a sleep and he stood up in the boat, calmed the storm and the winds, and the men wondered at this with fear, who is this that even the winds and the storms obey him? So we have a God who, who is uh, infinite, and eternal, and unchangeable in his power, who can rule and overrule those forces in nature. But I've got a question, maybe it's a contradiction of infinite: Is God infinite in his power? Jesus tells us in Matthew 19 verse 26, Mark 10:27, Luke 18:27, "for all things are possible with God," and Jesus tells us in Mark 9 verse 23 "all things possible to him that believes." But *are* all things possible with God? Are there things that are—another way to look at it—are there things that are *not* possible with God? Some were mentioned in the tape last week. What are some of those things?

SARAH: He cannot lie.

JOHN: He cannot lie. Have a verse for that?

DOUG: Titus 1:1 or 2. "God who cannot lie."

JOHN: Titus 1:1 or 2. Also we've got Hebrews 6:18, where "God swore by an oath, it's impossible that he should lie." What else is it impossible for God to do? What else is it *not possible* for God to do?

BRENDA: He cannot die.

JOHN: He cannot die. Can you think of a verse there?

DOUG: It's in the outline: 1 Timothy. [Laughter all around.] Are they all going to lie, are they all going to rhyme here lie, die, . . .

JOHN: Well in 1 Timothy 1 verse 17, Paul refers to God as the one who is infinite, eternal, immortal, the one and only true God, that God possesses immortality, he cannot die. What else can God *not* do?

How does it come about that people who claim to believe what the Bible says, and acknowledge that the Bible says "all things are possible for God," would then affirm that *not* all things are possible for God?

So blatant a contradiction was unusual. There were several times, in the course of my fieldwork, when I thought a class interpretation ran counter to the spirit of a passage, but seldom did an interpretation run counter to the very wording of a passage, as here. Nonetheless, the class discussion proceeded smoothly—without the awkward silence that greets a leader's blunder—and most of those present subsequently contributed to the discussion of things impossible for God, each limitation based on one passage or another from the Bible, and in this respect the class *was* typical. So how did it come about that their discussion combined a straightforward contradiction of one biblical passage with the equally straightforward acceptance of others?

The history of this particular interpretation is, in fact, fairly clear: the class had, on the previous Sunday, watched "Does God Have a Withered Arm? (God Is

Omnipotent)" from the popular evangelical theologian R. C. Sproul's video series, *One Holy Passion (The Attributes of God)*. In the video, Sproul had actually said very little about limitations on God's omnipotence:

> Oh, you know, you hear the question all the time when you teach seminary, the student comes up and asks, "Professor, do you believe that God is omnipotent?" "Yes, I believe that God is omnipotent." "Well, can God build a rock so big that he can't move it?" Now you've heard that, right? Can God build a rock so big that he can't move it? Now he's got me on the horns of a dilemma. If I say, "No, God can't build a rock so big that he can't move it," I've said that there's something God can't do. And if I say, "Yes, God can't build a rock so big he can't—er, yes, God can build a rock so big that he can't move it," I still have something God can't do—he can't move the rock. And so the student sits there and says, "I got him." But there *is* a correct answer to that question. The answer to the question is no, God cannot possibly build a rock so big that he couldn't move it, because for God to build a rock so big that he couldn't move it would mean that there would be some point that God had no more power over his creation. Let me say this: the term *omnipotent, omni-potent,* all potent, all-powerful, does not mean literally that God can do anything. The Bible tells us there are certain things that God can't do. He can't die. He can't lie. He can't be God and not be God at the same time and in the same relationship. And contrary to the credulity of certain Christians, God can't make a square circle. Lots of things that God can't do. And one of the things that he can't do is build a rock so big that he suddenly loses his authority and power over it. What *omnipotence* means is that God always has power over everything that he creates, including this rock he wants to build.

The accompanying study guide, which most of the participants had in hand, made a larger point of the limitations on God's omnipotence. It first raised the issue of limitations on God in a quotation from Augustine of Hippo:

> We do not put the life of God and the foreknowledge of God under any necessity when we say that God must live an eternal life and must know all things. Neither do we lessen His power when we say He cannot die or be deceived. We call Him omnipotent because he does whatever He wills to do and suffers nothing that he does not will to suffer. He would not, of course, be omnipotent, if He had to suffer anything against His will. It is precisely because He is omnipotent that for Him some things are impossible.

The study guide emphasized the limitations on God by including the "can God build a rock so large. . ." question as one of three that readers were to answer as they listened to the videotape, and as one of five points for review after the videotape was finished. It also asked readers to look up the limitations on God's power found in Hebrews 6:18 and James 1:13–17 and suggested for discussion the series of questions—"What are some things God cannot do? Why can't he? What in his character prevents these activities?"—a version of which was taken up by the Sunday school class.

Stephen Charnock's book, *The Existence and Attributes of God* (2002 [1853]), although not mentioned in the video, was quoted twice in the study guide and listed as a reference for further reading. John, the Sunday school leader, did in fact read Charnock's "Discourse X" and reproduced part of it in a handout he began distributing as he ended the class with a lengthy quotation:

> In the outline, one of the suggested readings that accompany this chapter is "Discourse X" from Charnock, on the attributes of God, this one dealing with the power of God. And the verse that [Charnock] uses to introduce this topic [is], "Lo! These are parts of his ways: but how little a portion is heard of him? But the thunder of his power who can understand [Job 26:14]?" And so Charnock defines God's power this way: "The power of God is that ability and strength, whereby he can bring to pass whatsoever he pleases, whatsoever his infinite wisdom can direct, and whatsoever the infinite purity of his will can resolve."
>
> And so the very things that we were mentioning here, he summarizes the same way. There are certain things that cannot be. And he [has] . . . a nice way of introducing it, "It's granted that some things God cannot do, or rather as Aquinas and others, it is better to say such things cannot be done than to say God cannot do them, to remove all kind of imputation of weakness on God, because the reason of the impossibility of these things is in the nature of the things themselves." So here we go.
>
> "Some things are impossible in their own nature." Some things are contradictory: vice and virtue, light and darkness, life and death, can't be the same things. They have to be opposite: for God to make this contradiction true is to make himself false. And my understanding . . . is that, you know, how opposite this is of the mindset behind some Eastern religions that yes, you can have light and darkness, vice and virtue be the same, on a continuum, not poles apart, but more a circular type of thing. Anyway, certain things, we say, they are impossible in their nature. They can't both be true at the same time.
>
> "Some things are impossible to the nature and being, being of God." Such as, God cannot die. 1 Timothy 6:16 also is there.
>
> "Some things are impossible to the glorious perfections of God." He can't do anything unbecoming of his holiness and goodness; anything unworthy of himself, or against the perfections of his nature. So, he cannot lie, he cannot sin, he cannot deny himself. The second or third line there in item three: "As he doth actually do whatsoever He doth actually will, so it's possible for Him to do whatsoever it is possible for Him to will. He doth whatsoever He will, and can do whatsoever He can will; but He cannot do what He cannot will; He cannot will any unrighteous thing, and therefore cannot do any unrighteous thing."
>
> And then finally, and one we can take great comfort in: "Some things are impossible to be done, because of God's ordination. Some things are impossible, not

in their own nature, but in regard of the determined will of God." And as you flip the page, the second line, "Though it was possible that the cup should pass from our blessed Savior,"—that's where Jesus was praying in Matthew 26, Mark 14, "If possible let this cup pass." Well it *was* possible that "the cup should pass from our blessed Savior," that is, possible in its own nature, yet it was *not* possible in regard to the determination of God's will, since he had both decreed and published his will to redeem man by the passion and blood of his Son. These things God, by his absolute power, might have done; but upon the account of his decree, they were impossible, because it is repugnant to the nature of God to be mutable. . . .

So the interpretation that God's power is limited is a traditional one, in the sense of being handed on through church doctrine, and, as presented here, has an explicit genealogy extending back from John, through R. C. Sproul to Stephen Charnock (1628–1680 AD), Thomas Aquinas (1226–1274 AD), and Augustine of Hippo (354–430 AD).

This history illuminates a central dynamic of evangelical Biblicism: the structure of evangelicalism as an interpretive tradition. The quotation from Augustine is taken from his *City of God*, volume 10, in which Augustine is discussing the freedom of the will, arguing that just as God's omniscience and foreknowledge, being necessary to his nature, cannot therefore be said to limit him, so the human freedom to will is necessary to the nature of willing itself. God's omnipotence and foreknowledge are mentioned as an illustration of how essential attributes cannot be said to put someone under necessity. Augustine's argument is philosophical rather than interpretive: he cites no scriptures in the entire chapter, preferring rather to argue on the basis of reason alone. He gives no indication of regarding the proposition "some things are impossible for [God]" as an *interpretation* at all.

By the seventeenth century, however, Protestants were framing the limitations on God's power as interpretations, the Reformation having cast doubt on all other paths to knowledge. Charnock begins his "Discourse X" by quoting Job 26:14 and casts his overall discussion as an exegesis of the chapter in which this verse is found. His ideas about the power of God are framed as an *interpretation* of Job 26. In regard specifically to the limitations on God's omnipotence, Charnock cites Ephesians 1:4–5, I Timothy 6:16, 2 Timothy 2:13, and Hebrews 6:18 (twice).

The Sunday school class replayed, in simplified, dialogical form, this general rhetorical strategy, citing verses from throughout the Bible—Isaiah 40:13–14, I Timothy 1:17, 2 Timothy 2:13, Titus 1:2, Hebrews 6:18—in support of the idea that not all things are possible for God.

Between Augustine and Charnock, a traditional *doctrine* was transformed into a traditional *interpretation*: the idea that God's power has limits came to be regarded as something the Bible says rather than as a proposition to be believed on rational grounds alone.

The transformation from doctrine to interpretation is possible because of the nature of interpretations. The statement "not all things are possible with God" is not *intrinsically* an interpretation. It is a proposition that someone might come to believe in any number of ways, and which someone might believe quite apart from consideration of the Bible. What makes this statement an interpretation is the assumption that it may be derived from verses in the Bible. Its status as an interpretation is part of its cognitive description, not a logical or semantic feature of the proposition itself. The proposition and its status as an interpretation may thus have different histories.

This highlights a distinction between *belief traditions* and *interpretive traditions*. A belief tradition is a tradition in which a community identifies certain propositions as truths to be believed. (Belief traditions typically also include morals, which I aggregate with beliefs here.) An interpretive tradition is a species of belief tradition, a tradition in which a community (1) identifies certain propositions as truths to be believed and (2) justifies those beliefs by reference to a text. In an interpretive tradition, the text is held to be true and authoritative, and beliefs are justified not in terms of their rational or intrinsic truth but in terms of their basis in a text.

In the Sunday school class, participants were given a proposition—"not all things are possible for God"—and the assumption that this proposition was an interpretation of Bible passages. Their task was then to find ways of supporting it, to think of passages that implied that something is not possible for God. This way of setting up the problem was explicit in the discussion:

JOHN: But *are* all things possible with God? Are there things that are—another way to look at it—are there things that are *not* possible with God? Some were mentioned in the tape last week. What are some of those things?

SARAH: He cannot lie.

JOHN: He cannot lie. Have a verse for that?

DOUG: Titus 1:1 or 2. "God who cannot lie."

JOHN: Titus 1:1 or 2. Also we've got Hebrews 6:18, where "God swore by an oath, it's impossible that he should lie." What else is it impossible for God to do? What else is it *not possible* for God to do?

BRENDA: He cannot die.

JOHN: He cannot die. Can you think of a verse there?

DOUG: It's in the outline: 1 Timothy. [Laughter all around.]

When the problem was posed this way, participants had only to draw on their Bible knowledge to come up with verses relevant to the topic at hand. In general, they had little difficulty in coming up with limitations on God's power and one or more citations to support them, despite the fact that no biblical text actually discusses the question.

The insistence on having a verse to support one's claims is critical for identifying this statement as an interpretive tradition as opposed to merely a belief tradition. It is therefore interesting to see what happened when once the request for a verse went unfulfilled.

> JOHN: What other things are not possible for God?
>
> DOUG: The outline says God cannot sin. [Laughter.] Well, I wasn't here last week, so I have to have some help. God cannot sin.
>
> JOHN: Okay. What else? By the way, can you think of a verse for that? Does the outline include a verse?
>
> DOUG: No, it doesn't, but all I can think of is his holiness, that his holiness would not allow him to sin.
>
> JOHN: Yeah, it won't allow iniquity.
>
> DOUG: That's right.
>
> JOHN: Alright. Other thoughts?

Here the limitation was that "God cannot sin." It is curious that John, the leader, initially accepted the answer—perhaps because "God cannot sin" is a truism, or because it was in the study guide—before thinking better of it and asking Doug for a biblical citation. But the study guide does not include a biblical citation on this point, and Doug, who has an impressive knowledge of the Bible, drew a blank as well. So he fell back on God's holiness, an attribute the Bible frequently ascribes to God, and suggested that the inability to sin is part of God's holiness. John then explicated Doug's answer, using a style of language that, as I suggested in chapter 2, often indexes biblical language: "allow" in the older, more formal sense of *accept* followed by a noun (JOHN: "allow iniquity") rather than the more common sense of *permit* followed by a sentence (DOUG: "allow him to sin"), and the archaic "iniquity," a word no longer used except in church hymns and, of course, Bibles. Table 3.1 gives the number of times "iniquity" is used in each of the seven most popular Bibles at Creekside Baptist. The archaic nature of "iniquity" is reflected by the fact that it is used much less in conscientiously modern language versions than in revisions of the King James tradition (NAS, RSV, NKJV, NRSV). In the absence of a direct citation, then, the interpretive nature of "God cannot sin" was indicated semantically by its consonance with the doctrine of God's holiness, and perhaps also indexically by the use of archaic language.

Evangelicals may thus be seen as inheritors of an *interpretive* tradition, a tradition in which beliefs are justified by their textual basis, and they are therefore keen

Table 3.1.   "Iniquity" in Bibles at Creekside Baptist

Version	Occurrences of "Iniquity"
The New International Version	25
The King James Version	334
The Living Bible	6
The New American Standard	256
The Revised Standard Version	220
The New King James Version	294
The New Revised Standard Version	192

to establish some kind of connection between their beliefs and the Bible. Two elements in this model—the role of the text and the nature of the connection—require closer examination.

The Text as Tool

The role of the text in evangelicals' belief tradition becomes especially clear in cases where the text is *re*interpreted. The following is drawn from an adult Sunday school discussion that took place in 1999, with about thirty people present. The class had begun a series of studies in the Epistle to the Ephesians only the week previously, with an introduction to its historical context. The passage under discussion that day was Ephesians 1:3–23, and discussion had gotten as far as verses 11–14 (NIV):

> In [Christ] we were also chosen, having been predestined according to the plan of him who works out everything in conformity with the purpose of his will, in order that we, who were the first to hope in Christ, might be for the praise of his glory. And you also were included in Christ when you heard the word of truth, the gospel of your salvation. Having believed, you were marked in him with a seal, the promised Holy Spirit, who is a deposit guaranteeing our inheritance until the redemption of those who are God's possession—to the praise of his glory.

The topic of discussion was predestination versus free will, one of the theological quandaries familiar (at least generally) to many evangelical Christians. The problem arises from two beliefs widely held by evangelicals: (1) that all individuals are free to choose to believe in Jesus and thus be saved and (2) that some, but not all, individuals are predestined by God for salvation. Ted, the middle-aged Sunday school leader, admitted up front that he did not understand how to resolve the seeming contradiction between free will and predestination, and then tried to focus discussion instead on the practical implications of this passage, but his admission triggered a round of speculation by class members. The speculation was inconclusive, and the class had just started to consider in what way predestination might be "to the praise of his glory," when a young man sitting in the back resumed the previous thread of conversation: "I see here that it says 'might' [verse 12]. That makes it sound like predestination doesn't make us saved, like, maybe it means we *can* be saved, and that's why it says 'might.' Maybe we're predestined, but there's still a choice we have to make."

Apparently, he had reread the passage with a different emphasis, trying out the indicative sense of "might" rather than reading "that we might" as a purpose clause. He was suggesting that if the passage is read in this way, the conflict between predetermination and free will could be resolved, at least in this passage. He implied that the text was ambiguous and that the other reading—the one the rest of the class had not noticed and that he was pointing out—made better theological sense. His use of the text was evidence for his interpretation: "maybe it means we can be saved and that's why it says 'might.'"

The passage is not genuinely ambiguous in this way, and his reading is very awkward even in English. (The underlying Greek—εἰς τὸ εἶναι ἡμᾶς εἰς ἔπαινον δόξης αὐτοῦ—sides decisively with the more natural sense of the English.) But this incident illustrates an important feature of evangelical Bible reading—its use of the text to establish an interpretation.

The role of the text for him, and for others in the class, was as *evidence* for an interpretation. They were not fixated on the text itself; rather, they were using the text teleologically, as a path to something beyond it. The text is a means to some other end, a tool for some epistemological work.

The epistemological work, in this case, was the reconciliation of two doctrines. His rereading of the text was neither random nor part of any systematic exploration of all of a text's possible meanings: like the rest of the class, he was disturbed by a doctrinal conflict, and this young man reread the text in an attempt to solve a doctrinal dilemma. The work being done was epistemological.

The use of a text as a tool for epistemological work ought not to be regarded as self-evident. Not all texts are taken this way: some texts are valued for the efficacy of their performance rather than for the content of what they say (cf. Denny and Taylor 1985, 7–9, on the performative function of scriptures). In addition to the fairly obvious example of amulets, some Buddhist texts, especially mantras, are regarded less as expositions than as verbal tools for the attainment of enlightenment or other effect, and the oral audition and repetition of some Buddhist texts, the Hindu Vedas, and the Muslim Qur'an are regarded as means for the transfer of knowledge even apart from reflection on those texts. Harold Coward (1988, 148) relates a case where a text was memorized *ten years* prior to reflection on its meaning:

Raised within the [Buddhist] tradition, the Rev. Y. Kawamura reports: "My father taught me scripture. I would repeat after him. After ten years he taught me how to read and what it meant. Later on in University I studied these texts." The order indicated has psychological importance. First the oral texts are learned by chanting; then comes the reading of the text, and finally study through rational analysis.

Coward emphasizes the internalization of the sounds of scripture, an emphasis Buddhist scripturalism shares with Vedic and Qur'anic scripturalism, and which is not entirely alien to the Biblicist tradition (Graham 1987).

When scripturalism is examined cross-culturally, Christianity—especially modern Protestant Christianity—begins to appear unusually obsessed with interpreting scripture, and unusually disinterested in other forms of scripturalism. In other major traditions, interpretation is one of the things scripturalists do with texts, but it is not the only thing and often not the primary thing. (Yet it seems never to be completely absent, either [Denny and Taylor 1985].) Evangelicals too do more with the Bible than merely interpret it, but there is no question that interpretation is the main thing they do with the Bible. Let us consider what they are after.

THE ASSUMPTION OF TRANSITIVITY. Underneath hermeneutic activity lies the assumption that there is (or can be) a transitivity from a text to ideas derived from it. Recall this chapter's opening Sunday school discussion, where Titus 1:2 was cited as evidence that God cannot lie.

> JOHN: Are there things that are—another way to look at it—are there things that are *not* possible with God? Some were mentioned in the tape last week. What are some of those things?
>
> SARAH: He cannot lie.
>
> JOHN: He cannot lie. Have a verse for that?
>
> DOUG: Titus 1:1 or 2. "God who cannot lie."

The transitivity presupposed in Doug's answer becomes clear when one compares the following two propositions:

1. Titus 1:2 says "in hope of eternal life which God, who cannot lie, promised before time began."
2. Titus 1:2 says that God cannot lie.

I say there is a transitivity operating here because the proposition embedded in point two, God cannot lie, is attributed to Titus 1:2 in the same way as the representation of the text in point one. Clearly, Titus 1:2 does not say "God cannot lie" in the same sense that it says "in hope of eternal life which God, who cannot lie, promised before time began." (I have thus put point two in the form of an indirect quote.) But "God cannot lie" is attributed to Titus 1:2 in just the same way as if the text of Titus 1:2 were "God cannot lie." The transitivity assumption is reflected in the fact that the *attribution of the text* is also the *attribution of the interpretation*, despite the intervening semantic processing.

In a case like Titus 1:2, this is barely remarkable—worth explicating for the sake of thoroughness perhaps, but bearing the stale aftertaste of scholasticism. Yet the assumption of transitivity is a general one, and interesting because it is necessary for hermeneutic activity and, as I will show later, also a destabilizing factor in interpretive traditions.

The assumption of transitivity makes interpretive traditions possible because it allows propositions to be regarded as interpretations of a text even when they are not identical to the text. As I showed above, propositions like "Not all things are possible with God" or "God cannot lie" are not intrinsically interpretations. They are interpretations because they are cognitively and discursively attributed to a text. But the moment this attribution ceases, these propositions lose their status as interpretations. The maintenance of the attribution is thus what distinguishes hermeneutic activity from reasoning more generally and what distinguishes interpretive traditions from the broader category of belief traditions.

And this raises a critical point: the goal of evangelicals' hermeneutic activity is to establish *transitivity* between the text and the reader's understanding. This is not necessarily identical with *interpretation* in the normal sense of the term. The means of transitivity is indeed sometimes what might be called the text's meaning: I Timothy 1:17 describes God as "immortal" and was used as evidence that "God cannot die"—a definition of "immortal" and thus a semantic representation of the text. But sometimes the object of reading is not what would normally be called the meaning of the text at all. Titus 1:2 (together with Hebrews 6:18) was offered as evidence that "God cannot lie." But "God cannot lie" is not a semantic representation of Titus 1:2. That God cannot lie is presupposed in this text, and therefore regarded as *part* of the meaning of the text, but it is not *the* meaning of the text, and any translation that replaced this verse with "God cannot lie" would be regarded as an inadequate translation. "God cannot lie" is not the *meaning* of the verse in the normal, semantic-equivalence sense of the term. It is an interpretation only in the weaker, broader sense that its justification or warrant—the evidence for it—is drawn from the Bible. Participants in the discussion were picking out Bible passages *relevant* to the question, "what can God not do?" but not necessarily *about* that question. The texts they cited stood in an evidential relation to the proposition "not all things are possible with God" without this statement capturing the meaning of any particular passage.

Table 3.2. The Changing Basis of God's Limited Omnipotence

	Charnock's "Discourse X"	Sproul's Study Guide	Sunday School
Ephesians 1:4–5	X		
1 Timothy 6:16	X		
2 Timothy 2:13	X		X
Hebrews 6:18	X	X	X
James 1:13–17		X	
Isaiah 40:13–14			X
1 Timothy 1:17			X
Titus 1:2			X

No *particular* connection to the text is required—only the general fact of *some* connection. In the discussion of God's limited omnipotence, participants were given an interpretive conclusion, and it was left to them to reinvent the interpretive basis. The shifting basis of this doctrine may be seen historically: while the specific limitations on God's power remained generally constant from Augustine to the present, the particular passages cited in support of the doctrine changed considerably, as shown in table 3.2.

Of the total eight passages cited in support of the limitations on God's power, only one was commonly cited by Charnock, Sproul, and the Sunday school class. In fact, the Sunday school came up with three passages not cited previously by either Sproul or Charnock. Far from merely rehearsing tradition, the Sunday school participants were recalling Bible passages on their own, and finding new ways of interpretively supporting a traditional doctrine. The biblical evidence for limitations on God's power was being partly recalled and partly reinvented that spring morning.

But the biblical basis for beliefs is not always made explicit. An interpretive tradition requires that the *fact* of a connection between the Bible and beliefs be conveyed, but not that any particular connection be maintained. Sometimes, particularly with children, the notion that there is *some* biblical basis for beliefs is conveyed in quite indirect ways.

"BIBLICAL" FOR CHILDREN. The children's Sunday school curriculum at Creekside Baptist is designed to acquaint children with the basic Bible stories that will form the framework of their adult knowledge of the Bible. Children's Sunday school classes, from the age of two, have a Bible story time. Although I observed Sunday school classes for most ages, my description here will focus on the two- and three-year-olds' Sunday school class, which I observed on numerous occasions. The general framework, however, was not greatly different for the four- and five-year-olds' class.

The Sunday school class opens with an initial craft project and free play time. The craft project is one of the class's thematic elements, and functions both to entertain children and to reinforce the lesson for the day.

After about half an hour, the children are called to Bible story time. The teacher sits in a chair in one corner of the room, and the children gather around her on a rug. For young children, the teacher begins with a song in which each child is welcomed to the class by name. For the two's and three's, other songs, to which the children play instruments or move about, follow. These activities sometimes conclude with prayer, but often the teacher moves directly into the Bible story time.

The children usually enjoy Bible story time. The teacher illustrates the stories on a flannel board, introducing each of the characters as she puts them up. Often several flannel board figures will portray the same character doing different things, and some skill is required to put up and remove figures appropriately as the story is told. As the teacher tells the story, she encourages children both to interact with the telling of the story (e.g., "Which one of these [flannel board figures] do you think is Samuel?") and to identify with the characters in it (e.g., "When her boy was very sick, how do you think the Mommy felt? How does your Mommy feel when you are sick?"). Story times are short—usually around ten to fifteen minutes—and the teachers are quite good at keeping the children's attention on most days. Having occasionally taught this class myself, I can attest to the regular teacher's high degree of storytelling skill.

Stories usually end with a bit of theology (e.g., "God created everything") or a moral (e.g., "be kind to others"). This lesson is often summed up in "Bible words," which the children are encouraged to memorize. The Bible words are short sentences, which the children can at least temporarily memorize with ease. In some classes, individual children are given stickers if they would voluntarily repeat the Bible words back to the teacher, although in fact so much help is provided that any attempt to repeat them to the teacher is assuredly rewarded.

The Bible story time is followed by a project involving use of child-safe scissors, crayons, and glue sticks. It usually consists of a scene from the Bible story just told, so as to provide further reinforcement for the story and lesson.

The story time is carefully framed. The stories are not merely taught as stories, but as *Bible stories*—stories that are *from the Bible*. This framing message is communicated in a variety of ways. Sometimes it is explicit, "The Bible says . . . ," but other times it is more subtle. One of the most prevalent signals is for the teacher to hold a Bible on her lap while she teaches the lesson. Seated in a chair, she holds the open Bible on her lap, glancing down occasionally at the lesson plan inside. The teacher then appears, from the children's vantage point, to be intermittently reading the Bible and telling the lesson, and my own children, at any rate, got the message that the story was from the Bible.

This mild deception is intentional: A small tear-out sheet, called a "Bible Tuck-In," is provided in the teacher's manual for this purpose. The curriculum guide says, "With the Bible Tuck-In™ your students will see that your teaching comes directly from the Bible, not a teacher's manual."

This framing message is reinforced by the Bible words. Sometimes a Bible reference is provided (though it is not expected to be memorized) for the Bible words. Since they never indicate from which version of the Bible they are taken, their precise relation to any actual Bible is difficult to ascertain. Thus, in a variety of ways, children are told that their Sunday school stories are in the Bible.

I suspect that what these children learn is that adults' God-talk and the morals adults teach are "in the Bible." The ideas are regarded as true not because they are evidenced from the text (as in adult classes), but because they are adults' ideas. As the children develop a richer understanding of what the adults think, they may well assume that all of the adults' religious views (or, when they reach school age, the adults of their church anyway) are "in the Bible." In this way children may come to associate a whole normative complex of beliefs and morals with the Bible, and to assume that—somehow—the Bible says all those things. Thus the beliefs of the interpretive tradition, and the nonspecific attribution of those beliefs to the Bible, may take root.

To recap this first part of my argument: evangelicals are inheritors of an *interpretive* tradition, a species of belief-tradition in which a set of beliefs is transmitted along with the attribution of those beliefs to a text, the Bible. The tradition presents the text as an object for hermeneutic activity, but the goal of that hermeneutic activity is not so much to establish the meaning of the text as to establish transitivity between the text and beliefs. The tradition emphasizes the *fact* of connection more than of particular connections. And thus a great deal of "what the Bible says" may be transmitted quite apart from actual exegesis.

But of course, evangelicals also read the Bible for themselves, and to that reading I now turn.

A Hermeneutic Tradition?

If the people of Creekside Baptist are recipients of an interpretive tradition, are they also recipients of a *hermeneutic* tradition, a socially transmitted set of special Bible-reading skills?

One might wish to count, as a hermeneutic tradition, the general beliefs that the Bible is the word of God, and that it is important for individuals to read the Bible. The people of Creekside Baptist do regard the Bible as inspired by God and think it is important that individuals regularly study the Bible for themselves. These beliefs entail some hermeneutic consequences, which will be explored in the next section. The question here is whether the people of Creekside Baptist bring to the Bible a special set of socially transmitted hermeneutic principles.

If they do, I saw no evidence of it: although hermeneutic instruction is available in evangelical literature, few people at Creekside Baptist seemed to have availed themselves of it; minimal hermeneutic instruction is given at Creekside Baptist, and I never heard people appeal to hermeneutic principles in their Bible study discussions.

There can be found a number of books at local Christian bookstores on how to interpret the Bible. They are not specialist texts, but guides for people who simply want to read and understand the Bible for themselves. They are highly readable and sometimes preface their instruction with lurid stories of Christians whose lives have gone awry because they misinterpreted some Bible passage. The instruction in such books mainly reflects the Renaissance commitment to reading the Bible as one would any other book, without special hermeneutic procedures such as were formalized in the early and medieval periods.

But, in talking to people at Creekside Baptist, I was not able to find more than a small handful of people who could recall having read this type of book. And those who had read one of these books had done so only after many years of individual Bible reading anyway.

No special training is needed to access the Bible. Especially if using one of the popular modern language versions, any reader can process the biblical text as they would any other. Bible reading requires no special orthography or grammar, and few additions to a common English lexicon. Most Bibles do, however, require some familiarity with their conventions of print. I realized this the first time my daughter Samantha read a Bible aloud. In much the way dictionaries have headers to indicate each page's place in the alphabetic organization, Bibles usually have the book and chapter marked in the heading of the page to indicate each page's place in the book and canon. These correspond to chapter and verse numbers marked throughout the text. She read straight from the top, beginning with the header and including the verse numbers. Bibles often also include cross-references, marginal notes, and explanatory annotations. In general, however, adult readers who have had experience with the formatting conventions of other genres have little difficulty navigating these. Bible reading, then, begins without any special skills beyond those generally involved in reading.

Little explicit hermeneutic instruction was provided at Creekside Baptist. In the time I was there, a short six-week class on Bible reading was also offered by the pastor, but it had to do primarily with special skills for dramatic readings in the church service rather than with private reading and interpretation. No classes covered the history or methodologies of biblical interpretation.

The subject of personal Bible reading was treated in the sermon of September 20, 1998. The pastor had just finished urging on the audience the importance of personal Bible study, and then addressed some of the practical issues of how to do it. His most basic advice was to pick a good, readable translation, to take advantage of the Bible study resources at local Christian bookstores, and to make a habit of reading:

> First of all, obviously, be sure you have a good, easy to understand version for your own study. Preferably you should have a version that's done with multiple scholars rather than one person. Let me explain that a little bit so that I make sure you know what I'm talking about. The NIV, which we often use here, is one of those where there were multiple scholars that worked on it so that you have the advantage of checks and balances. A better illustration: years ago, Living Bible came out. Now, there are many times when Living Bible is a good, worthwhile document to go to. It's a paraphrase and it can expose things but its weakness was that it was basically the work of one person. Within just the recent months, Tyndale House Publishers—the same people that put out Living Bible—have now come out with the New Living Translation and it is the result of the work of quite a number of scholars again. It has the advantage of the checks and balances of multiple scholars. Of the two, if I was going to use it for study purposes, I would certainly get the New Living Translation rather than the Living Bible. It will give you the better assurance that you have something that is as close to accurate as possible. And there is something to be said for having a more recent translation like that because new discoveries are constantly being made which allow scholars to tweak the accuracy of scripture. If you can think for just a minute, I don't know if you've ever played this game but you probably have heard of it, where you sit in a circle and start a secret around the circle and see how it ends up from where it started. I've done that and it can be kind of humorous: you say a sentence and then see where it ends up. Well that theory follows in biblical study. The idea would be that the closer you get back to the place where that sentence started, the more accurate it probably should be. Every time it's passed along there's a chance for inaccuracy to sneak in. And that's why, in doing Bible study, it's really better to get a translation that is most recent so that it has gone back picking up discoveries that weren't available, let's face it, in 1611 when [the] King James [Version] was put together. There was a lot of archeological material that wasn't available to people at that time. A lot that's been discovered, older stuff now that can help bring things into clarity.

> So get a good translation, one that you can follow, one that's easy to read, and then buy it in a form that you can mark up. You can get your fancy Bible to bring to church if you want to impress everyone else but for study purposes get something you can write in and underline and mess with. I would rather go through two or three paperback Bibles in the course of a few years than to have one real nice Bible that I wouldn't dare touch. Use it. You know, when something impresses you, write it in there. That's how you're going to learn, that's how it's going to come alive to you. Don't try to treat it as some sort of holy object that you dare not touch.

Now if it helps, you might also want to get some good study material. There are tons of these kinds of things available. Maybe too many. But all you've got to do is take a trip to a Christian bookstore and you can find a lot of good study material. The only thing I caution is just make sure that whatever you get allows you to do the discovery of truth, and isn't simply a regurgitation of somebody else's studies. I want to be able to dig in and find things myself too; I don't want to always have it just handed to me.

And then I would say establish a patient habit of study; as I've said before, you have a lifetime. Don't worry about what you don't know, work with what you do know. Be patient, but stick with it.

To this he added some more general principles about how to read:

You need to eventually, and somehow, get a feel for the flow of Bible history. Maybe it would be good to find a simple book or Bible survey or a Bible hand-book is what they are sometimes called. Something that you can find out where things fit. If you're going to start reading the book of Joshua, you can go to a Bible handbook and you can look it up and you can get an overview of where it fits to get its context. And it will make all the difference in the world in how you understand the book of Joshua. You'll be able to learn more from it that way.

Also, realize that there are different sorts of literature in scripture. Some of the biggest mistakes have been made when we try to take things out of their context. The Bible is inspired—it is true truth—but you also must realize what it is you are reading. For instance, sometimes you are reading things that are history. And not everything that happened in history should be copied. This is a report of what happened, it doesn't necessarily mean that it was good. Understand that you're reading history when you're reading those parts. There are parts that are poetry, and so when it talks about going to the four corners of the earth, don't come up with the notion that the Bible teaches a square earth or something. That's poetic. Take it for what it is. It's poetic language. Don't try to make it something it isn't. You're dealing with prophecy? You have to understand that prophecy is just riddled with symbolism. You may not understand—I don't understand—all of the symbolism of prophecy. I've never made it a particular area of specialty for me so there's a lot about that that I don't understand. But I know that a lot of it is symbolism and I have to be careful that I don't try to make what was intended to be symbol somehow concrete now. And then there are parts that are theological, are teaching portions. And you need to know which it is you are reading. I think there's been a lot of mistakes made, for instance, by people reading the book of Acts and trying to make theology out of the history of Acts. The book of Acts is a historical book. And we need to get our theology out of the teaching epistles. That's where the theology is. Now we may find it confirmed historically, in the book of Acts, but just be aware of what it is you are reading when you're studying.

I don't know if any of these are getting through to you but keep listening, I'm not done. You ought to tackle major sections or whole books, as opposed to individual verses, at least most of the time. Now I understand that individual verses can sometimes be just exactly what you need. But you want to see how it fits. I think a good example of what can happen if you don't do this is Philippians 4:13. I don't know how many of you have memorized that verse: "I can do all things through Christ who strengthens me." Bet you didn't know—well, maybe you do—but you need to know what the context of that verse is. You might not like it quite as well if you know what the context is. The context is in encouraging people to be generous givers. And in that context of generous giving Paul says "I can do all things through Christ." So you claim that verse, it ups the ante. [Pastor laughs.] But you take these major sections, you work with big bunches of it and see, that way you can learn the context even as you study. Read and reread. Memorize. Do you know that we have a lady at this church, bless her heart, I wish—she's always at the second service, but if you know Gwen Jones. Gwen has committed major portions of scripture to memory in her lifetime. I mean, we're talking entire books of the Bible that she can commit to memory. And even though her eyesight is gone now, she still listens on tape and I still have to be really careful when I preach because she catches me if I miss something. Believe me. You see, scripture is conversation between you and God. And if you ignore scripture, you've ignored one side of the conversation. And I don't think any of us likes one-sided conversations. So you say, "Well I pray." Well, that's one side of the conversation. Have you listened? Have you heard what God has to say? I've mentioned this before, but boy, it just fits, I've got to do it again. When John Stott was here three years ago to preach and we had the privilege of dinner with him afterwards, we asked him about his own devotional life. We were just curious, we got nosy. And he just put it so beautifully, I've never been able to forget it when he talked about this idea of conversation, he said that when he goes to scripture, he listens to what's there, he thinks about what's there, and that's where he starts praying. He starts praying back to God about what he just read. "'Cause," he said, "otherwise I would be rude. God speaks to me, and then if I change the conversation immediately, that's rude." And that has been just so helpful to me, to take scripture and read it with a view to saying, now, how am I going to pray back to God about this? What does he want to say? What do I need to say back to him?

And finally, be willing to file away questions. You're not going to know everything. There is going to be stuff that will come to you, you won't have the slightest idea what's going on. I have that happen too. And I was so encouraged when the dean of the college I attended, Kenneth Concer, who was probably one of the [godliest] scholars I've known in my life, Harvard PhD and the whole ball of wax. But he said to us one day in class, he said: Look, I still have a mental refrigerator where I store things. And he said, when something doesn't make sense and I don't have an answer I just tuck it away in my mental refrigerator. And he said it's amazing over the course of a lifetime how many things can come out of the refrigerator, and then how many things get put in again too. But it's a process. Put some in. Later: ahh, that's what it is. Take it out [laughs]. So don't get thrown by things you don't know, just keep pressing ahead, and letting scripture bleed into your lives.

What guidance is provided here—sensitivity to genre, attention to context—is of a very general sort, of precisely the same kind to be found in hermeneutic books at the local bookstore. While specifically addressed to the Bible, there is no suggestion that these principles are limited to the Bible. Quite the contrary: what the pastor is trying to do is to encourage people to read the Bible exactly the same way they would read other texts, though perhaps with greater regularity.

But does such instruction not *presuppose* that people are reading the Bible differently from other texts? Not necessarily. What it suggests is that churchgoers are sometimes deriving interpretations from the Bible that the pastor regards as misleading or wrong. But this is not necessarily evidence of a special biblical hermeneutic. They might well be reading the Bible in the same way they read textbooks or listen to their friends, but with different consequences because of the special authority of the Bible, the unfamiliarity of its contents, or difficulties in evaluating interpretations.

Finally, it is worth noting that I never heard anyone appeal to hermeneutic principles to settle interpretive disagreements such as sometimes arose in Sunday school classes. If churchgoers were being tutored in special hermeneutic principles for the interpretation of the Bible, it is hard to believe that they would never mention or appeal to them in Bible study discussions.

Therefore, while explicit hermeneutic instruction was available for those who are interested, I found that few people at Creekside Baptist had availed themselves of it, that those who did had already been reading the Bible for many years, and that seldom, if ever, did anyone appeal to hermeneutic principles in Sunday school discussions. If there is an explicit hermeneutic tradition, it is not being passed on at Creekside Baptist.

But what about literalism? Isn't literalism a hermeneutic tradition well known to characterize at least the fundamentalist wing of American Biblicism?

Literalism

Literalism is not a hermeneutic tradition. In this section I argue that literalism is more avowed than practiced, and that the term *literalism* is itself symbolic. By the end of this chapter it will be clear that claims of literalism are motivated precisely by the *denial* of any special biblical hermeneutic, but the burden of the present section is merely to show that claims of literalist interpretation do not amount to a hermeneutic tradition.

Literalism in biblical hermeneutics is often taken to be characteristic not so much of evangelical but of fundamentalist Christianity. Its contemporary American form has been the object of a small body of survey research (cf. Hunter 1981; Ammerman 1982; Jelen 1989; Dixon, Jones, and Lowery 1992; Smith and Emerson 1998), a couple of literature analyses (Bartkowski 1996; Boone 1989), and a recent ethnography by the anthropologist Vincent Crapanzano (2000). This research calls the conventional association between literalism and fundamentalism into question because literalism is not restricted to fundamentalists: religious conservatives in general—fundamentalist, evangelical, and others—affirm that "the Bible was written by Christians who recorded the actual word of God, and all it says should be taken literally, word for word" (Dixon, Jones, and Lowery 1992, 65). Fundamentalists do say they are literalists, but so do many people who do not identify themselves as fundamentalists.

Researchers over the last several decades have observed that even fundamentalists are not consistently literalist in their hermeneutics. Alan Richardson (1963, 309) writes:

> There is even a tendency in certain quarters [of conservative Christianity] to refuse to be pinned down to a literalistic type of exegesis; factual truths may be represented in a symbolic manner. Thus, it is argued, biblical references to the earth as standing on pillars above "the pit" to which the dead go down, or standing beneath the ceiling of heaven above which God and his angels dwell, need not be taken literally; these are only forms of speech, like our everyday references to the sun's "rising" and "setting," and are not to be taken as implying that the Bible upholds a cosmology at variance with modern science. . . . It would seem that many conservatives today are no longer severely literalist in the interpretation of cosmological texts in the Bible, and for that reason they resent the application of the word "literalist" to their type of exegesis; yet it would also seem that as far as historical texts are concerned their interpretation remains undeviatingly literalist.

James Barr (1978, 40):

> What is the point at which the fundamentalist use of the Bible conflicts with the use of it by other people? The "plain man," asked this question, will commonly say that a fundamentalist is a person who "takes the Bible literally." This, however, is far from being a correct or exact description. The point of conflict between fundamentalists and others is not over literality but over inerrancy. Even if fundamentalists sometimes say they take the Bible literally, the facts of fundamentalist interpretation show that this is not so. In order to avoid imputing error to the Bible, fundamentalists twist and turn back and forward between literal and non-literal interpretation.

Noel Coward (1988, 70):

> The fundamentalist approach to the interpretation of the Bible is based on two principles: (a) a very strong emphasis on the inerrancy of the Bible, the absence from it of any sort of error; and (b) a strong hostility to the methods, results, and implications of the modern critical study of the Bible. Of these two, the first, the idea of the inerrancy of the Bible, is the most important for fundamentalist exegesis. Contrary to popular belief, it is not the taking of the Bible literally that is basic to fundamentalists, but that it is interpreted so as to avoid any admission that it contains any kind of error.

Susan Harding (2000, 28) asserts:

> "The interpretive tradition is literalist in the sense that it presumes the Bible to be true and literally God's Word, but the interpretive practices themselves are not simply literalist."

Even fundamentalists are not, in practice, literalists. Yet this contradiction has never been taken seriously, or recognized as an important feature of literalism, worthy of analysis. One might well ask on what grounds these people are said to be literalists at all. If they are not actually literalist in their practice, why is it so commonly said that they are?

The most important reason for calling fundamentalists literalists is that literalism is often explicitly avowed in fundamentalist sermons and literature. Such avowals are so widespread that scholarly treatments of fundamentalists usually assume, rather than seek to demonstrate, that fundamentalists are literalists. This assumption is not exactly wrong—survey data show that many fundamentalists are willing, when asked, to say that the Bible should be interpreted literally—but, in the face of the consistent observation of nonliteralist practice, one might question whether such self-avowals ought to be taken at face value.

Self-avowal thus raises a problem having to do with the definition of literalism: *literalism* is itself a metaphor. Many self-avowed literalists are cautious about using the term. Stephen, a pastor at an Ann Arbor evangelical church other than Creekside Baptist, learned about the limitations of literalism in seminary:

> BRIAN: Do you know of cases where you would say Bible use has kind of gone wrong for someone?
>
> STEPHEN: Yes. And there is always that potential. Always. And what it stems from generally, speaking in my own experience from the last twenty, twenty-five years, is misunderstanding which results in misuse. For example, there are people who, you know, we will advocate a *literal* interpretation of the scriptures, so that, you know, it means what it says, it's as plain as the nose on your face or something, it's what

it says. So I still remember one of my, my New Testament professor trying to explain one day that the word "all" didn't always mean *all*. "Every" doesn't always mean *every*, okay? Working through a concordance, ad infinitum, helping us understand. "Forever" may not always mean *forever*. Okay? Like, "we're going to have this clock forever" or "that's going to happen in this church forever." Well, it won't be forever—eternity—but it will, you know, there's a content there, so whenever people misuse or misunderstand, and one of the big things I try to help people understand is that "literal" doesn't always mean *literal*. And that there are reasons, and part of what we need to understand is the significance and relevance of this. And so a typical example of this is you're sitting in the library one day, studying or working on your dissertation [gestures to me], and you smell smoke. And you glance over here in this utility or maintenance room and you see flames. And what do you do with that? Well, there's clearly a sign right near your little table or study center there that says "Quiet." Now what do you do? Do you violate the law and the rule or not? Well, what is the point of the sign that says "Quiet"? It's to facilitate effective studying for most people. Now personally I don't need quiet. . . . You yell "fire!" And does somebody come along and say "Bad boy! Don't you see the sign?" [laughs]. And sometimes people read the scriptures and they misunderstand and they say "fire" or not, and then somebody says, "You broke the rule." And so there's always been groups like that, and it comes from misunderstanding and misinterpreting, and, you know, so we guise it for some, we guise it with "literal." For example, you know, 2 Timothy 3:16, "All Scripture is inspired by God." Well, what was scripture when that verse was penned? Now that's 2 Timothy. That means that everything from that date, you know, it hadn't been canonized yet. I mean, basically the whole of the New Testament hadn't been canonized yet, so that refers to the Old Testament. Now if you go and you take that *literally*, [it's] a misuse. Just like in Revelation it says the reading of this book [brings a blessing on the reader and hearers (Revelation 1:3)], you know, and we misapply that, you know, and so there's always that kind of potential. And I've seen some, you know, there's some of the whole marriage, marriage–divorce issue that I think is misused. .

BRIAN: Could you develop that a little bit more?

STEPHEN: I'll make a long discussion short, but I think the New Testament says "What *God* has drawn together, let no man separate." Now some people have taken that and made an assumption, that every marriage that has ever been consummated is one that God put together. [Laughs.] I've seen some marriages that I *know* God didn't put together! [Laughing.] I just *know* he wasn't happy about that! [Laughing.] Right? And then somebody comes along and says "I know he's got a drinking problem, and I know he beats her on a regular basis, but 'What God joined together . . . ,' don't mess with it. She's got to stick with him." I think that's an abuse. I don't think every marriage has been joined by God, so whenever we misunderstand something then it has the potential to be misapplied. And so you can make a case from almost [chuckles] every situation you want. It's not a hard thing to do. . . . So discipline with children, you know, "Spare the rod, spoil the child." So don't spare the rod. What kind of rod? Well, the Bible said "rod." What kinds of rods do we have? Steel. [We both laugh.] Yeah. You better not spare the rod. See, it comes from a misunderstanding. You know, one of the abuses I've seen over the years too, Brian, is people want to take proverbs in particular and make them absolutes. A proverb is not an absolute. Now I think the Bible's still authoritative, but this section, this form of literature, is deemed to be, is called Proverbs [laughs]. Okay? Proverbs are general guidelines. And so one of the abuses I've seen is you know "Train up a child in the way he should go [and when he is older he will not depart from it]," and I've seen some fine people beat themselves up and feel guilty because "I didn't train him up in the way he should go because it says when he is older he won't depart from it. But he has departed, so I must have messed up." Instead of realizing that's a general guideline: if you generally do this, this will happen. If you generally work hard, you will prosper. Well here's a guy that worked hard, I mean he's a workaholic, and he's not a millionaire. How come? Because that's a general principle. So, you know, don't abuse the Bible that way, but I have, you know, seen those abuses.

Stephen made several revealing comments on the meaning of "literalism." He stated explicitly, "'literalism' does not always mean *literalism*. And . . . part of what we need to understand is the significance and relevance of this." His example of the person crying "Fire!" was designed to illustrate the limitations of a purely literal approach to the Bible, because such an approach would fail to take into account the full context in which the text appears. Most interestingly, he twice described the word "literalism" as a "guise," by which he seemed to mean that it was a pedagogical tool for helping people to understand the Bible properly. He even left open the possibility that it might be merely a pedagogical tool, as was suggested by his examples—the meaning of "scripture" in 2 Timothy 3:16 and "book" in Revelation 1:3—both illustrating how a modern, *literal* understanding of *scripture* and *book* fails to take into account the historical circumstances of the texts' composition.

He also used the term "literalism" to refer to a variety of different things. He gave three different kinds of examples of what literalism does or does not entail. In his description of one of his seminary classes, he gave examples of how literalism does not necessarily entail that words mean exactly what they say. Moments later, however, he insisted that the words "scripture" and "book" mean *exactly* what they say—when understood in proper historical context. But then he shifted again and, insisting on a fairly close reading of Jesus's statement about divorce, interpreted it in a thoroughly modern context, not taking into account the Jewish understanding of marriage or debates over divorce in terms of which the question was put to Jesus and Jesus's answer was framed. In the few minutes of conversation described here, the exact meaning of words and the necessity of historical context both came and went, all in the name of "literalism."

Stephen was not peculiar in his usage. I was not able to find, among evangelicals, an explicit theory of literalism. It was just not a topic that invited their attention: I never heard it discussed in naturally occurring contexts, and when I asked directly about literalism in interviews, laypeople would just shrug their shoulders or offer halfhearted comments like, "Well, I think the Bible is *true*, I mean that it really happened. . . ." They seemed more committed to the Bible's veracity than to glossing that veracity as *literal*. The pastors I interviewed were more prepared to give examples of literalism and its nuances than to discuss what it actually was and what understandings of language underlay it.

Finally, to verify that there was no consensus about what precisely literalism is, I sent out an inquiry to a Bible translation e-mail discussion list, asking if there were "classic" statements on literalism in translation. "Literalism" has been extensively discussed as a merit of Bible translations, and I hoped that this group of Christian scholars might point me to a widely accepted definition. With characteristic generosity, they gave better answers than I had hoped for. George Goolde, an exegetical consultant for New Tribes Mission, offered the following description (quoted with permission):

> I can't speak for all, but I think I can safely say that "literal" is used in two, slightly different, Bible-related contexts.
>
> In the theological, or hermeneutical (interpretation) context, "literal interpretation" is "normal interpretation." This means that one who follows this school of interpretation (I do and many others on this translation list do) believes that utterances found in the Bible have the same meaning as they would in an other-than-biblical context.
>
> In the translation context, "literal" is often used to refer to formal equivalent, or word-for-word, translation. This is an approach to translation that believes that the translator should attempt to substitute a word in the target language for each word in the source language. The alternative to this approach is "meaning-based translation" which believes that the meaning should be transferred from the source language to the target language, without necessarily retaining the form of the source language. With minor differences, this is sometimes referred to as "dynamic equivalence" as opposed to "formal equivalence."

The same distinction was mentioned by others. Literalism in hermeneutics is therefore understood in a different way than literalism in translation: literalism in hermeneutics has to do with a contextually sensitive preference for the normal or primary meaning of words; literalism in translation has to do with lexical correspondence between source and target texts.

Literalism, then, regularly refers to two recognizably different phenomena, but these are distinguished only by those people who have had particular cause to think systematically about it. Laypeople, who have cause to think of literalism only occasionally, do not seem to distinguish these two types.

Moreover, neither of the phenomena that go under the name of literalism really deserves the name. Strictly speaking, a *literal translation* would be a *transliteration*, a mapping from one *alphabet* to another, and not a translation at all. Bible translators do in fact alternate between translation and transliteration: in the first few chapters of Genesis, the Hebrew word אָדָם is sometimes translated as "man" or "humankind" and sometimes transliterated as a name, "Adam." The first four books of the Bible have titles taken from the Septuagint, but whereas the first three—Genesis, Exodus, and Leviticus—are *transliterated* from Γενεσις, Εξοδος, and Λευιτικον, the fourth, Numbers, is a *translation* of Αριθμοι. Other terms have also been alternately transliterated and translated over the last few centuries. In common parlance, however, a literal translation is a word-for-word translation.

As Stephen noted above, *literalism* in hermeneutics is also something of a misnomer. Evangelicals use *literal* interpretation to mean "normal" interpretation, in contrast to special figurative or rhetorical hermeneutics. There are many biblical passages that they interpret figuratively because there is textual or historical warrant for doing so.

Given this contextual sensitivity, the necessity of reconstructing the text's original context means that what is taken as literal—even among literalists—depends partly on how one has reconstructed that context. The revisability of literal interpretations was apparent in an interview with Ralph, one of the pastors at Creekside Baptist.

BRIAN: Do you consider yourself a literalist?

RALPH: Yeah, I do. I mean I think that virtually everything that is portrayed as literally happening literally did. Now, there are very few things that I don't think literally happened in the Bible, that maybe are portrayed in that way. There's been some debate about whether the magi actually were a group of people that actually came to visit Jesus, or whether it was a story, a kind of midrash, but I think if you look at the form I think it's a literal story that's being portrayed, but if you looked at it and you said, the form really is this kind of form, it's really meant to portray that it's a kind of a fictional event to portray another point, and if that was convincing, I would have no problem saying that that story wasn't a literal story. . . . When you look at Jesus' stories as parables, very few people think that these things literally happened—the sower went out to sow—that Jesus was looking at a literal sower and is portraying the story. He's using an event in that day and age to illustrate something else. Although people would have seen a sewer sewing or they would have seen someone going out and doing something in a wheat field—there's a number of different kinds of parables—but nobody doubts that those aren't literally true in the sense that they actually happened in the way Jesus is saying. And it's very easy to see: it's just like when you say "Once upon a time. . . ," for example; when Jesus begins a parable, you can identify pretty easily that it's not a literal event. There are harder things like the literal historicity of Job. Again, I think it literally happened but nobody really knows when, and nobody really knows in what place even, as far as I can tell. And so there's some debate there, and people of course fall on both sides of that. And by that I mean evangelicals fall on both sides of that. Some believe that it actually happened and some believe that it didn't. And I've met numbers of other evangelicals who have various views of things like Daniel in the lion's den, various views of what happens before Genesis 12 in particular. Once you get to Abraham, people are much less willing, after Genesis 12, to say that those things are somehow made up. They really have a sense that those things are anchored in history. But Genesis 1 through 11 sounds like mythology to people, and I think there's an open discussion there. Included in that is Noah's ark. I think if you look at the story of Noah's ark, it's just not portrayed as mythology, it's portrayed much more, almost down-to-earth I would say, outside of the fact that he builds this vast structure and gathers all these animals together there's interactions in the family structure that sound true to form. But, some people don't believe in a literal Noah's ark and one of the problems for that is the verification that is in our geological phenomena. There's a lot there, there's a lot literally, but for the most part I think the Bible . . . portrays itself as being literal, and that when it's not portraying itself as being literal it's fairly clear, like in the parables of Jesus. So the answer to whether I am a literalist is yes, just I'm literal where the Bible portrays itself as being literal.

Ralph considers himself a literalist, but makes it clear that his literalism depends partly on what biblical scholarship concludes about the meaning of biblical texts in their original contexts. His view of the historicity of the stories of Noah and Job is admittedly tentative. But what he is doing is interpreting the Bible in the same way he would interpret a conversation or another text. He is trying to take it as it seems intended: if as history, then as historical; if as allegory, then as allegorical; if as illustration, then as illustrative. But his interpretation hinges on what seems warranted by the text itself and its (reconstructed) context. Literalism in hermeneutics, then, involves the kind of textual (and contextual) sensitivity used in many other kinds of discourse, and for this reason some fundamentalists and evangelicals gloss *literal* as "normal." But, of course, *literal* does not mean "normal"—the two words are not synonyms.

The multivalence of the term literalism has sometimes infected analyses of the practice of *literalism*, as Kathleen Boone (1989, 45) notes: "[James Barr's analysis (1978)] trades on an equivocation all too common both in fundamentalism itself and in studies of the phenomenon. There are two senses of the word literalism. On the one hand, it can be taken to mean the disallowance of figurative or symbolic interpretation. . . . On the other hand, literal also denotes the empirical or ostensively referential." *Literal* has thus been used to mean "not figurative" and also "real" or "historical," to describe a hermeneutic preference and also beliefs that follow from reading an authoritative text with that preference. Indeed, the network of phenomena associated with literalism can be widened still further, as in Crapanzano's characterization of literalism (2000, 2–3):

> By literalism, I mean, roughly, a style of interpretation that shares the following ten features:
>
> 1. It focuses on the referential or semantic dimension of language—more specifically on the word—rather than on its rhetorical or pragmatic (that is, context relating) dimensions.
> 2. It assumes a simple, unambiguous correlation of word and thing.
> 3. It insists on the single, the essential, the "plain, ordinary, commonsense" meaning of the word.
> 4. It believes that the meaning of a text, at least a sacred or otherwise exceptional text, is ultimately decidable.
> 5. It finds figurative understanding distorting, even corrupting. Or it contains such figuration in special genres, like "poetry" or "parable," which limit its extension.
> 6. It stresses authorial intention—"original intention"—as an indicator of right meaning.
> 7. It views certain texts as fundamental—as grounding meaning.
> 8. Its practitioners are given to quoting or citing such texts on all manner of occasions.
> 9. It gives priority to the written—the text—over the spoken and in the case of sacred texts like the Bible, at times over experience.
> 10. Its proponents argue for the most part that a text must be understood in its own in [sic] terms before it can be applied to a particular situation. In other words, they tend to separate exegesis, interpretation, and application from one another rather than conjoin them in a single, mutually enriching movement.
>
> Of course all these features are not necessarily present in all literalist interpretation. They are united by what the philosopher Ludwig Wittgenstein called family resemblance. They form a constellation rather than a list of essential features shared by all.

Although Crapanzano lumps in with literalism a number of features that I would associate with authority rather than literalism per se, he recognizes in literalism elements of epistemology, hermeneutic preferences, and linguistic ideology. My impression is that all of literalism's meanings—textual sensitivity, dispreference for figurative interpretations, referentialism—run together in fundamentalists' discourse, and that the term has sometimes been adopted for analytic use without sufficient reflection on its presuppositions, its multiple facets, and the political loading it carries.

The very term *literalism*, then, is symbolic. It is not taken literally: "'literal' doesn't always mean literal." It is rather a symbol with one meaning when talking about translation and quite another when talking about hermeneutics. And, even if restricted to a hermeneutic context, the term literalism has a multivalent structure incorporating metacognitive and heuristic aspects. Metacognitively, *literalism* refers to belief in the referential truth of the biblical text: it is not a statement of beliefs, but a statement about what constitutes adequate ground for belief. Heuristically, *literalism* refers to phenomena of two logical types. On one hand, it refers to contextually sensitive recovery of a text's original intent, whether that intent is literally or figuratively expressed by the text. On the other hand, it refers to a selective dispreference for figurative interpretations, even where they might seem warranted.

Literalism, then, is not really a hermeneutic tradition, inasmuch as no single, coherent way of reading is practiced or transmitted. Literalism is rather a multivalent symbol with vague and unsystematic referents. This is not to say that there is no phenomenon of interest here—quite the contrary, I will examine the assumptions that underlie the avowal of literalism below, because they reveal an important way in which interpretive traditions are unstable—but use of this term does not indicate the presence of a hermeneutic tradition.

The absence of a hermeneutic tradition carries a significant implication for the way the interpretive tradition propagates. Given the general principle that doctrines are somehow connected to the Bible, and an absence of formal rules to determine those connections, the interpretive tradition can harness evangelicals' hermeneutic imagination anew in every generation. This, I will argue below, is key to the Bible's ongoing influence.

In denying the presence of a hermeneutic tradition among evangelicals, I hasten to add that it is quite possible for special biblical hermeneutics to be reproduced without constituting a true tradition. Some of the people I talked to admitted, when asked, that they had tried what is sometimes called "Bible dipping," flipping open their Bible randomly and looking for instruction in whatever passage fell open. One woman described it thus: "Sometimes when I'm tired, and I want to read something inspirational, I just open the Bible and begin reading. Sometimes I flip around between chapters a little bit, and just begin reading at random. And sometimes I find peace and satisfaction from what I'm reading and sometimes I don't."

Although many people had engaged in this simple exercise (I did too, as a teenager), the people to whom I talked clearly found it embarrassing—the person just quoted wanted to be sure that she would be quoted anonymously, so that she would not "look like an idiot"—and I never heard specific instances discussed in any kind of group setting, though many people seemed to have heard of the procedure.

Although such practices may go back as far as the medieval period (Metzger 1988), there is no compelling evidence that it is a tradition. A friend of mine, who had grown up Catholic, emphasized that, as a girl, she hit upon that method for herself:

> My parents were pretty devout Catholics who went to church every Sunday, had gone to Catholic schools themselves, etc. They considered it their duty to make sure their kids went to Mass every week and they sent me to Catholic school too. The Bible was not a big part of it though. There was one Bible in our house, a huge thing bound in red leather that my parents had gotten as a wedding gift I think, that they kept their marriage license and our birth certificates in. I don't remember ever seeing my mother open it except to get one of those documents out, and I don't think my father ever touched the thing at all.
>
> Anyway, I went through a brief period of religiosity around late elementary school/junior high where I started saying the rosary every night and doing the stations of the cross. . . .
>
> So anyway, another little ritual I invented was one that I would do at school sometimes when I was upset. I would get terribly emotional and overwrought about problems with friends or boys or whatever, and I would go to the little chapel in my school because it was always empty, cool and quiet, and clean, and I found it extremely comforting and I could be alone there where no one would bother me.
>
> Up at the front of this chapel there was a big pedestal with a big Bible on it, and I got the idea that I could search for an answer to whatever particular problem was bothering me by looking in the Bible. Sort of like a magic 8-ball—you ask it a question, and God will send you an answer. Only the Bible didn't give yes or no answers so I had to be more creative. But anyway, I would go up to the huge Bible and close it so that it was sitting on its spine (it was really heavy!) and then close my eyes and try to open the Bible to any random page and I would put my finger down on the page and then open my eyes, and that was going to be my answer.
>
> I only did it on maybe two or three occasions, and I remember feeling kind of confused and annoyed with God for mocking me because the passages I pointed to appeared at first to have nothing whatsoever to do with my problem. But I would think about it and think about it, and eventually manage to make some long, circuitous connection between them, and then I just felt ecstatic. God had spoken to me, and I had heard it! And now I knew what to do. (The answer was always to be more generous or forgiving or something like that.)
>
> It sounds silly, but the effect was real. I really did feel better. I really did go back and deal with those problems in a better way. I no longer believe there was any

divine intervention going on, but you know what I was basically doing was meditating. I was sitting for a long time in a quiet place reflecting on what was essentially a Zen koan (How does "Make it twenty-four cubits high by eight cubits wide" relate to my best friend saying *she* likes Jeremy when she knows that *I* like Jeremy already?) and so it's not surprising that I would come out of it with an increased sense of peace and well-being.

Bible dipping is afforded simply by the codex design of books, and its rate of reinvention is probably high enough that no tradition need be postulated to account for its recurrence.

In the next section I will examine actual hermeneutic activity, and how special assumptions about the nature of the Bible can give rise to interpretations that would be quite unusual in the absence of those assumptions—that is, for any other text. But first a brief recap of the argument thus far:

1. Evangelicals are inheritors of an interpretive tradition, a species of belief-tradition in which a set of beliefs is transmitted along with the attribution of those beliefs to a text, the Bible. The tradition presents the text as an object for hermeneutic activity, but the goal of that hermeneutic activity is not so much to establish the meaning of the text as to establish transitivity between the text and beliefs. The tradition emphasizes the *fact* of connection more than of particular connections. And thus a great deal of "what the Bible says" may be transmitted quite apart from actual exegesis.

2. Evangelicals are not inheritors of a hermeneutic tradition, a socially transmitted set of methods for reading the Bible. Evangelicals' and fundamentalists' widespread avowal of literalism is not evidence of a hermeneutic tradition. Rather, in each generation, the interpretive tradition mobilizes individuals' hermeneutic imagination anew.

Hermeneutic Activity

The absence of a hermeneutic tradition does not necessarily mean that evangelicals are reading the Bible as they would any other book. In interviews, I asked people whether their Bible reading differed from the other kinds of reading they did, and if so, how. The following is from my interview with Ann, an older woman in the congregation who had attended church her whole life.

> BRIAN: Do the times you sit down and just pick up a Bible and read out of that, do those times differ in some way from the times you're picking up *Cry of the Soul* [a devotional book she had mentioned] and reading out of that? Or is it pretty much the same kind of thing?

ANN: Actually no, it probably is different. It probably is different. When I pick up the Bible and start reading, I'm looking for something specific, I'm looking for God to talk to me. Sometimes I hear it and sometimes I don't. But I think that's kind of my motivation. The other is intellectual curiosity, seeking knowledge in a broader sense.

BRIAN: When you're reading *Cry of the Soul*, are your expectations different?

ANN: Yes, maybe so. Kind of the focus. I tend to read that faster. Like I would read any other book. Not *pondering* as I go.

Other people responded similarly. The following is from a conversation with Greg, a man in his late thirties, who had been attending Creekside Baptist for almost ten years.

BRIAN: Can you describe what you do, what's your procedure. Do you do it in the morning?

GREG: No, I do it at bedtime. I'm not a morning person. I'm lucky if I can drive a car in the morning [laughs].

BRIAN: Okay, so you get into bed, or . . . what?

GREG: Usually, boy, I'll tell you, my routine has gotten sloppier since I got married [laughs]. What I usually do now is I sit down for a Quiet Time about the time my wife is getting ready for bed. I start with some prayer to kind of put my heart and my mind in the right attitude, to kind of get rid of all the distractions, any, especially any sinful or hateful attitudes I've fostered during the day, just to try to put myself in the right frame of mind. I don't spend probably as much time at that as I should, generally no more than a minute, and then I just plunge in and start reading. I mean I read the Bible pretty much cover to cover. I don't jump around looking for opportunities. I think some of that goes back to my desire to take things in context. When I read one chapter I want to know how it's building on the chapter that came before.

BRIAN: Do you prefer to contextualize a book of the Bible in terms of the rest of the Bible, or in terms of that book's historical context, or both, or . . . ?

GREG: Both. I mean, every part of the Bible . . . the whole thing is God's word. It all has to be internally consistent. But yeah, the specific background, the specific audience matter because they can help bring clearer meaning to what you are reading.

BRIAN: Okay, so you pray, now you're reading. How long do you read?

GREG: Fifteen or twenty minutes a night. I think especially because the Bible I'm reading at a deeper level than other casual reading. I mean, really trying to figure out what things say and where they're coming from. I think I would be hard-pressed to keep at that for like a whole hour.

BRIAN: But you do read other things longer, for more than fifteen or twenty minutes at a time [I knew him to be a voracious reader]. . . .

GREG: Oh, yeah, there's other books I can sit down and read for two or three hours at a time, but I'm usually not trying to take them apart the way I do the Bible.

BRIAN: How would you describe your Bible reading? How exactly is it different from this other reading?

GREG: I guess one of the biggest differences is, in my ordinary reading, if there is something I don't follow or doesn't seem to make sense, I'm perfectly willing to say, "Okay, fine" and move on. Whereas with the Bible I don't like settling for that. If something bothers me, if something strikes me as interesting, I may jump around to other parts of the Bible, or I may pull out a set of Bible notes and try to read exactly what is all the meaning behind it. Yeah, most other books I sit down and read with, I just read straight through. Actually, I'm a really anal reader, I guess [laughs], even in a history book if I find something I think is wrong, I'll probably go off and try to settle it in my own mind. But somehow there's a big difference in attitude. With the Bible I know I'm dealing with weighty material. Now, that doesn't mean everything in the Bible is massively important. I've recently been reading Numbers. I don't see much spiritual importance in the census data. . . .

As Ann and Greg report, Bible reading is distinguished from other reading by its daily pattern and the expectation that God might speak to the reader through the text. When evangelicals approach the Bible, they do so with the expectation that God will speak to them, either corporately, as part of the universal church, or individually, in the particular circumstances of their lives. And they expect that God will say things that are important, in one sense or another. The question they ask of the ancient text is not "Does this have anything to do with me?" but rather, "How does this apply to my life?" They take its relevance to their lives for granted. While they may approach it for ritual or even magical reasons, what they make of the text turns on considerations of relevance.

Relevance

Evangelicals' Bible-reading practices may be partly explained by relevance theory, an account of language processing proposed by Dan Sperber and Deirdre Wilson (1995). According to Sperber and Wilson, flexibility in human communication (our ability to understand, in a contextually sensitive way, simultaneous, partly tacit messages in multiple, partially known symbol systems) is made possible by precisely the same processes that make normal cognitive processing flexible. Sperber and Wilson (1995, 260) note that "Human cognition tends to be geared to the maximisation of relevance": people tend to allocate their attention to those trains of thought that they anticipate will produce the most extensive or important information relative to the cost of processing—cognition is geared to get the most informational bang for its energetic buck. Sperber and Wilson (1995, 260)

argue that human communication is founded on this tendency: "Every act of ostensive communication communicates a presumption of its own optimal relevance." They argue that when a speaker produces an utterance (or any other
ostensive, communicative act), he is giving an implicit promise to the recipient
that the message is a relevant one—one worth the effort to process. This promise then provides the recipient with an important key to interpreting the signal so
as to recover the message. This guidance is necessary because signals almost never
encode messages completely: they are better understood as coded bits that are
(the speaker thinks) sufficient guidance for the recipient to form an appropriate
notion of the intended message. The recipient then, on the strength of the
speaker's implicit promise, uses his normal (relevance-guided) cognition to infer
the speaker's intended message. The recipient settles on an interpretation when it
is sufficiently relevant to him and might plausibly be intended by the speaker.
Relevance theory suggests that people will, when interpreting a communicative
signal, try to find the most relevant interpretation within the bounds of what the
signaler might plausibly intend.

The degree of relevance a person expects from an utterance and the ways in
which that relevance might be sought out are strongly affected by the speech register in which the utterance is thought to be. Some speech registers are reserved for
humor, others for business, still others for philosophy. And it is a special register
indeed when you expect God Almighty to speak to you personally through his inspired word. This register is set off from others in a variety of ways—many of my
informants told me that they did their devotional reading at different times,
places, and frequencies than they did their other reading—but all of these features
are subservient to the heightened expectation of relevance. Evangelicals expect the
Bible to be profoundly relevant to them in their individual circumstances. They expect it to say especially important things about their contemporary needs and con-
cerns. As another of my informants told me, in response to the question "Does
your Bible reading differ from other reading you do?":

> Yeah, I read the Bible differently. It's to understand the significance of what it says
> and how it relates to me today. And that's why it's so fascinating, 'cause it's so rel-
> evant, it's just so profoundly relevant, so yeah, I read it differently. I mean I can
> read other stuff about the Bible and learn from it . . . but I take the Bible also as
> authoritative, so I don't take the other stuff as being authoritative.

The Bible need not say something evangelical readers necessarily like, but they believe it should be highly relevant to them, and they try reading it in different ways
to see how it might be.

To this end they are willing to devote quite a lot of energy, in comparison with
other interactions. Like Ann, evangelicals read the Bible meditatively, spending

time sifting through the text for the way in which it might be relevant to them. Greg mentioned his earnestness in researching anything about the Bible that he didn't understand, and contrasted it with his less meticulous approach to histories (and I can vouch for Greg's impressive and exact historical knowledge). The search for relevance, while still limited by energetic considerations, finds those constraints much loosened, and is permitted to explore possible avenues of relevance more freely. One might expect, then, that biblical interpretations would be, in comparison to other kinds of readings, relatively imaginative.

The claim that evangelicals read for relevance receives some support from their devotional habits. In talking with people about their devotional reading habits, I inquired how they decided to stop reading for the day. How did they decide that they had read enough? I found that devotional reading is often brought to a close by mundane external factors such as the clock, or by convenient divisions in the text, but people also stop reading when something strikes them, when they come across something especially meaningful. This latter sort of voluntary, motivated cessation suggests that devotional reading is at least partly a goal-directed process that is terminated when its objective is achieved. Its objective is an interpretation that achieves a high degree of relevance. When you suddenly see the importance of a passage for your life, God has spoken to you.

Close questioning indicated a slight asymmetry in the sort of relevance sought. I posed the following question: "Suppose you set down to read your Bible for fifteen minutes. And you're reading along, and after ten minutes you encounter a verse that strongly convicts you of some sin in your life. Would you stop reading or continue?" Most informants responded that they would stop reading and pray about whatever they had been convicted about. I then posed a variant of the question in which, instead of being convicted of sin, they were strongly reminded of God's love for them. Again, they said they would stop reading. I then asked the convicted-of-sin version again, but this time the conviction came after only three minutes of Bible reading. They seemed less certain of their answers this time, but they generally said they would stop reading and pray. Finally, I posed a version in which they were impressed with God's love, but after only three minutes of reading. All agreed that in this last scenario they would keep reading. This pattern could be understood in several ways, but my sense is that conviction stops reading, even after only three minutes, because it calls for a response. The reader then has "enough to do" and has no need to read further—full relevance has been achieved.

From the perspective of relevance theory, the problem of the Bible's durability, of its continuing ability to hold an audience, changes. The question is no longer how the Bible maintains its relevance: modern evangelicals just assume it is relevant, and read the Bible in ways that deliver the expected relevance. But how do they manage to keep finding relevance in it? I suggest that they do so by framing

Bible reading as a dual-context communication event and by using a suite of hermeneutic tools to move beyond the text as given.

Dual Contexts

Like other English speakers, the people of Creekside Baptist use the term *meaning* for the object of reading, and so I set out to explore what they meant by this. In interviews, I examined people's theory of meaning by inquiring about whether biblical passages might have multiple meanings. I approached the problem this way because I knew that most people thought the answer varied from passage to passage, and I wanted to observe how informants would reason through the question. Their answers were indeed instructive, particularly those of Greg, the history enthusiast, who talked about the different ways a passage might mean something:

BRIAN: Does the Bible have one and only one meaning?

GREG: [Long pause.] No. [Laughs.] I mean it's about one and only one God, and in terms of how he relates to humanity, I think there's only one way and one meaning, but the Bible also includes just lots about people, human feelings. I mean, the Song of Solomon I don't think is, I mean, I know there's been attempts to spiritualize it, to say it's about the [universal] church, but I think it's a love song.

BRIAN: Would you be willing to say it's not about the church?

GREG: [Long pause.] I'm not a scholar but I would say, I don't think it is. I've heard some arguments saying it is, and they seem weak to me.

BRIAN: Does it have one meaning, which some people have got wrong, or does it have two meanings, and some people think it means this, and other people think it means this?

GREG: You know, a lot of things can be used for allegory, other than what they were originally intended. I don't doubt some people may have drawn some meaning related to the church out of it. It's entirely possible. But I think it was written as a love song.

BRIAN: Okay, so you're distinguishing between meaning and intent. So it was intended as a love song, but people may have drawn presumably romantic meaning out of it but also this spiritual allegorical meaning out of it.

GREG: I think so. Now, it wouldn't surprise me that the nature of love could be consistent. I mean, we have a God of love. So, I could easily see where you could draw parallels from romantic love to God's love for us. So that makes good sense. But like I said, I think it was written to be a love song.

BRIAN: Would you say that the people who have drawn meaning from it, who have seen it to be, the people who have found meaning in it as an allegory, are *wrong*? Is that meaning *wrong*?

GREG: It depends on how serious they are about it. No, I mean basic. . . . I think they're wrong, I mean, if they insist that that's what it was meant to be.

BRIAN: Okay, so basically if they turn it into a historical claim, you say they're wrong. If their claim is that that's what it meant, they're wrong.

GREG: Right.

BRIAN: But what if the meaning they draw from it is, this just makes me feel so loved, makes me feel God's love so much. So would that be a meaning?

GREG: Yes, that would be a meaning. I wouldn't argue with that.

BRIAN: And, could that be wrong? Would that be wrong?

GREG: When you're dealing with things on an emotional level, it's hard to quantify. Like I said, it depends on how serious they are about it. If they're going to turn around and say this is absolutely what this book means, then I would challenge them. I would say I don't think that's what it means. You know, maybe some Hebrew scholar can come along and prove me wrong, but I don't think it's meant to apply to that. But at the same time it's great if it helps you in some way to understand God's love.

BRIAN: Could God use it that way?

GREG: Oh, definitely.

BRIAN: So that could be God speaking to them, even if it's not historically right.

GREG: Yeah, I think that's true.

BRIAN: You think that's possible?

GREG: I think that's possible.

Greg determines the text's meaning by reference to its history, its (reconstructed) authorial intent. The Song of Solomon is a love song because it was intended, by its author, at the time of its composition, as a love song. The event of composition fixed its meaning once and for all.

Yet other meanings are possible too, meanings that derive from God's actions through the text in the reader's life. At another point in the interview, he talked about this kind of divine communication through the Bible:

BRIAN: Who is the audience of the Bible? Who is the Bible to?

GREG: The broad answer would just be it's written to God's people. You can narrow that down. The Old Testament was written primarily for Jews, for ancient Israel. The New Testament, the books vary somewhat. Some of them are clearly written more for new Jewish believers, others are written for Gentile believers. Ultimately, the New Testament is written for people who follow Jesus, or wish to follow Jesus. I think it's written in a way that nonbelievers and new believers can find instructive, and it's also written in a way that longtime believers can still draw a lot of meaning out of.

BRIAN: Some people feel that God speaks to them now through the Bible. Other people feel that God spoke in the Bible, and we can try to get that message, but we have to try to reconstruct the people to whom it was given and figure out what it meant to them. And other people seem to have this kind of in-between view that I don't know exactly how to describe. Can you comment on that? I guess I don't have a well enough formulated question here, but. . . .

GREG: Right, right. I may be sort of in between, although I probably side a little bit more with who was it originally written for, what was the original intent. I love history, not just the Bible, I love all kinds of history, so it's very important to me what the context was, what the original meaning was. And that I think is where you find the best interpretation or the best meaning, is to put it in its proper context. Now there have certainly been times when I read the Bible, and I suddenly saw something, and I had—geeze, I wish I could think of a concrete example of this—but there's times I read things that I'm not at all sure I was reading things the way it was meant to be written, but I still was able to take some encouragement from it. I would be very suspicious of someone who tries to draw meaning of something totally out of context. But I guess it's still possible to get meaning without knowing all the background.

BRIAN: I hope so.

GREG: [Laughs.] Yeah, since we're often not given all the background. It is a hard question.

BRIAN: Have you ever felt that God spoke to you, directly, through the Bible, personally?

GREG: Right, right. No, I understand. Not that I can think of. I mean I've certainly had events in my day-to-day life where scripture was suddenly brought to mind that answered a question on how I should respond to something. I feel that's God or the Holy Spirit, however you want to phrase it, working in my heart. Of course a lot of people would also say it's just because I've read the Bible a lot, it's what I'm thinking, but . . .

BRIAN: Would you thank God for that?

GREG: Oh yeah.

BRIAN: Okay, so you credit that to God. I mean no matter what other people say, *you* credit it to God.

GREG: Yes. Whether it's because he actually brought the verse to mind, or he gave me the discipline in the first place to read it, either way I credit that to God.

BRIAN: And just it coming to you, at that moment, helps. . . .

GREG: You know, I *do* think that's from the Holy Spirit. 'Cause there's any number of times you get into a really good argument and you can't come up with that best answer you need at the time, but when it comes to spiritual issues, I find usually the biblical or godly answer does present itself at the opportune time.

Greg's comments reveal a fascinating model of Bible reading. Greg treats Bible reading as part of a communicative process, but a communicative process with a double structure. On one hand, he maintains that the Bible is written by a human author, and that the human author's intent fixed the Bible's meaning once and for all. That meaning is intended, generally, for God's people: the Old Testament for ancient Israelites and the New Testament for Christians, whether Jewish or Gentile. One the other hand, he also maintains that God, in the person of the Holy Spirit, may speak to an individual, in the particular circumstances of that individual's life, through some passage from the Bible.

The incessant complaint of scholars—Christian and other—is that laypeople are always taking passages "out of context." What they mean is that laypeople develop understandings of particular passages that do not make sense, or are very improbable, in those passages' historical contexts. But the criticism is misplaced, inasmuch as the critic is recognizing only one of two simultaneous frames for Bible reading. On the model held by Greg and other evangelicals, each text has—or can have, anyway—both historical and devotional contexts. And when they are actually reading, both contexts are available for interpreting a passage.

The devotional context has special hermeneutic implications. The relevance of the ancient text is not limited to its most general messages, such as "God loves humanity." Relevance may also be found in the timing of an individual's encounter with a particular text: if a reader comes across Romans 8:28, "For all things work together for the good of those that love [God]," he or she may feel that God is bringing this verse to my attention at this time to remind me of his love in the face of an unexpected layoff or the death of a child. Framed devotionally, the *timing* of the words can be significant—even though the words have been around for two millennia.

Devotional framing sheds light on Bible dipping. The behavior of randomly opening a Bible and pointing to a verse might be interpreted in several ways: (1) it might be one way of beginning systematic Bible reading (after all, one has to start somewhere); (2) it might be a way of randomly accessing the Bible's general historical messages; or (3) it might be a way of intentionally creating a context in which any relevance the passage might have can be attributed to God speaking to the reader as an individual, at that particular moment. While I have heard of instances of all three motivations, my impression is that the third is the most common, as Bible dipping is often carried out in addition to systematic reading, and people often look not for a passage's historical significance but for ways in which the passage is relevant to their particular circumstances. This path to relevance is opened by devotional framing, the expectation that God continues to speak through his word.

Beyond the Text

In the quest for relevance, readers are not strictly limited to the text as given. Rather, evidence suggests that evangelicals take the biblical text, as given in one of the versions, and try out different permutations to see if they can establish transitivity between the text and their lives. Along the way some aspects of the verbal pattern are dropped out, and other elements—e.g., story lines, motivations, inferences—are filled in.

On Sperber and Wilson's model, some permutation of verbal stimuli is always necessary, if only to transform a text into something more cognitively useful. The amount of transformation that is required depends on what a person is reading, and on the degree to which he expects it to be relevant to his life. For Bible reading, genealogies are probably the limiting case: evangelicals usually read them quickly and usually take them at face value—*x begat y*—because they expect them to be only indirectly relevant to their lives. To note that a genealogy links King David to Jesus (e.g., Matthew 1) is merely to note that Jesus is the rightful and true King of Israel in the Davidic line: a nice little tidbit for worship perhaps, but not really all that interesting to most Christians today. At the other extreme stands the Sermon on the Mount (Matthew 5–7), which was studied at Creekside Baptist three times in 2000, in three different adult Sunday school classes. While this frequency of study is somewhat unusual, there is no question that the Sermon on the Mount is one of the most widely studied passages today (it was studied again at Creekside Baptist in 2003). It is mined for all kinds of moral and spiritual instruction. Its hyperbolic language invites the reader to look beyond its face value, and evangelicals do, though somewhat selectively.

There are many different ways in which the biblical text might be transformed. For the sake of illustration, I will examine several as they occurred in a particular sermon.

Part of the genius of a good preacher is to figure out a way to mine new insight from a seemingly mundane passage. The lead pastor of Creekside Baptist, Ted Williams, was skillful at this, as may be seen in his sermon of December 20, 1998. He began:

> Well, believe it or not, Christmas is a tough time for being a pastor, because it's hard to know what to say that's new. This is one story pretty much everybody knows. And of course there's the temptation that we do succumb to kind of a sentimental approach, "Awww, isn't that nice" kind of reaction to Christmas. By the way, it wasn't really that nice, when you stop to think about the actual details [laughs] of what happened that night, it was anything but nice. But there's a lot more going on here, and today's passage, which again comes out of the lectionary, and which I wondered about at first, has some interesting thoughts, I think, that confront us.

The reason he wondered about the lectionary's selection of scripture is that it recommended—on the Sunday before Christmas—the introduction to the book of Romans. The scripture passage he was to explicate—Romans 1:1–7—had just been read aloud by a female layperson:

> Paul, a servant of Christ Jesus, called to be an apostle and set apart for the gospel of God, the gospel he promised beforehand through his prophets in the holy scriptures regarding his son, who, as to his human nature, was a descendant of David, and who, through the spirit of holiness, was declared with power to be the son of god by his resurrection from the dead, Jesus Christ our lord. Through him and for his name's sake, we received grace and apostleship to call people from among all the gentiles to the obedience that comes through faith, from faith. And you also are among those who are called to belong in Jesus Christ, to all in Rome who are loved by God and called to be saints, grace and peace to you from God our father and from the Lord Jesus Christ.

When one thinks of Christmas, this is not a passage that springs to mind. But the pastor found a way to link this fairly standard introduction to an ancient letter to the themes of Christmas, and along the way to make it pointedly relevant to his audience.

Williams' first technique is to extend the semantic field of a word beyond what it has in the text as given.

> The early verses are introducing Paul to these people in a very real sense so let's look at them that way. Verse 1: "Paul, a servant of Christ Jesus, and called to be an apostle, and set apart for the gospel of God." Now believe it or not, that verse is rich with information about Paul. For instance, he gives us two descriptions of himself that on the face of it seem like they might be somewhat contradictory. *Servant* and *apostle*. As a matter of fact, the word for *servant* here is really the word that in other places is translated *slave*. So on one hand he describes himself as a *slave*, and yet on the other hand it's like he pulls rank, I mean *apostle*—whoa! You know, these were important people. These were special people with a very special designation, a very special mission, to this day we are the beneficiaries of their ministry through the written word. And so, to say *apostle* was to claim a level of authority that was very, very real. But it's interesting that he combines those two— *apostle*, yes, but in attitude, slave, *servant*. He's not going to use his position of authority to lord it over them, to try to be dictator; rather he's going to come to them as a *servant*, a *slave of Christ*, one who has that spirit of service.

The Greek word δοῦλος is indeed variously translated as *servant* or *slave*, though these words have quite different valences in English. Here Williams takes *servant* from the text and, by glossing it with another term—*slave*—extends its semantic field so as to accentuate the contrast with *apostle*. There is nothing exegetically improper here, but it does demonstrate how an interpreter can go beyond the text as given.

Another technique is to paraphrase the passage, adding in remarks that expand on what is actually in the text.

> He also is very clear in this verse to tell us that this is not something he has con-jured up himself, for two different times he makes very clear the fact that this is something he has been entrusted with. He says "I was *called to be an apostle*" and "I was *set apart for the gospel of God*. I didn't come on this myself. I didn't ask for this. This isn't something where I worked my way up the ladder of authority or some-thing like that—no, these were designations that came from God himself, I have simply accepted his call. I have acknowledged the fact that I am set apart for his purposes."

Here Williams reads a great deal out of two adjectival phrases. His exegesis is con-sistent with the story of Paul's conversion and calling as related in Acts 9, but he supplies contrast cases—"I didn't come on this myself. I didn't ask for this."—that bring an emphasis to *called* and *set apart* that they do not have in the text as given.

A few sentences later he uses the same technique again, to emphasize Paul's claim that the gospel message was implicit in the earlier Hebrew prophets:

> [Paul] says, "This gospel is the one that *God promised beforehand through his prophets in the Holy Scriptures*. It's not something new that I've created, I'm not just pulling this out of thin air, even I would have seen it had I understood, because it was there. It had been predicted, it had been, the plan had been laid out already in the scrip-tures which we knew," which would be the Old Testament scriptures. He says, "And this isn't created out of whole new cloth or something. It's in continuous flow from what God has put before us for years if we had just seen it."

The notion that Paul might have simply invented the gospel is introduced by way of contrast to bring fresh life to Paul's claim that the gospel antedates him.

A third technique—elaboration, or adding specifications to what the text says—comes to the fore in his discussion of Jesus's dual nature:

> And in verses 3 and 4 he lays out for us several important facts about Christ. He tells us that Jesus is both human and divine, for he says he was a *descendant of David* but also *the Son of God*; *Son of David*; *Son of God*—that great mystery of the two na-tures of Christ—human; divine. To have lived back in those days to see Jesus walk-ing down the street you could have said "There goes a man" and you would have been accurate. You could have said, "There goes God," and you would have also been accurate. Do we understand that completely? No. But it's clearly outlined for us not just here but in many places through the New Testament.

Here Williams takes a passing reference to Jesus's dual nature and expands it by proposing a scenario in which Jesus's fully divine and fully human natures are explicitly articulated, in a version—fully human, fully divine—that goes considerably beyond the text, reading into it several points of orthodox Christology:

- Human. Early Christians entertained many different understandings of Jesus's human nature: partial and complete, apparent and real, integrated with the divine nature or separate. To say of Jesus, with respect to his nature, that he is a man is to affirm the orthodox conclusion that Jesus's nature is complete and real. (It does not necessarily entail any claim about integration.) But such an affirmation goes considerably beyond the text's reference to Jesus as "a descendant of David."
- Divine. Early Christians had similarly diverse views of Jesus's divine nature. Was Jesus always God? If not, when did he become divine? Was he fully divine? To whom did he pray? Paul says here only that Jesus was God's *Son, declared with power to be the Son of God*—a statement that suggests, if anything, an adoptionist Christology, as will be seen below.
- Mystery. Christological doctrine has traditionally been regarded as a mystery, a divine truth that defies full human understanding. In characterizing the orthodox doctrine this way, Williams anticipates and defuses a series of objections to it. However, he recognizes the difficulty here, and asserts that the full weight of scriptural authority supports it: "It's clearly outlined for us not just here but in many places through the New Testament." But to claim that the divine incarnation is a mystery is to go well beyond what is in Romans I.

My point is not that these variations were necessarily present among Paul's earliest Roman readers, but that Paul's statements are ambiguous, and that Williams, in expounding them, is adding to them a great deal of specificity and orthodox expansion.

The text, in fact, is perfectly consistent with an adoptionist Christology. Williams continues:

We also see that there were human ways this came about. As to his human nature he was or became *a descendant of David*, but there is also a divine intervention, for *through the spirit of holiness he was declared or appointed with power to be the Son of God*. Now, we need to be a little careful here. I don't know if anybody thought of this or not, but in case [laughs], we'll stop at this moment just for a little bit. We want to be careful to understand that Jesus didn't *become* the Son of God at this point. That isn't what he is saying. We have to read on to understand that this declaring or appointing of Jesus to be Son of God by power is something that was declared to us, it was for our benefit. So how did he do that? How did God do that? How did God demonstrate to us that he was the Son of God? Well, Paul says, *by his resurrection from the dead*, that's how. So, he was *a descendant of David but through the spirit of holiness he was declared with power to be the Son of God by his resurrection from the dead.* He was *declared* to us to be the *Son of God* in that way.

One variant of adoptionism, attested from after the time of Paul, is that Jesus was a man until his death, at which time he was adopted as God's son and hence received immortality. Well aware of this history and recognizing its consonance with what this particular passage says, Williams takes care to "disambiguate" the text by simply stating that the idea here is that Jesus's divine nature was merely evidenced—not established—by his resurrection.

These techniques—expansion of a term's semantic field, paraphrase, and elaboration—all serve to connect the text with the reader's linguistic horizon, to modify the text so as to establish transitivity between the ancient text and the modern reader's beliefs.

These are not the only ways in which the text may be made to connect with its readers. A good preacher has a large repertoire of techniques for making a text relevant to his audience. One of the most common was next illustrated by Williams:

> Then this important phrase that ends verse 4. Who are we talking about here? And Paul is clear, *Jesus Christ our Lord.* Now don't miss that [laughs], that's key in what we're going to be looking at as we go through this. *Jesus Christ our Lord.* What effect did that have on Paul? Verse 5, he tells us. *Through him*, that is, through Christ, through the power which he gave him, and *for his name's sake, to the glory of Christ*, then Paul uses the editorial "we"—*we received grace and apostleship to call people from among all the Gentiles.* The word there could just as easily by the way be translated "nations." This is a missionary verse. *To call people from all the nations to the obedience that comes out of faith.* We call them to place their faith in this Son of God and to follow it with obedience, an obedience that grows out of that faith. And that was the task that drove Paul from the moment that he had met Jesus on that road to Damascus and understood that this was the person who was both man and God, the one who was declared to us as God through the resurrection. Once he caught on to that he was then driven to take that message of grace and declare it to all the nations.
>
> Now, the clincher, and here's where we've been heading. Verse 6: *you also.* Bingo. This isn't just about Paul. It's about the people who are reading this and it's about us. *You also are called to belong to Jesus Christ.* Wow. What in the world does that mean, *to belong to Jesus Christ?* Well, the *you also* [laughs] just keeps pointing us right back to where we've been. What did it mean for Paul? It meant that he had a sense of mission, of call. It meant that he went with a spirit of service, to be a slave to

Christ. It meant that he focused his life on the gospel of God regarding his son, the message of the Son of God. It meant that he had confidence in who Christ was, his Lord. It meant that he was driven to share that message with all the nations, wherever in whatever way he could. That was what drove him. You also are called to belong to Jesus Christ. So it means all of those things for us as well. Do we sense a call to be involved in what God wants us to do? Are we willing to approach it with a spirit of service? Do we have that same confidence in Jesus Christ as our Lord? Do we have the heart for the nations that he had?

Here Williams does more than semantically transform the text: he uses the text (modified, even in this short passage, by semantic expansion, paraphrase, and elaboration) to construct a rich image of Paul, and to suggest that his listeners ought to mimic Paul in these respects. The text gets arranged into a psychological profile of Paul's focus, motivation, and attitude, and that profile in turn becomes the basis for his exhortation, that his audience ought to sense God's call, to have a heart for service, and to spread the gospel to those who have not heard it. The hinge point in connecting Paul and his modern audience is the *you also*, where the *you* is understood not in Paul's context, as a reference to the early Roman church, but to a modern congregation.

The techniques analyzed here, while common, are intended to be illustrative only. They reflect the workings of the hermeneutic imagination, the inference system that enables us to contextualize utterances and extract their significance for social interaction. The point, however, is that Bible readers, in searching to find a text's relevance to their lives, can go beyond the text as given. Not only can they contextualize it either historically or devotionally, but they may also employ the hermeneutic imagination—expansion of a term's semantic field, paraphrase, elaboration, folk psychology—to go beyond the text as given and to establish the relevance of the text to their lives.

Despite the flexibility with which people find relevance in the Bible, the search is not in fact always successful. The people with whom I talked had all had times when the Bible seemed "dry," and didn't speak to their needs. Most people, however, seem to have succeeded in establishing the text's relevance often enough to keep them reading.

Evangelicals' hermeneutic activity is driven by the expectation that the Bible will be highly relevant to their lives, and this search for relevance is facilitated by the availability of both historical and devotional contexts for reading and by techniques for going beyond the text as given. The structure of their hermeneutic activity thus goes a long way toward explaining the special hermeneutics that evangelicals bring to the Bible. But there is another factor operative here too: the influence of the interpretive tradition.

Influence of the Interpretive Tradition

Evangelicals' use of special hermeneutics for the Bible is sometimes inferred from their interpretations rather than observed in their actual practice of reading. It is tempting indeed to think that if evangelicals attribute an unexpected meaning to a biblical text that it is because they read the text in some special way to come up with this meaning. But I have shown already that this need not be so: the "meaning" may well be part of the interpretive tradition, and may have been learned indirectly rather than being inferred from the text at all. The interpretive tradition exerts a very powerful influence on how evangelicals understand the Bible: the doctrine of God's limited omnipotence was strong enough to override even Jesus's very words.

The influence of the interpretive tradition on hermeneutic activity is multifaceted and complex. First, the interpretive tradition specifies interpretations for some passages. Romans 3:23 is the first stop on the "Romans Road"—an often-memorized sequence of verses from the Epistle to the Romans, used to outline people's sinfulness, the availability of forgiveness through the death of Jesus, and the need to believe in his name. Romans 3:23 is used to establish the fact that everyone has sinned and thus needs salvation. It and the following verse read: "for all have sinned and fall short of the glory of God, and are justified freely by his grace through the redemption that came by Christ Jesus." The NIV faithfully reproduces a problem that goes right back to the Greek text: the subject—"all [people]"—of "have sinned" is the same as the subject of "are justified freely." The same text that says people have need of justification also says they are in fact justified. The normal use of verse 23 is thus rendered inappropriate by verse 24: everyone has sinned, but everyone is also justified. I have heard countless discussions of this verse, and this difficulty is almost never noticed. Having grown up with the traditional interpretation of the verse, I didn't notice the problem myself until it was pointed out as a puzzle in a grammar of New Testament Greek. Even though the problem is perfectly apparent in English translations, the interpretive tradition specifies that this passage means that everyone has sinned, and this interpretation so guides hermeneutic activity that almost no one notices that the text does not fit terribly well with this doctrine.

Second, the interpretive tradition serves as a guide to context. Jesus's statement that all things are possible for God was not directly overridden by a doctrine. Rather, the doctrine served as a guide to other passages, some of which explicitly mentioned things God could not do. The doctrine invoked these other passages both through references and by posing the question of limitations in such a way that class participants could recall passages on their own.

Third, the interpretive tradition creates new conditions of relevance. The biblical text functions as evidence for or against an evangelical reader's beliefs—and achieves relevance either way. The more ideas a person has about what the Bible says, the more opportunity there is for biblical passages to confirm or disconfirm those beliefs. The biblical text does cognitive work either way.

Thus the interpretive tradition influences the ways in which evangelicals encounter the Bible, and gives rise to interpretations that stand in a relation to the Bible in ways that would be unusual between other texts and their interpretations.

Before moving on to the final step in this lengthy argument, it is helpful to recapitulate the main points so far:

1. Evangelicals are inheritors of an interpretive tradition, a species of belief-tradition in which a set of beliefs is transmitted along with the attribution of those beliefs to a text, the Bible. The tradition presents the text as an object for hermeneutic activity, but the goal of that hermeneutic activity is not so much to establish the meaning of the text as to establish transitivity between the text and beliefs. The tradition emphasizes the *fact* of connection more than of particular connections. And thus a great deal of "what the Bible says" may be transmitted quite apart from actual exegesis.

2. Evangelicals are not inheritors of a hermeneutic tradition, a socially transmitted set of methods for reading the Bible. Evangelicals' and fundamentalists' widespread avowal of literalism is not evidence of a hermeneutic tradition. Rather, in each generation, the interpretive tradition mobilizes hermeneutic imaginations anew.

3. Evangelical Bible reading is driven by a search for relevance, much the way other communication is. However, dual contextualization of the act of Bible reading, use of heuristics for moving beyond the text as given, and the influence of the belief tradition combine to make interpretations of the Bible unlike interpretations of other texts.

In outlining the various ways of establishing the relevance of the Bible, I have perhaps given the impression that, in evangelical hermeneutics, anything goes. In a sense, this is true: at the level of the local congregation, no hermeneutic technique is absolutely proscribed. Particular interpretations may be disputed, but general hermeneutic methods are hardly discussed.

Yet such flexible hermeneutics are a threat to an interpretive tradition, because, if hermeneutic activity is not constrained, it might allow almost any proposition to be attributed to a text. The interpretive tradition, I suggest, is caught in a bind.

Between Irrelevance and Anarchy

The evangelical interpretive tradition is a set of beliefs that derive their validity from the Bible, that is, from being "what the Bible says." The interpretive tradition's appeal derives from evangelicals' respect for the Bible and the plausibility of the claim that the beliefs specified are indeed "in the Bible" in some reasonably determinate sense. This tradition is fed by evangelicals' actual hermeneutic activity, in which they find the Bible highly relevant and do indeed find support for evangelical beliefs in the Bible. (The general human tendency to perceive support for prior beliefs more than evidence against them is called the *confirmation bias* in psychology.)

Yet the flexibility of hermeneutic activity, I suggest, poses a serious threat to the interpretive tradition by undermining the determinacy of traditional interpretations. If the traditional beliefs are not "what the Bible says" any more than a host of alternative beliefs, then they lose their appeal. One might expect evangelicals and fundamentalists to manifest some awareness of this threat, and I suggest that it is precisely this that motivates the avowal of literalism.

Literalism

My argument in this section refers entirely to the hermeneutic theory held by evangelical and fundamentalist Bible scholars well versed in the history of interpretation. It is they, not the average churchgoer, who most clearly perceive the threat that hermeneutic flexibility poses to the interpretive tradition, and it is in their statements that this threat is explicitly addressed.

My suggestion is that Bible scholars conceptualize hermeneutics as an algorithmic process involving the application of a series of rules for deriving meaning from a text. The conception of hermeneutics as the application of an algorithm to a text makes it possible to compare alternative hermeneutics. When hermeneutics are compared, literalism emerges as a highly reliable principle of interpretation. The avowal of literalism, then, is a consequence of the epistemology of an interpretive tradition, and is less a model of reading than a model of knowledge.

There are other possible hermeneutic models. Evangelicals frequently speak of having a "biblical basis" for their beliefs and practices. "Basis" is a dead metaphor nowadays, but the term was originally from Greek anatomy—"foot"—which is presumably the source of its use in geometry. This suggests at least the possibility of an alternate conception of the place of the Bible in Bible-oriented Christianity. Rather than conceiving beliefs as derived from the Bible, one might envision them as organically or even dynamically connected to the text. (In some respects the latter metaphor might even be more descriptively accurate.) In principle, a text might be related to its interpretive tradition in a great variety of ways. The algorithmic model—its depth in the Western tradition notwithstanding—is a choice from among a wider range of alternatives. Once chosen, however, it has consequences. A closer look at the formal properties of the algorithmic model will set the stage for examination of avowed literalism as one of those consequences.

THE ALGORITHMIC MODEL. Paul Ricoeur (1971, 529) characterized hermeneutics (*Auslegung*) as "the rules required for the interpretation of the written documents of our culture." In fact, however, the problem of hermeneutics— the problem of how texts ought to be interpreted—arose originally for the interpretation of written documents that were historically/culturally distant from the reader. The Alexandrian Greeks seem to have been among the first to wrestle with the problem, and they influenced the Jewish interpreter Philo, who influenced, in turn, the early Christian church.

The problem confronted by Philo, who left one of the earliest treatments of hermeneutic theory, was to respect the Septuagint (at the time regarded as one of the forms of Jewish scripture) while simultaneously embracing Platonic philosophy. He sought to reconcile these two commitments by reinterpreting the Septuagint so as to make Platonic philosophy the proper understanding of the text. To this end he formulated a series of hermeneutic rules. These rules were a series of statements that told the reader how a given passage should be understood. Some of them were conditional, and made the application of a particular hermeneutic principle contingent upon the text in some way (Ramm 1970, 27): "[According to Philo] there were three canons which dictated to the interpreter that a passage of Scripture was to be allegorically interpreted: (i) If a statement says anything unworthy of God; (ii) if a statement is contradictory with some other statement or in any other way presents us with a difficulty; and (iii) if the record itself is allegorical in nature." These rules were intended to enable the reader, confronting the ancient text, to derive from it its "correct" meaning. In this theory, hermeneutics is envisaged as the application of a set of rules to a text.

I call this the *algorithmic model* of interpretation because it sets out a procedure that anyone should be able to use. The possibility that anyone could use it requires the set of rules to be as complete and explicit as possible. If it is to be universally used, nothing must be left to the judgment of the interpreter: the process of interpretation must be tightly controlled by the rules. Most popular guides to Bible study today are based on the algorithmic model (McDowell 1982; Arthur 1994; McArthur 1997; LaHaye 1998). They set out a series of rules, or principles, designed to guide the reader into a fuller, richer understanding of the Bible while also preventing misguided or heretical interpretations.

David Olson (1994) has characterized literalism as an algorithmic approach to reading. My account differs from Olson's in distinguishing sharply between hermeneutic theory and hermeneutic practice: whereas Olson seems to suggest that a person might "read algorithmically"—that is, in accordance with the rules laid down by a hermeneutic theory—I regard hermeneutic theories alone as being algorithmic, in the sense that they take the form of rules for reading. On my account, hermeneutic practice—reading itself—is a relevance-driven search process that, if algorithmic at all, is guided by rules largely unknown.

The term *algorithmic* may seem inappropriate because hermeneutic rules do not really amount to a proper algorithm. They are not fully explicit. They are not exhaustive. The reader is not envisioned as an automaton slavishly following the rules. The rules are offered rather as advice to help the reader steer clear of common interpretive mistakes, and more fully to appreciate the text's meaning. But it is clear that the rules are algorithmic in tendency, just as are recipes, computer tutorials, and assembly instructions—all seek to delineate a widely understandable step-by-step process for achieving a goal.

Explicit algorithmic models of hermeneutics open up an interesting possibility: a set of rules might not only function as a *procedure* but also be examined for its *relative adequacy* in comparison to alternative sets of rules, for its presuppositions about language, and for its empirical adequacy. The rules might be evaluated. One way of directly testing a set of rules is to apply them to a text that has an established interpretation and to see whether they produce that accepted interpretation. Another more philosophical approach has been to articulate one's hermeneutic rules in the context of a theory of signs, such that the rules are motivated by the theory. Both of these methods have, historically, been tried at various times. But even prior to analysis, one can often tell, simply by inspecting the rules, what sort of interpretations they are likely to generate.

The possibility of evaluating hermeneutic algorithms also gives rise to an apologetic strategy: my interpretation is superior to yours if mine is the product of better hermeneutics. The rules can be used to evaluate interpretations.

It is in precisely this context that literalism is championed by evangelicals and fundamentalists. Within the algorithmic model, many view literalism as a particularly reliable principle of interpretation. Bernard Ramm (1970, 30) criticizes the unreliability of allegorical hermeneutics:

> The Bible treated allegorically becomes putty in the hand of the exegete. Different doctrinal systems could emerge within the framework of allegorical hermeneutics and no way would exist to determine which were the true. This was precisely one of the problems in refuting the gnostics. The orthodox wished to allegorize the Old Testament, but not the New. The gnostics accused them of inconsistency. The only method of breaking an exegetical stalemate created by the use of the allegorical method is to return to the sober, proper, and literal interpretation of the Scriptures.

According to Ramm, the strength of literalism is its reliability. Evangelicals are well aware that the Bible has been said to mean many different things. The acknowledgment of such wide variation threatens to make any particular interpretive tradition seem arbitrary and unfounded. In principle literalism is said to keep readers from wildly varying interpretations of the text, and to eliminate the arbitrariness of the literalists' interpretive tradition.

Note that interpretive variation is no threat to the *textual* tradition, the tradition of producing and disseminating Bibles. In fact, the Bible's history as a book suggests that the text has benefited from being, to borrow a biblical phrase, "all things to all people."

Interpretive variation is a threat rather to the *interpretive* tradition because it threatens the ability to extend the authority of the text to its interpretation. Ramm's criticism of allegorical hermeneutics is that they could arbitrarily extend biblical authority to any doctrinal system. The transitivity must be constrained, so that one is able to decide which doctrinal system is correct. He is less worried about which doctrinal system is validated than with the possibility of validating one or another of them. For people who locate themselves inside an interpretive tradition, wide interpretive variation is a threat because transitivity from the text to its interpretation is a plank in their epistemology, and if this transitivity applies equally to all interpretations, then their particular set seems arbitrary.

The avowal of literalism, then, as a hermeneutic theory may be seen as a response to the fear that the Bible's authority could be extended willy-nilly to any and all propositions, and indicates an awareness that the transitivity implicit in hermeneutic activity, left unregulated, has the potential to destabilize the interpretive tradition. So why not solve the problem by actually being strictly literalist? Why not emphasize a thoroughgoing literalism in one's use of the Bible not just in academic centers but also in the churches?

Scylla and Charybdis

The interpretive tradition, I maintain, is perennially caught between the Scylla of hermeneutic freedom and the Charybdis of irrelevance: too much hermeneutic freedom and the tradition disintegrates, loosing its epistemological appeal; too little interpretive freedom and the Bible becomes merely an irrelevant historical artifact, rather than the ever-living word of God. The interpretive tradition, by its very structure, needs both hermeneutic freedom and determinacy.

At present, the evangelical tradition solves this problem by maintaining fairly rigorous standards of exegesis in its scholarship and quietly ignoring those standards in the churches. There is no hermeneutic tradition at Creekside Baptist or any other church I have seen, but there is a hermeneutic tradition in Bible colleges

and seminaries. I suggest that this is a very practical response to the conflict between maintaining ongoing biblical relevance in the pews and hermeneutic determinacy in the classroom.

Synopsis

The various strands of the present analysis may now be tied together, to form a
new, empirically driven model of evangelical biblical interpretation.

1. Evangelicals are inheritors of an *interpretive* tradition, a species of belief-
    tradition in which a set of beliefs is transmitted along with the
    attribution of those beliefs to a text, the Bible. The tradition presents the
    text as an object for hermeneutic activity, but the goal of that
    hermeneutic activity is not so much to establish the meaning of the text
    as to establish transitivity between the text and beliefs. The tradition
    emphasizes the *fact* of connection more than of particular connections.
    And thus a great deal of "what the Bible says" may be transmitted quite
    apart from actual exegesis.
2. Evangelicals are not inheritors of a *hermeneutic* tradition, a socially
    transmitted set of methods for reading the Bible. Evangelicals' and
    fundamentalists' widespread avowal of literalism is not evidence of a
    hermeneutic tradition. Rather, in each generation, the interpretive
    tradition mobilizes hermeneutic imaginations anew.
3. Evangelical Bible reading is driven by a search for relevance, much the way
    other communication is. However, dual contextualization of the act of
    Bible reading, use of heuristics for moving beyond the text as given, and
    the influence of the belief tradition combine to make interpretations of
    the Bible unlike interpretations of other texts.
4. The interpretive tradition is perennially caught between the Scylla of
    interpretive freedom and the Charybdis of irrelevance: too much
    hermeneutic freedom and the tradition disintegrates, loosing its
    epistemological appeal; too little interpretive freedom and the Bible
    becomes merely an irrelevant historical artifact, rather than the ever-living
    word of God.

This model shows how the standard question, "How do evangelicals interpret the
Bible?" is quite misleading, because it presupposes that evangelical interpretations
are derived from some special method for reading the Bible. What I have shown is
that evangelical interpretations are sometimes derived from the Bible and sometimes merely attributed to it, that there is no special method for reading the Bible,
but instead that normal communicative competency is deployed with some special

parameters. I have further suggested that the contradiction between proclamations of literalism and nonliteralist practice is not merely a failure of consistency but instead reflects a deep contradiction in evangelical Biblicism.

Indefinite Interpretability

I would like to conclude by examining a consequence of the foregoing model for the general shape of interpretive practice: the Bible's indefinite interpretability. Consider a scenario described by Roy Zuck (1996, 5):

> Imagine a small Bible study group meeting in the living room of a nice home every Thursday evening. The group has no designated leaders other than the host and hostess. Each week they study a passage in the book of Romans.
>
> As they come to a difficult verse or group of verses, they each give their opinion on what it means. Their views differ and even conflict with each other. Having no way of determining which view is correct, they move on to another passage in the chapter, and again voice differing ideas. The so-called Bible study concludes with each having shared varied opinions but with no sense of whether the verses mean all those things shared, one of them, or none of them.
>
> Why do informal Bible study groups face this problem?

Actually, they don't. I participated in just such a study for two years, and have talked with people involved in many more. In general, such studies transpire very much the way Zuck describes, although the discussion is not necessarily so orderly and people's commitment to their individual interpretations varies quite a bit.

But the problem Zuck describes seldom arises. Participants seldom spoke about *the* meaning of a passage. They tended to talk rather about what impressed them out of the passage, what it meant for their lives. Their interpretations were usually expressed with some degree of tentativeness, and were framed as observations on the passage rather than as expressions of "the meaning." They did say that the text had a meaning—and a real, definite one—but none of them pretended to know it exhaustively. Their claims, at most, were to know *part* of the meaning of a passage. They seemed untroubled when different people took away different lessons from the discussion—after all, the Holy Spirit might say different things to different people. Their attitude toward the text was much less exclusive than Zuck—a professor at a conservative seminary—describes.

So it is with pastors too, at least in their sermons. One exceptionally well-educated pastor shared with me his way of preparing topical sermons:

> I think when a pastor has to preach something sometimes they have a topic they want to preach. I'm facing this right now because I want to preach on community, and there's a number of texts that you could preach from but somebody was

reading out of John 17. There's a number of things that are said in there that are about the community of God, relationship with God, and how that influences our relationship with each other and then our relationship with each other, how that influences our relationship to the world, which is pretty much the flow of what I want to say. Well, the danger is always to then get in, you kind of determine what text you want to say, you get into the biblical text and it doesn't quite say it the way you want it to say it, or it doesn't say it in the way you want to go. And that's hard. There comes a moment where you have to make a decision about how you're going to say it. So I just try to be careful not to exhaust the text, not to say that I'm saying everything that can be said about the text, but to say something out of the text that is actually there.

His problem was to preach a relevant, topical message without a fully appropriate text. His solution was to take a passage and read it in such a way as to serve his homiletic ends, but to hedge his message by not excluding other readings, by not exhausting the text. My interview with him took place on a Thursday before he was to preach, and earlier he had mentioned the time pressure he was facing. For preachers producing sermons under a deadline, the freedom to give *a* reading, rather than *the* reading, of a passage is a practical necessity.

Moreover, partial, nonexclusive meanings fit rather cleanly within the devotional frame for Bible reading. What impresses a person out of the text need not be God's message for everyone at all times, but only God's message for that particular person, or that particular church, at that particular point in time. Part of the meaning will do: no more definitive exegesis is usually needed.

The phenomenon of indefinite interpretability thus arises out of the way Bible reading is framed, the exigencies of preachers' time and goals, and the practical needs of Bible readers. Indefinite interpretability is important because the interpretive tradition requires the ongoing relevance of the Bible. In an interpretive tradition, the text is needed to stand above the beliefs—the text is the ground of their authority. But what grounds the authority of the text?

Biblical Authority 4

The Problem of Biblical Authority

PART OF THE SCHOLARLY DEFINITION of evangelicalism is that evangelicals regard the Bible as the authoritative word of God (Ammerman 1982; Bebbington 1989; Hunter 1981; Noll 2001). The purpose of this chapter is twofold: (1) to explore, more precisely than has been done in the past, the nature and shape of biblical authority in an American evangelical church; and (2) to propose an explanation of this authority, that biblical authority is tied to evangelicals' definition of their institutions and thus disseminated as part of the process by which these institutions reproduce themselves.

The proposition that evangelicals regard the Bible as authoritative is so widely acknowledged that the actual evidence for it has never, to my knowledge, been marshaled. I thus begin by examining several sorts of evidence that American evangelicals regard the Bible as authoritative. The purpose of this review is not to establish the veracity of the proposition, but to see whether consideration of the evidence for biblical authority does not provide some clue to its structure.

Evidence

Survey research provides one important source of evidence for biblical authority. According to a 1996 survey, 100 percent of self-described evangelicals and 99 percent of self-described fundamentalists say that the Bible is true (Smith and Emerson 1998). One hundred percent of the respondents to my survey at Creekside Baptist affirmed that the Bible is inspired by God, and the majority—69.5 percent—said that the Bible was inerrant even in matters of science and history. Survey research shows that American fundamentalists and evangelicals, when individually asked, strongly affirm the authority, divine inspiration, and truth of the Bible.

Another source of evidence is the doctrinal statements of evangelical and fundamentalist institutions. The following is from the constitution of Creekside Baptist, as the first item in article 3, "Affirmation of Faith": "We believe that the Bible is the Word of God, fully inspired and without error in the original manuscripts, written under the inspiration of the Holy Spirit, and that it has supreme authority in all matters of faith and conduct (II Timothy 3:15–17; II Peter 1:16–21; 3:14–18; Luke 24: 36–49)."

In its emphasis on the "supreme authority" of the Bible, Creekside Baptist is squarely in the evangelical tradition. The historian Mark A. Noll (2001, 59–60) reviewed statements of faith by three denominations in the American evangelical tradition, six evangelical parachurch organizations, and documents from the 1974 and 1989 International Congresses on World Evangelization:

> Convergence in these evangelical statements of faith begins with the *Bible*. Eight of the ten begin with a statement on Scripture (for the other two—Wheaton and Lausanne—Scripture comes second). All of them speak in unison by affirming that the Bible is infallible (it does not let people down) and inspired (its writing reflects the direct influence of God). They are equally in agreement that Scripture is the ultimate authority for beliefs and practices. The InterVarsity statement puts it most economically in affirming belief in "the unique divine inspiration, entire trustworthiness and authority of the Bible." The Lausanne Covenant expands matters considerably, but much along the lines of the other statements: "We affirm the divine inspiration, truthfulness and authority of both Old and New Testament Scriptures in their entirety as the only written word of God, without error in all that it affirms, and the only infallible rule of faith and practice. We also affirm the power of God's word to accomplish his purpose of salvation. . . . Through it [Scripture] the Holy Spirit still speaks today. He illumines the minds of God's people in every culture to perceive its truth freshly through their own eyes and thus discloses to the whole Church ever more of the many colored wisdom of God."

Evangelicals have traditionally affirmed the authority of the Bible in their doctrinal statements, and this tradition continues today.

Some consideration of context, however, is worthwhile here. The constitution of Creekside Baptist, while available in printed form, in practice gets cited only to define issues of official procedure: never once did I hear the "Affirmation of Faith" ever quoted in sermon, Sunday school, or Bible study. Rather, the constitution is distributed to new members when they join the church, and they are given to understand that this document defines church polity and procedure. Once part of the church, they use the constitution seldom if at all: the Bible rather than the constitution functions as the touchstone document in most discourse. And this pattern is generally the same in most churches and other evangelical institutions I have encountered: the statement of faith is of interest mainly to new recruits because it is part of the institution's self-definition, but plays a rather small role in discourse within the institution.

Particularly in the Baptist tradition, the role of statements of faith is often recognized in relations between the institution and the larger public (North American Baptist Seminary 2003):

> Baptists, since their beginnings, repeatedly have composed confessions which expressed the doctrinal consensus among related churches. In principle, however, Baptists always have insisted that no statement of faith can be considered creedally binding even upon concurring congregations. The purpose of their doctrinal summaries was to explain to other Christians and to the larger society what Baptists believed and practiced. Within and among Baptist churches, statements of faith also provided a standard for instruction, counsel, and fellowship.

The function of statements of faith, as described here, is to define for outsiders what the people of a church or association believe, and to serve as a standard for what teaching is permitted within the church or association. In short, it marks an institutional boundary.

Thus it is that faculty and other employees of some evangelical colleges (e.g., International School of Theology, Calvary Bible College, Grace University), seminaries (e.g., The Master's Seminary, Reformed Theological Seminary, Grace Theological Seminary), and mission organizations (e.g., Fellowship International Mission, World Radio Missionary Fellowship, InterVarsity Christian Fellowship) have been required to sign annually their agreement with the institution's statement of faith. This practice has been instituted in many places to prevent theological deviation from evangelicalism's understanding of Christianity. In these cases, the statement of faith is an ongoing part of community life, but it still takes place at an institutional border inasmuch as signing is a condition of continued employment at the institution.

A third source of behavioral evidence for evangelicals' view of biblical authority lies in their discursive practice. Recall from chapter 3 how Sunday school participants structured their discussion as an exegesis of the Bible. The insistence on having a verse and the citation of Biblical passages seems to suggest, I argued, that the text is being used as *evidence*, and that part of what is being established in Bible study conversations is *transitivity* between the Bible and evangelical beliefs, such that evangelical beliefs can be attributed to the Bible.

The consistency and pervasiveness of this discursive pattern is such that *one cannot help but* infer (1) that evangelicals regard the Bible as authoritative and (2) that evangelicals assume that other evangelicals do too. I do not mean merely that their discursive behavior is compelling evidence that they regard the Bible as authoritative: I mean rather that the attribution of this belief to them is *conversationally necessary*, that one *cannot understand* their conversation, much less actively participate in it, if one does not assume that they regard the Bible as authoritative. The assumption of biblical authority is part of the ground of evangelical discourse. I will return to this point below, but for now it suffices to note that evangelicals' belief in the Bible's authority explains their use of it as evidence and their motivation to ascribe beliefs to the Bible, to ensure that their beliefs are "biblical."

A final source of evidence is the sharp separation that evangelicals maintain between the biblical text and all other texts. The biblical canon was formally defined, in the fourth century, by lists of which works were considered scripture. Today, the canon is dictated, for the ordinary evangelical, by the conventions of print. The artifactual boundary defines the canon, and serves as a convenient point of reference for the many evangelicals who could not, if asked, pick out the canonical books from a lineup of ancient literature. A boundary around the canonical books, once supplied by definitive lists of which books were included, is now supplied implicitly through modern binding practices.

Canon, therefore, if understood only as a list of which books are included in the Bible, might seem to be a dead issue. But if canon is understood as an issue of boundary, then there remain boundaries in need of active maintenance. Biblical text is bounded off from all other texts by distinctions in both print and performance.

If the artifactual nature of Bibles has afforded a convenient means of signifying a boundary around the books included, it has also introduced complications at another level. Bibles have long contained more—sometimes a great deal more—than biblical text. In addition to the Bible text, they may contain prefatory material of various kinds: dedication pages, family records, church records, chronological charts, a table of contents, a list of maps and figures, one or more prefaces, one or more introductions, and notes on the text and translation. Once one is past the front matter, the page still presents titles, page numbers and indexical headings, numbered verse and chapter divisions, cross-references, alternate readings, and often, commentary. At the back of a Bible one often finds tables of weights and measures, a subject index, maps, a concordance, and a dictionary.

What is interesting about these additional materials is that many of them are of a factual nature: family records, cross-references, concordances, maps, dictionaries all may be absolutely factual. Others, such as the annotations, are either historically factual or interpretively accurate from an evangelical point of view. In short, their truth-value differs little from that with which evangelicals regard the Bible. In a very practical sense they might be viewed as extensions of the Bible. And it is with respect to these materials that it becomes clear that canon is not a dead issue.

Most modern Bibles sharply separate the biblical text from accompanying apparatus. Figure 4.1 shows a page from the *NIV Study Bible*, the most common

The Beginning

1 In the beginning[a] God created[b] the heavens[c] and the earth.[d] **2**Now the earth was[a] formless[e] and empty,[f] darkness was over the surface of the deep,[g] and the Spirit of God[h] was hovering[i] over the waters.

3And God said,[j] "Let there be light," and there was light.[k] **4**God saw that the light was good,[l] and he separated the light from the darkness.[m] **5**God called[n] the light "day," and the darkness he called "night."[o] And there was evening, and there was morning[p]—the first day.

6And God said,[q] "Let there be an expanse[r] between the waters[s] to separate water from water." **7**So God made the expanse and separated the water under the expanse from the water above it.[t] And it was so.[u]

8God called[v] the expanse "sky."[w] And there was evening, and there was morning[x]—the second day.

9And God said, "Let the water under the sky be gathered to one place,[y] and let dry ground[z] appear." And it was so.[a] **10**God called[b] the dry ground "land," and the gathered waters[c] he called "seas."[d] And God saw that it was good.[e]

11Then God said, "Let the land pro-

1:1 *Ps 102:25;
Pr 8:23;
*Isa 40:21; 41:4,
26; Jn 1:1-2
*ver 21,27;
Ge 2:3 <ver 6;
Ne 9:6; Job 9:8;
37:18; Ps 96:5;
104:2; 115:15;
121:2; 136:5;
Isa 40:22; 42:5;
51:13;
Jer 10:12; 51:15
*Ge 14:19;
2Ki 19:15;
Ne 9:6;
Job 38:4;
Ps 90:2; 136:6;
146:6;
Isa 37:16;
40:28; 42:5;
44:24; 45:12,
18; Jer 27:5;
32:17;
Ac 14:15;
17:24; Eph 3:9;
Col 1:16;
Heb 3:4; 11:3;
Rev 4:11; 10:6
1:2 *Isa 23:1;
24:10; 27:10;
32:14; 34:11
*Isa 45:18;
Jer 4:23

*Ge 8:2; Job 7:12; 26:8; 38:9; Ps 36:6; 42:7; 104:6; 107:24;
Pr 30:4 *Ge 2:7; Job 33:4; Ps 104:30; Isa 32:15 *Dt 32:11;
Isa 31:5 1:3 *ver 6; Ps 33:6,9; 148:5; Heb 11:3 *2Co 4:6*;
1Jn 1:5-7 1:4 *ver 10,12,18,21,25,31; Ps 104:31; 119:68;
Jer 31:35 *ver 14; Ex 10:21-23; Job 26:10; 38:19; Ps 18:28;
104:20; 105:28; Isa 42:16; 45:7 1:5 *ver 8,10; Ge 2:19,23
*Ps 74:16 *ver 8,13,19,23,31 1:6 *S ver 3 *S ver 1; Isa 44:24;
2Pe 3:5 *ver 9; Ps 24:2; 136:6 1:7 *Ge 7:11; Job 26:10;
38:8-11,16; Ps 68:33; 148:4; Pr 8:28 *ver 9,11,15,24 1:8
*S ver 5 *Job 9:8; 37:18; Ps 19:1; 104:2; Isa 40:22; 44:24;
45:12; Jer 10:12; Zec 12:1 *S ver 5 1:9 *Job 38:8-11; Ps 33:7;
104:6-9; Pr 8:29; Jer 5:22; 2Pe 3:5 *Ps 95:5; Jnh 1:9; Hag 2:6
*S ver 7 1:10 *S ver 5 *Ps 33:7 *Job 38:8; Ps 90:2; 95:5
*S ver 4

*2 Or possibly *became*

1:1 A summary statement introducing the six days of creative activity. The truth of this majestic verse was joyfully affirmed by poet (Ps 102:25) and prophet (Isa 40:21). *In the beginning God.* The Bible always assumes, and never argues, God's existence. Although everything else had a beginning, God has always been (Ps 90:2). *In the beginning.* Jn 1:1–10, which stresses the work of Christ in creation, opens with the same phrase. *God created.* The Hebrew noun *Elohim* is plural but the verb is singular, a normal usage in the OT when reference is to the one true God. This use of the plural expresses intensification rather than number and has been called the plural of majesty, or of potentiality. In the OT the Hebrew verb for "create" is used only of divine, never of human, activity. *the heavens and the earth.* "All things" (Isa 44:24). That God created everything is also taught in Ecc 11:5; Jer 10:16; Jn 1:3; Col 1:16; Heb 1:2. The positive, life-oriented teaching of v. 1 is beautifully summarized in Isa 45:18.
1:2 *earth.* The focus of this account. *formless and empty.* The phrase, which appears elsewhere only in Jer 4:23, gives structure to the rest of the chapter (see note on v. 11). God's "separating" and "gathering" on days 1–3 gave form, and his "making" and "filling" on days 4–6 removed the emptiness. *darkness . . . the waters.* Completes the picture of a world awaiting God's light-giving, order-making and life-creating word. *and.* Or "but." The awesome (and, for ancient man, fearful) picture of the original state of the visible creation is relieved by the majestic announcement that the mighty Spirit of God hovers over creation. The announcement anticipates God's creative words that follow. *Spirit of God.* He was active in creation, and his creative power continues today (see Job 33:4; Ps 104:30). *hovering over.* Like a bird that provides for and protects its young (see Dt 32:11; Isa 31:5). The imagery may also suggest the winged sun disk, which throughout the ancient Near East was a symbol of divine majesty.
1:3 *God said.* Merely by speaking, God brought all things into being (Ps 33:6,9; 148:5; Heb 11:3). *Let there be light.* God's first creative word called forth light in the midst of the primeval darkness. Light is necessary for making God's creative works visible and life possible. In the OT it is also symbolic of life and blessing (see 2Sa 22:29; Job 3:20; 30:26; 33:30; Ps 49:19; 56:13; 97:11; 112:4; Isa 53:11; 58:8,10; 59:9; 60:1,3). Paul uses this word to illustrate God's re-creating work in sin-darkened hearts (2Co 4:6).
1:4 Everything God created is good (see vv.

10,12,18,21,25); in fact, the conclusion declares it to be "very good" (v. 31). The creation, as fashioned and ordered by God, had no lingering traces of disorder and no dark and threatening forces arrayed against God or man. Even darkness and the deep were given benevolent functions in a world fashioned to bless and sustain life (see Ps 104:19–26; 127:2).
1:5 *called.* See vv. 8,10. In ancient times, to name something or someone implied having dominion or ownership (see 17:5,15; 41:45; 2Ki 23:34; 24:17; Da 1:7). Both day and night belong to the Lord (Ps 74:16). *first day.* Some say that the creation days were 24-hour days, others that they were indefinite periods.
1:6 *expanse.* The atmosphere, or "sky" (v. 8), as seen from the earth. "Hard as a mirror" (Job 37:18) and "like a canopy" (Isa 40:22) are among the many pictorial phrases used to describe it.
1:7 *And it was so.* The only possible outcome, whether stated (vv. 9,11,15,24,30) or implied, to God's "Let there be."
1:9 *one place.* A picturesque way of referring to the "seas" (v. 10) that surround the dry ground on all sides and into which the waters of the lakes and rivers flow. The earth was "formed out of water" (2Pe 3:5) and "founded . . . upon the seas" (Ps 24:2), and the waters are not to cross the boundaries set for them (Ps 104:7–9; Jer 5:22).
1:11 *God said.* This phrase is used twice on the third day (vv. 9,11) and three times (vv. 24,26,29) on the sixth day. These two days are climactic, as the following structure of ch. 1 reveals (see note on v. 2 regarding "formless and empty"):

Days of forming	Days of filling
1. "light" (v. 3)	4. "lights" (v. 14)
2. "water under the expanse . . . water above it" (v. 7)	5. "every living and moving thing with which the water teems . . . every winged bird" (v. 21)
3a. "dry ground" (v. 9)	6a₁. "livestock, creatures that move along the ground, and wild animals" (v. 24)
	6a₂. "man" (v. 26)
b. "vegetation" (v. 11)	b. "every green plant for food" (v. 30)

Both the horizontal and vertical relationships between the days demonstrate the literary beauty of the chapter and stress the orderliness and symmetry of God's creative activity. *kinds.* See vv. 12,21,24–25. Both creation and re-

Figure 4.1.   Text and Apparatus in the *NIV Study Bible*

annotated Bible at Creekside Baptist. The *NIV Study Bible* contains extensive apparatus: annotations in smaller print at the side of the page, cross-references in the center column (and spilling over into the foot of the second column of biblical text), translators' notes following the biblical text, and superscripted verse numbers. This apparatus embodies, in extremely condensed form, a long tradition of scholarship. Yet the apparatus is not regarded as the word of God, but the word of scholars. And so biblical text—God's word—is made to dominate the page, despite the fact that the apparatus occupies more space. The format of the page distinguishes the two kinds of text and juxtaposes them in a hierarchical relationship.

Scripture reading, in the Sunday morning service, is also set apart and overtly marked as scripture. The scripture reading is marked as such in the bulletin, is often carried out by a layperson, and is often further set off with explicit scripture references and introductory ("Hear the word of the Lord") and concluding ("This has been the word of the Lord") phrases.

These conventions in print and performance indicate that evangelicals regard the Bible as distinct from all other texts, but the evidence reviewed in chapter 2 suggests an even stronger claim—that the Bible is regarded as *stereotypically* distinct from all other texts. It is one thing to say that evangelicals maintain a boundary between the Bible and all other texts; it is quite another to say that this boundary is regarded as intersubjective.

I showed in chapter 2 how Bibles are thought to have a distinct appearance, and the text a distinct sound. The stereotypical appearance of Bibles (leather bound, gold lettering on the cover, etc.) is impressed on youngsters from at least the age of two—even though the actual Bibles they will use look nothing like this. The stereotypical sound of scripture (lofty, archaic diction and grammar) is reproduced through the recitation of the Lord's Prayer—even though the form of the prayer recited occurs in no actual Bible. I argued in chapter 2 that these practices enrich the Bible concept and give (somewhat fictive) substance to the category "Bible." Here I want to point out the Bible's social nature, the fact that not only are individuals' Bible concepts enriched with descriptors unique to the Bible, but that they are enriched *in stereotypical ways*, ways that each individual can reasonably expect others to recognize too.

Four sorts of evidence—surveys, the doctrinal statements of evangelical institutions, evangelicals' discursive practices, and evangelicals' maintenance of a boundary between the Bible and all other texts—suggest that evangelicals regard the Bible as authoritative. The purpose of my review, however, has been more than merely to establish this decidedly unstartling conclusion: along the way I have noted features of each that will serve as the evidential basis for a theory of biblical authority. But first it is worth examining the closely related doctrine of biblical inspiration.

The Doctrine of Inspiration

The following is from my discussion with Chris, a middle-aged man who had attended Creekside Baptist for nearly a decade.

> BRIAN: Is the Bible the word of God?
>
> CHRIS: Boy, you're asking a lot of . . . now if we define what is the word of God. . . .
>
> BRIAN: I'll let you define it however you like.
>
> CHRIS: You know, for me it *is* the word of God, it's the inspired word of God. Is it affected by who wrote it? Yeah, I think it is. I think . . . but it is the inspired word of God. I believe, you know. And it is inerrant, in things spiritual.
>
> BRIAN: Is anything *but* the Bible the word of God? Anything other than the Bible?
>
> CHRIS: No, I don't think so. I don't think revelation comes to us in that form in any other you know, like Joseph Smith or anyone else, I don't buy it. I don't think we can add to it. I think it is the only word of God. I think it's unique. I think we could say revelation is a picture of God, you know, it's a graphic description. Creation, you know, that to me is revelation. But it is not the word. It's not a word. A word is a little more definitive. It's not so general, it's more specific. Words are very thoughtfully chosen and picked and selected and used. Hopefully [laughs].
>
> BRIAN: What does it mean to say the Bible is inspired by God?
>
> CHRIS: Well, to me it means that the person who wrote it is basically—I don't know how to say this—is mentally stimulated through a spiritual force, the Holy Spirit, and that that is in them, and they are attuned so much when they are writing this, or God has them attuned so much, that it would be as if he were writing it. That's what I think the inspiration of the Holy Scriptures is, is that they sat down to write this, and they could do nothing else but write what they wrote. It was inspired by God.

Chris's answers are useful to consider because they are among the most explicit that I received, and they agree in most points with the answers of other informants. Chris was not raised in a Christian environment, but converted while in college. When I initially asked whether the Bible is the word of God, he paused momentarily to ask about how I define "word of God." However, when I invited him to define it, he instead answered the original question, taking "word of God" as a reference to the Bible and contrasting it with revelation in nature. Along the way he added the word "inspired" and noted that it is "inerrant, in things spiritual." My other informants also affirmed that the Bible is the word of God, and, like Chris, introduced the notion of inspiration in this context.

The doctrine of biblical inspiration has been a fundamentalist and evangelical mainstay. Reacting against the "low" view of the Bible implicit in much "higher criticism," fundamentalists articulated very clear and precise statements about biblical authority, inspiration, and inerrancy in *The Fundamentals* (Torrey and Dixon 1993 [1909–1917]). Evangelicals have agreed about the Bible's inspiration, but have disagreed about the extent of its inerrancy, whether it is inerrant in all matters or only in spiritual matters (cf. Geisler 1980; McKim 1985; Ryrie 1981; Youngblood 1984), with both sides claiming to represent orthodox tradition (essays by Edwin Blum, Robert Preus, and John Gerstner in Geisler 1980; Rogers and McKim 1979; Woodbridge 1982; Woodbridge 1986). Analysis of the various views of evangelical theologians would require a book-length treatment in its own right: here I will merely summarize some of the more widely held elements of the doctrine of inspiration, and discuss the degree to which each was reported by my informants.

"INSPIRATION." The word *inspiration* is derived from the Latin "breathe into," and it appears in 2 Timothy 3:16 (KJV, Living Bible, RSV, NAS, NKJV, NRSV, et al.) as a translation of the Greek θεόπνευστος, a compound word "God-breathed" (NIV). None of my informants mentioned the etymology of *inspiration*, but two mentioned the underlying Greek word, and a couple more mentioned the literal translation "God-breathed."

But informants were quite vague about the process. Just as Chris talked vaguely about the writers being "mentally stimulated through a spiritual force" and God having the writers "attuned," other informants glossed inspiration with phrases like "God guided their thoughts" or "impressed their minds." When I pressed for further details, most informants said that they did not know. I eventually thought to ask a few informants whether it bothered them that they did not know, and, as one man told me, "Not really. I mean, I probably should find out, just so I would know what to tell people, but I'm not worried about it."

It is important to note that my informants' responses were quite variable in their wording. Apart from those few who used the words θεόπνευστος and "God-breathed," they did not seem to be drawing their answers from any common source. And indeed this may be the case because, although there are frequent allusions to the doctrine of inspiration at Creekside Baptist, I never heard it explicitly discussed.

PLENARY INSPIRATION. The doctrine of the Bible's plenary inspiration holds that divine inspiration extends to the whole of the Bible—no part is uninspired. On my survey, 84 percent of respondents (n = 81) agreed with the statement "The *entire* Bible is inspired by God," with 6 percent disagreeing and 10 percent marking "undecided."

Formal doctrinal statements often leave unspecified whether any texts other than the Bible might also be inspired, and less consensus on this point was reflected in my survey: only 31 percent of respondents (n = 80) agreed with the statement "*Only* the Bible is inspired by God. No other book is inspired by God," with 53 percent disagreeing and 16 percent marking "undecided."

Further kinds of variation were evidenced in interviews, where some informants said that no other book was inspired; some thought that there were degrees of inspiration, and that other texts might be inspired, but less so than the Bible; some thought that there were kinds of inspiration, and in this way differentiated between biblical and other inspired texts. All informants, however, agreed that the Bible is inspired differently than any other text. One of the most interesting notions came from a man who, in addition to differentiating the Bible with respect to extent of inspiration, also said, "Other texts *might* be inspired, but we *know* the Bible is inspired."

VERBAL INSPIRATION. Many fundamentalist and evangelical theologians say that the inspiration of the Bible extends to the words, that the Bible has the *ipsissima verba*, the *very words*, of God. This view is sometimes dogmatically asserted and supported with formal arguments (e.g., Gray 1993 [1917]; Ryrie 1981).

On my survey, 86.3 percent of respondents (n=80) agreed with the statement "The *words* of the Bible are inspired." Of the rest, 10 percent marked "undecided" and only 3.7 percent disagreed. Yet in interviews, few of my informants expressed strong views on this, and several said that it did not make any practical difference whether the words or the ideas were inspired. Some sense of what a nonissue this is may be seen in the following interview:

> BRIAN: You've mentioned a couple of times believing the Bible as the literal word of God, and I want to inquire a little bit further what you mean by that. What does it mean to say the Bible is the literal word of God?
>
> SANDRA: That it [was] inspired by him, has been protected by him through the ages, and tells it like it is. It is not a series of fairy tales.
>
> BRIAN: Would you say that every word of the Bible is inspired and is supposed to be just the way it is?
>
> SANDRA: I don't think I'd go that far.
>
> BRIAN: For some people that's what literal means, and I wanted to be sure I understood you.
>
> SANDRA: Yes, literal in my sense is broader.
>
> BRIAN: Would it be fair to say the Bible is true?
>
> SANDRA: Yes.
>
> BRIAN: Okay, to put it negatively, it's not corrupted in any way?
>
> SANDRA: I think overall, no. What I consider to be the basic Bible—if you start looking at varieties of translations, while the verbiage may vary depending on

the bent of the publisher or the translator—the basic ideas are pretty much there, I think.

BRIAN: Is it the ideas that are inspired?

SANDRA: Yes.

BRIAN: Some people say it's the ideas of scripture that are inspired. Other people say it's the words that are inspired—not that the ideas aren't, but the inspiration extends to the words. Do you have an opinion about that?

SANDRA: I would probably be inclined to think that's true of the original. But as you come down through the ages, as it's come to me, obviously the original's several iterations back.

Sandra's closing reference to "the original" reflected a long-standing fundamentalist insistence that the autographs, at least, were verbally inspired, even if errors might have crept in over the centuries. Yet she made no strong claim in this regard—like my other informants, she regarded the details as of little import.

The Nature of Biblical Authority

When informants said that they did not know exactly how inspiration worked, I followed up with questions about the implications of the doctrine: Does it entail that God is the author of the Bible? Does it entail that the Bible is true? Does it entail that the Bible is authoritative? Each of these questions received an unhesitating, confident *yes* from all interviewees. Whatever uncertainty they had about the nature of inspiration did not extend to its implications.

Now it is a curious situation when an unclear idea has clear consequences. As I showed earlier in this chapter, the Bible's authority is often presented, in evangelical doctrine, as a *consequence* of its divine inspiration, and this same premise→ consequence relation is apparent also in the interviews reported above. The doctrine of inspiration is indeed often invoked as a justification and explanation of the authority that evangelicals attribute to the Bible.

Yet the relative certainty and uniformity of informants' views of biblical authority suggests that it is in fact biblical authority that is primary, and that the doctrine of divine inspiration functions psychologically as a *rationale* for *prior* belief in the Bible's authority. Psychologically, it is authority, not inspiration, that is the premise, and inspiration, not authority, that is the consequence.

In fact, practically speaking, there is no need for *any* theory of biblical authority. At the beginning of his argument for a postmodern theology of biblical authority, Darrell Jodock (1989, 5) writes:

A worked-out view [of biblical authority] is important in order to discern appropriate implications and explain them to others but is not required in order to make the Scriptures significant for Christian living. On the contrary, individuals or groups can experience the claim of the scriptural message without thinking through all the ramifications involved in their approach to the Bible; they need not, in this sense, possess any *theory* of biblical authority. If persons can find the Bible useful without having any theory of its authority, then surely agreement among Christians about a single theory is not necessary either.

Jodock's observation is stated without evidence, but aptly synthesizes the results of my empirical work: the people of Creekside Baptist can and do "experience the claim of the scriptural message" without having a clear, well-developed, or uniform theory of biblical authority. They are able to do so because the practice of biblical authority turns on psychological mechanisms that are quite different from those involved in speculative theology.

Dialogical Biblicism

It is now possible to synthesize the empirical work reported above and to construct a theory of biblical authority. In doing so, I will draw on models proposed by Emile Durkheim and Roy Rappaport, modified as necessary by recent work in cognitive and linguistic anthropology.

Durkheim (1995 [1912]) famously proposed that sacredness accrues to objects insofar as they function as symbols of society, on the ground that the attributes of "the sacred" correlate with the attributes of society. A direct extension of Durkheim's ideas to Biblicism would hold that evangelicals regard the Bible as sacred because it symbolizes evangelical society. Yet the dissimilarities between the Bible and the church far outnumber the similarities, particularly with respect to the core, definitional features of the Bible reviewed in chapter 2. Evangelicals themselves have far more often suggested analogies between the Bible and Jesus Christ (both called the word of God) or between the Bible and creation (both forms of revelation) than between the Bible and the church. In its direct form, this hypothesis has little to recommend it, even if one would like to preserve its core intuition that the Bible's authority is somehow social in origin.

A more sophisticated model was developed by Rappaport (1979; 1999). Rappaport argued that all human societies involve several distinct kinds of "understandings" distinguished by formal and semantic properties. These understandings are arranged in an adaptive hierarchy, such that those that are lower in the hierarchy are more variable both within society and over time, serving as mechanism of adaptation for the understandings at higher levels.

In Rappaport's model, the most fundamental premises of a society are its "ultimate sacred postulates" (USPs). USPs are distinguished from the other understandings present in a society in that USPs are nonempirical, beyond the reach of logical refutation, and regarded as unquestionable. Examples of USPs given by Rappaport are the Shema of Judaism and the Shahada of Islam. Such postulates have an important social function in that they define a community and thus serve as a kind of core around which the community can transform and adapt to circumstances while preserving its essential identity. It is important for this function that they be neither empirically nor logically falsifiable, because this shelters them from ever having to change. Their nonempirical, often nearly tautologous nature makes them ideal foundations for community identity.

The notion that at the core of community identity might lie ideas with special properties was prefigured by Durkheim, but whereas Durkheim sought to explain these ideas' special status by their representational (symbolic) function, Rappaport tried to explain their special status as an adaptive necessity. Rappaport pointed out that adaptation requires some stasis in the midst of change, and claimed that USPs, because of their nonempirical status and perceived importance, are ideally suited to remain constant no matter what challenges a society's environment presents.

Less central than the USPs is another class of ideas, what Rappaport calls "cosmological axioms." These are basic premises about the structure of the universe, the core categories of a worldview. Rappaport identified these with the kinds of binary oppositions revealed by structuralist analysis. Among evangelicals these would correspond to basic oppositions between God and humankind, good and evil, right and wrong, and heaven and earth.

The cosmological axioms form the logical basis for the next set of understandings—rules. Rules "transform cosmology into conduct" (Rappaport 1979, 120) by articulating the shoulds and should-nots that arise from a particular worldview. Rules are less central than cosmological axioms because rules can change while maintaining the basic categories in terms of which those rules are cast.

Rappaport described several other levels, less central than rules, but his thoughts on these were less developed and, in any case, the distinction between USPs and other understandings is the key one for this analysis.

As it stands, there are three related problems with Rappaport's model. First, anthropologists have largely abandoned the notion, implicit in Rappaport's proposal, that members of a society substantially share a coherent worldview. The older view of culture as a shared worldview is largely dead today, replaced by the recognition that different cultural elements may have different distributions in a given population.

The second problem is that there is little reason to believe that "understandings" are organized in the way Rappaport described. The cognitive structures uncovered by cognitive anthropologists and psychologists do not map at all to Rappaport's proposal.

Finally, there is no compelling evidence that the hierarchy Rappaport proposed is really a means by which societies adapt. The general architecture appears to be adaptive, but Rappaport provided no extended case studies showing that any society ever actually adapted in the way he described. (His ethnography of the Maring [Rappaport 1984 (1968)] showed only that the Maring ritual cycle could be understood as cybernetic, not that its adaptation was structured by the hierarchy he later proposed.) So it seems that a society *could* adapt in the way he described, but there is no evidence that any have.

In light of these problems, I will modify Rappaport's model in a way that rescues, I think, its most insightful elements. I propose that Rappaport's model may be usefully reinterpreted dialogically not as a model of culture, but as a model of culture making, an unpacking of some of the cognitive elements required to form a community. Specifically, I want to preserve three key insights of Rappaport's theory:

1. The notion that at the core of community identity may lie deeply held beliefs that are enigmatic or mysterious.
2. The notion that these USPs are logically and empirically disconnected from the assumptions implicit in a community's actual practice.
3. The notion that USPs and cosmological axioms are not merely descriptions of the world, but also values.

I will argue that these features of USPs may be usefully understood as consequences of community making, with reference to biblical authority at Creekside Baptist.

The doctrine of biblical inspiration may be usefully regarded as an ultimate sacred postulate. This identification captures the fact that interviewees not only didn't understand it but also were relatively unconcerned about not understanding it—it is regarded as unquestionable, a fundamental postulate within the community, and so there is no practical need for them to have a well-developed theory of biblical authority. Such an identification captures the place of statements about biblical inspiration at the beginning of doctrinal statements, often coming even before the doctrine of God: the doctrine of inspiration is among the *most fundamental* of beliefs.

This identification also captures a curious feature of doctrinal statements about biblical inspiration: their use of scripture to justify belief in scripture. Just as the doctrinal statement of Creekside Baptist justified its regard for scripture by reference to 2 Timothy 3:15–17, 2 Peter 1:16–21, 2 Peter 3:14–18, and Luke 24:36–49, so evangelicals' doctrinal statements in general justify their belief in biblical inspiration in terms of the text itself. The use of the Bible to justify Biblicism makes these statements tautologous in just the way Rappaport described.

An objection: evangelical theologians have in fact advanced empirical and logical arguments for biblical inspiration. If the belief is really beyond empirical and logical confirmation or refutation, why would they do so? Several answers are possible here. Evangelical theologians might advance arguments just because a modernist epistemology requires that beliefs be objectively assessed if they are to be respectable, and they are able to put together essays that have at least the form of objective assessment, even if the proffered arguments were not the *cause* of their own beliefs. Evangelical theologians might also advance arguments because they do not *recognize* that their belief is nonempirical—all rationalization, after all, presupposes that the thing rationalized is really a consequence rather than an antecedent. (Some such story is suggested by what seems to me the remarkably uncritical nature of the arguments they set forth.) Or it might be that theologians entertain a more empirical form of this belief than do the regular attendees of Creekside Baptist.

The doctrine of biblical inspiration has the characteristics Rappaport proposed for USPs. Yet the identification of biblical inspiration as a USP does not in itself explain these characteristics. Rappaport had explained the properties of USPs as an adaptive necessity, but, as I noted above, there is no compelling evidence that this explanation is correct. My proposal is instead that the properties are a result of community formation. This requires some explanation.

Community members cannot be assumed to share common views about any specific feature of the world except one: if they are to form a community, they must at least share some common assumptions about their community. This is, I should emphasize, a *practical* necessity. Church members need not share a common *theory* of the church, but only common expectations about how to interact with other church members. A community requires a discursive ground, even if that ground is occasionally subject to renegotiation.

Biblical authority—as manifest in the discursive practice of framing one's speech in relation to the Bible—is one of the foundational assumptions of evangelical communities, one of the practices in which community members, in order to *be* community members, participate. It is, as I noted above, quite impossible to understand much evangelical discourse without attributing to evangelical speakers the assumption that the Bible is authoritative. In order to participate in evangelical conversation, one must treat the Bible as authoritative. One might distinguish—and I will below—between the rule-governed practice of Biblicist framing and the abstract belief in biblical authority (i.e., between Rappaport's rules and his cosmological axioms), but it should be understood that they are intertwined on the ground: the performance of biblical authority in dialogue reinforces the abstract belief in biblical authority and the abstract belief in biblical authority motivates and shapes the discursive convention.

The classification of biblical authority as a cosmological axiom captures the importance attributed to biblical authority in evangelicals' formal doctrinal statements and evangelicals' interest in establishing transitivity between the Bible and their beliefs. Evangelicals do indeed take biblical authority as axiomatic in their communities, and place great importance on making sure that what they do is "biblical."

It also explains the importance assigned Biblicism by individual evangelicals in the process of selecting a church. In interviews, I asked what people looked for in a church. The following is from my conversation with Greg:

BRIAN: What do you look for in a church?

GREG: Well, initially I think the most important thing is doctrine, that they believe Jesus Christ is the only way to God. Something I don't think I mentioned in my definition of Christian—maybe it was implied—but just that Jesus is the only way [and] the Bible is the word of God.

BRIAN: That's part of being a Christian?

GREG: [Nods.] [Pause.] It may not be a key part of becoming a Christian. It's definitely possible to accept Christ while there's still areas you don't understand or things you don't get. . . . But a church should definitely hold to the Bible as the word of God, [and] Jesus [as] the only way—I think those are kind of the first things you can check up on. I think you pretty much have to sit through a service to figure out if their style is going to be something you enjoy. And that can mean a lot of different things, everything from the type of preaching to the type of music, to how friendly the people are. To an extent, I feel like I settled for a church that was not my first choice, or it was not a perfect choice I should say when we came here. Just because Creekside Baptist did not measure up in every way that I considered important. I mean, significantly, the music I find tedious and boring. Although it has improved lately, there is no guarantee that would happen at the beginning. But the teaching, the doctrine seemed solid, and I found people I liked fairly quickly. We knew another couple going to the church right from the beginning, which helped.

Greg mentions a number of considerations, prominently among them regard for the Bible as the word of God. Another respondent also regarded Biblicism as a primary consideration in choosing a church:

Flat off, the assumption that they believe in the Bible. . . . Those type of things. So it would have to be a Christian church, it would have to believe that the Bible is the word of God, and seek to do that evangelism we spoke of. But are you looking for. . . what are some more peripheral type of things? In more detail, I would look for the preaching, programs for kids, the type of participants and what do they do with their kids, things like that.

In general, I found that the people who attended Creekside Baptist were attracted to the church in part by its Biblicism. So biblical authority is part not only of how churches define themselves but also how some individuals select churches.

Given evangelicals' axiomatic regard for the authority of the Bible, it is possible to see how the doctrine of biblical inspiration might come to be entertained as an ultimate sacred postulate. The practice of biblical authority invites the question, Why is the Bible authoritative? Why should this ancient text be regarded as so important? It does not demand that this question be answered, but it does create an interest in hearing what answers might be available. More precisely, it creates a situation in which justifications of biblical authority are relevant enough to be attended to and repeated.

The doctrine of biblical inspiration is just such an answer. The average layperson does not know what it means, but is nonetheless very sure that, whatever it means, it explains the Bible's authority: the Bible is authoritative because it is the inspired word of God. The implication is clearer than the premise because the premise came to be entertained precisely to provide an explanation for the "implied" belief.

It might be objected that a mysterious answer is not really much more satisfactory than no answer at all. Epistemologically, this is true—but practically, it is not. The mysterious answer has three practical advantages over no answer at all.

1. It defers the problem by one inferential step. Rather than having the mystery rest on the doorstep of an institutionally foundational belief, it is moved at least as far as the front sidewalk. As I pointed out above, the doctrine of biblical inspiration is seldom discussed at Creekside Baptist, and people are free to get on with using the Bible as an authority without immediately confronting the mysterious nature of that authority.

2. It changes the critical term. The question "Why is the Bible authoritative?" focuses attention on the Bible: What about the Bible makes it authoritative? A direct answer to this question must turn on distinctive and relevant features of the Bible, and this list—probably quite short—would have to justify adequately all community uses of the Bible. But if one says that the Bible is authoritative because God inspired its human authors to write his message for humanity, attention focuses on the term *inspire*, which can be left mysterious without threat to the community, and which, precisely because of its vagueness, can justify many different uses of the Bible.

3. Finally, it distances the problem. Rather than explaining present biblical authority by reference to the changeable present, the justification is pushed into a closed and inaccessible past: it is simply impossible now

to know how inspiration might have taken place, and its location in the past makes any expectation that one *should* be able to know unreasonable.

In brief, the doctrine of biblical inspiration is nearly an ideal rationalization, socially and psychologically speaking, for biblical authority.

It has another benefit, too, in that it connects biblical authority with the hermeneutic expectations that make the Bible so powerful. Belief that the Bible is inspired by God helps to raise expectations of the text's relevance and suggests that God may be particularly likely to speak through this very special work. These expectations do not, strictly speaking, depend on the doctrine of inspiration, but they resonate with it and give it additional relevance.

(The functionalism implicit in this account does not run afoul of the standard objection to social functionalism—that individuals seek their own interests rather than the interests of the group— because there is minimal conflict here between the interests of the individual and group: just as it is in the group's interest to preserve this rationalization, so the rationalization permits the individual to remain a member of the community, a desire which, in a religiously pluralist society, may be reasonably attributed at least to adult community members.)

In summary, on the model proposed here, the felt authority of the Bible for evangelicals is derived from the discursive practice of biblical authority as a condition of participation in evangelical institutions. Biblical authority is axiomatic in evangelical communities like Creekside Baptist Church. Biblical authority is thus spread as these institutions reproduce themselves through time. The axiomatic status of biblical authority is protected, to some degree, from curiosity, because the doctrine of biblical inspiration defers, shifts, and distances the problem. This doctrine functions as an ultimate sacred postulate because it is taken to imply the Bible's authority, though the precise shape of this justification is not clear.

Principle vs. Practice

One of the implications of the proposition that evangelicals regard the Bible as authoritative is that evangelicals will do what the Bible says. Yet it is curiously easy to find examples of perfectly clear biblical injunctions that are uniformly ignored by large communities of people who claim to believe the Bible. I have in mind texts like Romans 16:16, "Greet one another with a holy kiss" (repeated in I Corinthians 16:20, 2 Corinthians 13:12, I Thessalonians 5:26, and in another form in I Peter 5:14). When I inquired about this command of a few people at Creekside Baptist, informants concurred (1) that its meaning is quite clear, (2) that it is in the Bible, and (3) that they are not going to do it.

My informants' explanations were that this particular command is "cultural." In the words of one woman: "Well, in their culture that was how people greeted each other, you know, a kiss on each cheek. It would be weird if you went to church and just started doing it." But of course, this rationale could be used to get one out of nearly *any* biblical command, and my informants were unconvinced by the parallel argument that what was objectionable about homosexuality was the particular way it was practiced in biblical times. It is an ad hoc argument, widely endorsed because it has the convenient consequence of exempting evangelicals from an inconvenient command.

The existence of this rationalization, however, points up an important distinction between two kinds of biblical authority. On one hand, the *principle* of biblical authority is avowed in statements of faith and assessed by surveys. This is an abstract principle that defines a community in relation to a text concept and stipulates a community ideal: belief that the Bible is authoritative in principle creates a situation in which actual community practices may be compared to the text. This principle contributes to a dynamic of renewal and reformation.

The *practice* of biblical authority, on the other hand, is the discursive practice of establishing transitivity between Bibles and beliefs outlined in chapter 3. This responds to different dynamics than the principle of biblical authority suggests. Transitivity is driven by relevance: the task of the expositor is to make the text meaningful within the lives of modern evangelicals. This does not necessarily entail that the whole Bible is expounded or that all texts are subjected to the same hermeneutic processes. It leaves room both for selectivity and for ad hoc hermeneutics.

Ad hoc explanations develop when the results of the practice of biblical authority conflict with the principle of biblical authority. In principle, the whole Bible is authoritative, but in practice, in a community like Creekside Baptist, commands like "Greet one another with a holy kiss" are not, because unrelated midwesterners *just do not* walk up and kiss each other. The "cultural" rationalization finds an audience because it defers the conflict and changes it into an abstract hermeneutic one. The audience is susceptible to it because they are caught between the principle and the practice of biblical authority.

The Structure of Biblicism   **5**

A New Model

IN THE LAST THREE CHAPTERS, I have argued for a new model of American evangelical Biblicism. The main claims of the model may be summarized as follows.

1. "The Bible" is a *category* designating a set of books bounded by conventions of print (e.g., leather bound, sober color, ribbon marker), language (i.e., formal, archaic), and naming (i.e., use of "Bible" in the title). This boundary is stereotyped, and is regarded by evangelicals as common knowledge. The existence of a strong boundary allows evangelicals to assume that there is something called "the Bible" despite significant variation in actual Bibles, especially children's Bibles.

2. The boundary is important because a major feature of evangelical communities, part of their very *self-definition*, is the authority they ascribe to the Bible. Evangelicals regard the Bible as authoritative both in principle and in practice, but the principle of Biblical authority and the practice of Biblical authority are distinct processes.

3. The *principle* of Biblical authority is part of the evangelical community's self-definition in a pluralist religious environment. Statements of this principle are cast abstractly, stipulating relations between "the Bible" and broad categories like "belief" and "practice," and occur mainly on institutional borders. The abstraction and normative nature of these statements sometimes puts them in tension with the selectivity of evangelicals' actual biblical interpretations.

4. The community's self-definitional use of biblical authority is protected, to some degree, from its arbitrariness because the doctrine of biblical

inspiration defers, shifts, and distances the problem. The doctrine of biblical inspiration functions as an ultimate sacred postulate because it is taken to imply the Bible's authority, though the precise shape of the rationale is not clear.

5. Evangelicals' *practice* of Biblical authority consists in the maintenance of their interpretive tradition. The interpretive tradition is a species of belief-tradition in which a set of beliefs is transmitted along with the attribution of those beliefs to a text, the Bible. Evangelicals' tradition presents the text as an object for hermeneutic activity, but the goal of that hermeneutic activity is not so much to establish the meaning of the text as to establish transitivity between the text and beliefs. The maintenance of transitivity between the Bible and a set of beliefs is the core of the interpretive tradition.

6. The transitivity is sometimes established implicitly, particularly with children. The interpretive tradition emphasizes the fact of *some* connection more than particular connections. And thus a great deal of "what the Bible says" may be transmitted quite apart from actual exegesis. When this practice is combined with the definition of "the Bible" by its meaning, there may develop considerable differences between evangelicals' idea of the Bible and actual Bibles.

7. Transitivity is greatly facilitated by evangelicals' hermeneutic flexibility. Evangelicals are not inheritors of any socially transmitted set of methods for reading the Bible; rather, evangelical Bible reading mines the riches of individuals' hermeneutic imaginations. Like other communication, evangelicals' Bible reading is driven by a search for relevance. However, dual contextualization of the act of Bible reading, use of heuristics for moving beyond the text as given, and the influence of the belief-tradition combine to make interpretations of the Bible unlike interpretations of other texts.

8. The interpretive tradition is perennially caught between the Scylla of interpretive freedom and the Charybdis of irrelevance: too much hermeneutic freedom and the tradition disintegrates, loosing its epistemological appeal; too little interpretive freedom and the Bible becomes merely an irrelevant historical artifact, rather than the ever-living word of God. The avowal of literalism, being motivated by the need to limit hermeneutic freedom, thus conflicts with any actual restriction to a text's historical meaning, which would severely constrict the Bible's ongoing relevance.

These are the main claims. This model, it will be noted, is distinctly anthropo-logical. I have not appealed to sacredness, ultimacy, or special insight in order to explain the ways in which people handle, read, and cite the Bible. The terms that bear analytic weight are social and psychological notions like *category, context, relevance, community, discourse, identity,* and *interaction.* However problematic some of these terms may be, they are located in theories that are at least ideally empirical.

Comparison to the Commonsense Model

The new model is in some ways familiar, in other ways quite different from the "commonsense" characterization of scriptures given in the introduction (Smart and Hecht 1982, as summarized by Levering 1989, 8–9):

- There are often beliefs that the text is of divine origin, or the product of special insight.
- Whatever their origin, they are regarded and treated as sacred, that is, powerful and inviolable, to be treated with respect.
- They are regarded and consulted as normative, authoritative for a community in various aspects of its religious life: for worship, doctrine, and behavior.
- The texts, whether written or oral, are regarded as closed and fixed, not to be added to or subtracted from. In other words, they are treated as a canon.
- When the sacred text is in the form of a book, it is regarded as complete. It contains everything of importance, and can be applied to all aspects of human life.
- The texts are used by members of the community in religious and ritual contexts.
- Sacred texts testify to that which is ultimate.

If, in the words of Miriam Levering (1989, 9), these statements "belong to the widely shared common sense characterization of the Bible" and are "weakly true, and far less significant (or significant in a different sense)" as characterizations of texts other than the Bible, it is clear now that they miss key aspects of Biblicism, at least in its evangelical form, as well. In this section, I show how the new model of evangelical Biblicism contrasts with this commonsense characterization of the Bible, both substantively and as a basis for cross-cultural comparison.

Divine Origin

The commonsense formulation includes an *interpretation* of the doctrine of inspiration: it takes Christian statements about the Bible's origin and incorporates them into its model of scripture.

In order to facilitate comparative studies, it makes this interpretation less tradition-specific by use of a broad notion of "divine origin" and throwing in "or special insight" to account for cases such as the *Dhammapada* in Theravada Buddhism, which is regarded as originating not from any divinity, but from the Buddha's special insight. Yet this is still not broad enough: some Hindu schools regard the Vedas as uncreated, as part of the sound of the universe (Coward 1988). The comparative strategy used for Buddhism was essentially to take the Christian model, to subtract out any specifically Christian elements, and to add any substantive differences. But this will not work for Hinduism, because one would be forced either (1) to subtract out *all* of the semantic content of the Christian doctrine of inspiration, in which case the result would not be in any meaningful sense true of the Bible; or (2) to add another disjunction, such as "or uncreated," in which case the characterization is no longer really general, but amounts to a list of the different ways the scriptures' origins are described. With this strategy, comparison ends up using either semantically empty descriptors or a list.

A different strategy is suggested by the present analysis. The model presented here focuses on the social and cognitive function of beliefs about the Bible's origin. What is important about the doctrine of inspiration is not its *semantic content*—evangelicals themselves are uncertain about what its semantic content might be. What is important about the doctrine of inspiration for evangelicals are its implications, the beliefs it is felt to justify. These supposedly derivative beliefs appear, on closer analysis, to be in fact primary.

Proper cross-cultural comparison of the doctrine of inspiration thus may turn not on its semantic content, but on its social and cognitive functions. On the model presented here, the doctrine of biblical inspiration functions to rationalize biblical authority's place at the center of community identity. This model has several implications for a comparative study of scripturalism.

Most scriptures, it seems, are tied more or less directly into some community's identity. In the evangelical case, this tie is accomplished primarily by lay Biblicism, but secondarily by the widespread assumption that an evangelical community ought to have some kind of pastor who is an expert on the Bible. In other traditions, the connection may be primarily through religious officials who define their authority in relation to a text. Something of the latter case seems to be true in Hinduism, where the laity know little about the Vedas, but consult Brahmins, who ostensibly derive their authority from their knowledge of these texts. Comparison of traditions should therefore specify whether and by what means a text is tied to a community's self-concept.

A second implication is that stories of a text's origin ought to be clearer in their implications than in their content. Again, the Hindu case is instructive: while the laity regard the Vedas as given by the gods, some philosophical schools regard them as uncreated (Coward 1988). Yet both stories have similar implications for practical use of the Vedas: these texts are expected to be efficacious on the tongue of a knowledgeable Brahmin. The differences between the origin stories have little consequence for practice. Comparison should therefore focus not on the content of stories about various scriptures' origins but on the social and cognitive roles of those stories, and one might expect more variation in rationalizations than in practices.

Sacred

Scriptures are often revered as objects. Protestant Biblicism is often seen as an exception to this rule, as Protestants tend toward iconoclasm, but I have shown that even evangelicals are susceptible to special ways of handling the Bible. I have argued that this susceptibility arises from the dual nature of texts as bearers of meaning on one hand and as physical artifacts on the other, and that this dual nature is a deep part of evangelicals' Bible concept, because the text is defined by its meaning but identified by its physical characteristics.

This model suggests that scripturalists everywhere will be susceptible to inferencing between the physical and artifactual nature of their scriptures, and that this may be reflected in special handling practices and special decorative or formatting conventions for scriptures. Muslims' treatment of the Qur'an, for instance, is the subject of extensive rules, like "always set a Qur'an upright (so that no other book will be set on top of it)." The development of these traditions around scriptures may be attributed to the conceptual representation of scriptures and the particular historical circumstances of the tradition. It is important to describe this as a susceptibility because it is just that: a potential that is variously expressed, but that may be elicited even in the absence of a tradition, as I argued in chapter 2.

Authoritative

The characterization of scriptures as authoritative must, on the model presented here, be divided into two statements:

1. Scripturalists say (and believe) that their scriptures are authoritative in principle.
2. Scripturalists cite their scriptures to demonstrate/signal that an idea or practice is authoritative.

Statements one and two are quite different, in the evangelical case. Statement one is a normative generalization, something that evangelicals say in order to capture the importance of the Bible for their communities. Statement two is a description of their discursive convention of justifying ideas and practices in terms of the Bible, and does not necessarily mean either that everything the Bible says is actually practiced or that all practices may be found in the Bible in any obvious sense. The second statement allows a great deal more flexibility in the relation between evangelical beliefs and the Bible than the first would seem to suggest.

Moreover, these statements require different sorts of explanations. The first is motivated by the community's self-understanding as a Biblicist institution, and its articulation is necessitated by the evangelical institution's need to define itself in a religiously plural environment. The second statement is motivated by the interpretive tradition (which could occur apart from an avowedly Biblicist institution), and is structured by the quest for transitivity between the text and beliefs.

It is sometimes possible to find a general principle of scriptural authority in the absence of actual interaction with the scripture. This can occur in contexts where people believe that their ideas are derived from a text but in which the text is the responsibility of religious specialists, as in the Hindu case. Comparative studies must distinguish the general principle of a text's authority from the practice of authorizing beliefs by reference to a text. These are distinct processes that are mutually reinforcing in the same environment but that can occur separately.

Moreover, on the model I propose, the idea of a text, and of what a text says, may diverge markedly from what copies of the text in question actually say. Such divergence is attested ethnographically in societies where illiterate people may develop an extensive lore about a text they never actually encounter (Burdi 1993), and can even lead to striking contradictions: C. J. Fuller (1984) reports that priests in a southern Hindu temple memorize ritual texts while ascribing to those texts instructions that they do not actually contain.

Canon

The process of determining the precise set of texts to be included in the New Testament has loomed large in scholarship on early Christianity, and the Christian example led some to think that in each scriptural tradition the texts must form a well-defined, closed set.

The model presented here points to a slightly different conclusion. Evangelical Christians do indeed maintain a sharp boundary between the Bible and all other texts, and a stereotypical one at that: they maintain a boundary around the Bible that they expect to be recognized as such by all evangelicals. This suggests the comparative hypothesis that in every scripturalist tradition the set of texts that count as scriptures will be set off from other texts in ways that are regarded as common knowledge by community members.

This conventional boundary affords a different kind of flexibility. By demarcating the boundary of scriptures very clearly, the *content* of the texts can be left unspecified. So long as evangelicals can know what counts as a biblical text, they do not need to have a very elaborate knowledge of what is in those texts. Their practice turns on establishing links between their ideas and some biblical text or other, and this can be done in ad hoc ways so long as one has some way of knowing what counts as a biblical text. The *closure* of the canon affords *openness* in interpretation.

Completeness and Ultimacy

The impression that a scripture "contains everything of importance, and can be applied to all aspects of human life" and the similar claim that "scriptures testify to that which is ultimate" must be divided into several different claims.

1. All important things may be found in a scripture.
2. Everything a scripture says is important.
3. A scripture may be relevant to any aspect of human life.
4. A scripture is relevant to all aspects of human life.

In a given scripturalist community, points one and two may both be true, but point three is a weaker alternative to point four.

The model presented here suggests that what is important is defined for the majority of evangelicals as children, and is attributed to the Bible in a fairly general way. In this sense, all important things are found in scripture simply because establishing transitivity between beliefs and the Bible is a key Biblicist practice. I saw no evidence that evangelicals regard *everything* the Bible says as of importance, though I doubt they would say that any particular part is definitely unimportant—the flexibility and open-endedness of interpretation is such that the text always has more potential meaning.

Point three has to do with the scope of a scripture's potential relevance, and I think it is true that evangelicals are very flexible in their search to establish the relevance of the Bible to their lives. This flexibility is, as I showed in chapter 4, greatly aided by the dual contextualization of the act of reading, evangelicals' ability to move beyond the text as given, and the positive role of the interpretive tradition in illuminating otherwise obscure paths to relevance.

Point four is the sort of thing scripturalists sometimes say to express point three, but I know of no evidence that it is actually the case that any particular scripture is taken as relevant to *all* aspects of life, from tying one's shoes to selecting one's casket. Of course, it *could* be, but that is the premise of point three. To evidence point four one would have to show that a scripture is taken as relevant to *absolutely everything* some scripturalist does. I do not think this can be done even for someone in a monastic community.

Ultimacy, I suggest, is a by-product of the heightened expectation of relevance that evangelicals bring to the interpretation of the Bible. The way they contextualize their hermeneutic activity biases the results by ratcheting up their expectations.

Ritual Contexts

To say that members of a scripturalist community use their text in ritual contexts is mainly, I think, to suggest that they are doing things with the text that defy the modern Western expectation that one reads a text for its meaning. If a Muslim carries a Qur'an reverentially, or recites it in a language unknown to either reciter or audience, the modern Western observer sees superstition or ritual. Yet, on the model adopted here, a text is just a thing, and it has many possible uses. There is nothing especially problematic about uses other than reading for meaning.

The problem is rather why evangelical Christians are so obsessed with interpreting the text, to the relative neglect of many other possible uses. The answer, I suggest, is that Christianity is, unlike many other traditions, structured as an epistemology—that is, as a system of knowledge or belief. In Christianity, *orthodoxy* or *right belief* has long functioned as a core metaphor for the way Christians ought to be (Ruel 1982). (In many other traditions, *purity* is the core metaphor.) An implication of this metaphor, however, is that right belief is determinate and, in Protestantism, that means determinate *from the Bible*. The assumptions of evangelicals' interpretive tradition—(1) that a particular set of beliefs are true, and (2) that they are found in the Bible—arise from a core metaphor of Christianity, and this metaphor entails that ritual or magical functions of the Bible are secondary to its core epistemological function as an *interpretandum*.

The new model thus shows how many assumptions about Biblicism have been inadequate, and offers new axes of comparison for comparative study. The implicit "commonsense" model of scripture has been a distorting influence on past comparisons of scriptures and has also failed to capture the structure and dynamics of Bible use. This new, more empirically grounded model of Biblicism may provide a more useful standard of comparison.

The Epidemiology of American Evangelical Biblicism

The foregoing chapters have also shown how the cultural transmission of evangelical Biblicism is a complex process involving, at every point, the interaction of cognitive and historical factors. By way of conclusion, I will highlight the roles these different sorts of factors play.

Cognitive Factors

Whereas mimetic accounts of culture focus on our ability to imitate others, and existing epidemiological accounts focus on specific, evolved cognitive predispositions, I suggest that evangelical Biblicism involves both general cognitive abilities and at least one specific cognitive predisposition. Among the domain-general cognitive abilities must be counted the need for an epistemology, the drive for relevance, and the abilities to search for deep similarities between unlike things. We have a specific cognitive predisposition, I suggest, to form certain types of assumptions about stories. I will examine these in turn.

NEED FOR EPISTEMOLOGY. Lacking armor, claws, or fangs, and possessed of only inferior speed and strength, we humans, more than any other species, stake our survival on our minds. As part of our rather cerebral existence, we instinctively search for knowledge about our surroundings, accumulating far more knowledge than we have practical need of. As much as eating and sleeping, exploration and experiment are part of our nature, particularly evident in children. And of course, being highly social creatures, we depend on each other for information.

Because we are so very cognitive, and because we acquire so much of our knowledge socially rather than through direct experience, it is not surprising that a number of cultural traditions have developed in response to the human inclination toward knowledge. Around the world, the transmission of knowledge is a key metaphor in many cultural traditions, from initiation rites, to the many kinds of master–disciple relations, to Western science. All these cultural forms are putatively about knowledge, and each offers some guarantee of its own validity, whether in the social status ascribed to the initiated, the intellectual lineage or experience of the master, or the accumulation of empirical studies. Evangelical Biblicism is just such a tradition: it offers spiritual knowledge underwritten by an inspired text.

DRIVE FOR RELEVANCE. Part of being a heavily cognitive creature is sorting out what knowledge is relevant to a situation and bringing the appropriate inferences to bear. How we achieve this is not fully known (and the known bits are quite technical), but it does empirically seem to be the case that humans have the ability to sift relevant from irrelevant information much of the time, and that we are inclined to seek out information known to be relevant. It is not too much of a stretch, I think, to call this general orientation a drive.

Evangelical Biblicism feeds and exploits this drive for relevance. Evangelicalism includes several beliefs and practices that help readers to find the Bible relevant.

- Exposition. In sermons, Sunday school lessons, books, and study Bibles evangelicals are presented with ready-made, relevant messages. Through a number of devices, evangelicals are encouraged to regard these messages as *interpretations* of the Bible.
- Inspiration. Belief in the Bible's divine inspiration provides, as we have seen, two contexts in which any Bible passage may be interpreted: a text

may be understood either as God speaking to humanity once for all, or as the Holy Spirit speaking to the reader in the moment. The doctrine of divine inspiration leads evangelicals to expect great relevance from the Bible. The two contexts provide distinct but overlapping paths for finding the promised relevance.

- Meditative reading. The practice of reading the Bible slowly and meditatively increases the chance of finding relevance in the text.
- Traditional conditions of relevance. The belief-tradition supplies a number of ideas (salvation, character of God, morals, church life) to which a Bible passage may then be found relevant. The tradition thus provides beliefs that, once adopted, can serve as fonts of relevance when an evangelical reads the Bible.

The evangelical Biblicist tradition, then, is structured so as to co-opt individuals' drives for relevance. Once people are drawn into the tradition and accept a few basic premises about the Bible's inspiration and the nature of interpretation, their innate drive for relevance draws them further in, and the Bible's archaic text opens up like a flower to reveal new levels of meaning.

Of course, what is relevant varies, to some degree, from person to person, and the specific conditions of relevance change with time and circumstances. It is difficult to predict very specifically what will be relevant to a person next week, much less twenty or fifty years from now. And the evangelical Biblicist tradition does not try to: instead it emphasizes continuing exegesis—a constant return to the text—and allows evangelicals to seek out their own relevance in it. This is something they are cognitively well equipped to do.

PATTERN MATCHING. Humans' regular use of analogies and figures of speech shows that we intuitively conceptualize our environments at many levels of abstraction simultaneously. We are capable of seeing very subtle and indirect similarities between things that, on the surface, appear quite dissimilar. Our ability to detect similarities is called *pattern matching* because we usually focus in on important structural properties—similarities in relations between features—rather than similarities between individual features themselves.

Evangelical Biblicism exploits this cognitive ability by allowing readers to find their own resonances between the Bible and their lives. When they find in Abraham an impressive example of the faith they themselves should have, it is because they have perceived a relation between Abraham's faith-driven actions in his discouraging circumstances and their own, less faithful actions in their circumstances. They have looked past the surface dissimilarities between themselves and Abraham to find an analogy of personal faith and commitment in difficult circumstances.

In letting readers find their own relevant connections, the evangelical Biblicist tradition gains the dynamic ability to adapt to changing times. As the conditions of relevance change, so too will the ways in which the Bible is relevant. By not prescribing these in advance, the tradition remains fluid and adaptable.

CONCEPTUALIZATION OF STORIES. One specific cognitive predisposition that is co-opted by evangelical Biblicism is our tendency to identify texts by their stories or meanings. As described in chapter 2, people expect the Bible to be a text, but they differentiate this text from all others by reference not to its words (a necessary property of texts) but to its meaning (a nonnecessary property of texts). Consider: differences between texts are sometimes regarded as differences between *stories* (as when one text is the book of Genesis and the other text is *The Cat in the Hat*) and other times as differences between *versions* (as when one text is the NIV Genesis and the other is the NAS Genesis). This is not merely a matter of degree of textual difference: *West Side Story* is considered a version of *Romeo and Juliet* though the actual texts are very different. Rather, people seem to make the story/version distinction based on abstract features like plot, structure, and meaning. This is true even in oral cultures, where people distinguish between tellings of a story by the same reciter, versions by different reciters, and the different stories a reciter might tell (Goody 2000).

This way of organizing texts should not be taken for granted. After all, it is *texts* (written or—more transitorily—spoken), not *stories*, that have material existence. One could imagine a world in which texts were related by their material similarities. The way we organize texts is as yet little understood, but I think it likely that we bring to the organization of texts some very specific predispositions to focus on "deep" properties of story rather than "surface" textual properties.

This cognitive predisposition allows evangelicals to move interchangeably between different Bibles and even between adults' and children's Bibles. The text is permitted some degree of flexibility by the human cognitive predisposition to lump together textual variants of the "same" story.

I think it also underlies the transitivity of attribution that is so essential to evangelical Bible interpretation. If texts were thought of as *just* texts, then there would be no possibility of forming alternate representations of textual "meaning." Interpretation would be either impossible or irrelevant. Evangelical Biblicism would grind to a halt, for, as shown in chapter 3, transitivity between text and beliefs is essential to the interpretive tradition.

The cognitive factors described here are not incidental to evangelical Biblicism: they are important functions on which the tradition depends and which it exploits in different ways than other cultural traditions. They cannot be ignored in any account of evangelical practice. But, of course, they are somewhat ahistorical: while they adapt to changing circumstances, the basic cognitive abilities have presumably remained unchanged for thousands of years. I turn now to the more historical social and material factors that shape the tradition.

Historical Factors

American evangelical Biblicism has roots of various depths in Western history. An understanding of this root structure is necessary to any model of evangelical Biblicism because many features of American evangelical Biblicism are derived from the broader social, cultural, and material context in which American evangelical Biblicism developed. The factors I note here are religious voluntarism, individualism, Bible production, and, a central feature of Christianity, the emphasis on "belief" and "interpretation." Of course, each of these has its own epidemiological story to be told, but for the purpose of the present analysis, they may be taken as givens. I do not here attempt to give the histories of these factors, but merely to show how they are important causal factors in the shaping of American evangelical Biblicism.

RELIGIOUS VOLUNTARISM AND INDIVIDUALISM. Religious voluntarism and individualism are linked inasmuch as religion is widely regarded in the West as a matter of individual choice. The unit of religiosity here is the individual, and it is generally assumed that individuals are religious because they choose to be. These notions pervade evangelicalism, with its emphasis on individual salvation as a matter of personal faith.

The flip side of religious voluntarism is that churches compete for the allegiance of individuals and families. Because evangelicalism is understood as a property of individuals rather than churches, and because it is not even associated with any particular denomination, individuals and families will move on to a different church if they feel that their needs are not being addressed in their current one. This increases the selection pressure against ineffective churches.

In such a context evangelical Biblicism must "work" for individuals: it must help in some way to satisfy individual needs and to enrich individual experience. It does so largely, I suggest, through the production of authoritative messages that are relevant to the individual in all the particulars of his or her circumstances. The individual is further aided in finding Biblical relevance through the expositions of preachers, Sunday school teachers, Bible study leaders, and the many sorts of Christian literature.

Biblical authority is also an important tool for churches, in two ways. First, a church's emphasis on the Bible serves to attract some people to the church. Many of my informants indicated that Creekside Baptist's emphasis on the Bible was a key factor in their selection of the church, and said that, if they ever need to find another church, it will be a necessary property of any new church. Second, appeals to the Bible are rhetorically effective in that they give church teachings an apparent timelessness and divine authority. The Bible is not seen as some arbitrary text, custom-designed to serve the preacher's agenda. Rather, it is idealized as an objective standard available to all.

THE BIBLE AND BIBLE PRODUCTION. An obviously historical factor in evangelical Biblicism is their inheritance of the Bible, the collection of texts produced in the ancient Near East, defined by early church councils, copied by monks and scribes, translated (repeatedly) into English, and mass-produced for a highly competitive market by multiple publishers. American evangelicals thus live in a relatively wealthy society where a great variety of highly affordable Bibles is readily to hand. The variety of Bibles available has had three consequences, I think, for evangelical Biblicism.

- An abstract Bible concept. As I showed in chapter 2, American evangelicals regard the Bible as a text, but no particular text: they define the text by its meaning, and are aided in recognizing it through the use of a Bible stereotype. If there was only one variety of Bible available, I doubt such a complex concept would have developed.
- Personalized Bibles. Bibles may become very personal partly because they are either selected as a reflection of preference, when purchased by the individual user, or received as gifts on special occasions from friends, relatives, or institutions. In either case, people are likely to associate their Bible with some event or relationship, and treasure it the more for the association.
- Tight competition among Bible publishers has also given rise to the study notes and suggested applications that help guide Bible readers to the text's relevance. In this way preexisting Biblicism creates market conditions that reward products that further promote Biblicism.

Thus the material conditions in which American evangelicalism thrives have an influence on the forms evangelical Biblicism takes.

"BELIEF" AND "INTERPRETATION." Christianity has been a belief-oriented and interpretive tradition from its earliest days. The Bible, and evangelicals' notions of how to think about it, have been inherited by American evangelicals as part of this tradition.

Evangelicals maintain the Bible's relevance by finding in it relevant *interpretations*. Evangelicals' focus on interpretation rather than other textual activities is a consequence of the institutional role assigned to the Bible, the fact that evangelical institutions are built around and defined by relating ideas to the Bible's text rather than any of the other activities that might be performed on it. American evangelical communities are defined in terms of the Bible's *authority*, and so they provide contexts in which the Bible is *interpreted*. Interpretation is not a necessary feature of text use, but a consequence of encountering the text in a certain kind of community, the kind of community that defines itself in terms of the production and regulation of knowledge. In this respect, evangelical Biblicism is much like other literary and legal traditions in the West, and the similarities between Christian conservatives' use of the Bible and legal conservatives' use of the U.S. Constitution have often been noted (Crapanzano 2000).

But there are other ways a text may be relevant. A text might be relevant as a template for learning to read or write, for pronunciation, or for recitation. Such uses are all afforded by texts, and indeed the Bible has served at various points as a school text and as a source of ritual utterances. These uses turn on features of a text other than its meaning, but all can—and have—served to prolong a text's use long after its original relevance as a communication device has passed. In their focus on interpretation to the exclusion of other textual affordances, evangelicals seem closer to academics' use of well-established literary classics than to, say, Hindus' use of the Vedas or even medieval Europeans' use of the Bible. In historical perspective, a text is best viewed as an aggregate of affordances, a set of susceptibilities that are variously exploited in different sociocultural settings.

The Bible works, for American evangelicals, because American evangelicals work too. They conceive of their communities in relation to the Bible. They encourage, challenge, and persuade each other through appeals to the Bible. They search the Bible for messages from God, bringing to this search a criterion of success—relevance—and contextual assumptions that vastly increase the likelihood of finding such messages. And they are guided to such messages by study Bible notes, Bible study guides, sermons, and Sunday school lessons. The Bible works, but only at the end of a great deal of cultural and cognitive preparation.

References

1611. *The Bible: Translated according to the Ebrew and Greeke, and conferred with the best translations in diuers languages. With most profitable annotations vpon all the hard places, and other things of great importance, as may appear in the epistle to the reader. And also a most profitable concordance for the ready finding out of any thing in the same conteined.* Imprinted at London: By Robert Barker printer to the Kings most Excellent Maiestie.

1952. *The Holy Bible: Revised Standard Version.* New York: T. Nelson.

1971. *The Holy Bible: New Living Translation.* Wheaton, Ill.: Tyndale House.

1973. *New American Standard Bible.* La Habra, Calif.: Foundation Press.

1984. *The Holy Bible: New International Version.* Colorado Springs, Colo.: International Bible Society.

1987. *The Amplified Bible.* Grand Rapids, Mich.: Zondervan Corporation/Lockman Foundation.

1989a. *The Holy Bible: Containing the Old and New Testaments.* New York: Oxford University Press.

1989b. *The Revised English Bible.* Oxford: Oxford University Press.

1990. *The Revised English Bible.* Oxford: Oxford University Press.

1994. *Holy Bible: New King James Version.* Nashville, Tenn.: Thomas Nelson.

1996. *The Holy Bible: New Living Translation.* Wheaton, Ill.: Tyndale House.

Aland, Barbara, Kurt Aland, J. Karavidopoulos, Carlo M. Martini, and Bruce M. Metzger, eds. 1993. *The Greek New Testament.* London: United Bible Societies.

Aland, Kurt, and Barbara Aland. 1987. *The Text of the New Testament: An Introduction to the Critical Editions and to the Theory and Practice of Modern Textual Criticisms.* Grand Rapids, Mich.: W. B. Eerdmans.

Aland, Kurt, Michael Welte, Beate Köster, and Klaus Junack. 1994. *Kurzgefasste Liste der griechischen Handschriften des Neuen Testaments.* Berlin: W. de Gruyter.

American Bible Society. 1976. *Good News Bible: The Bible in Today's English Version.* Nashville, Tenn.: Broadman Press.

Ammerman, Nancy T. 1982. "Operationalizing Evangelicalism: An Amendment." *Sociological Analysis* 43 (2): 170–171.

Arthur, Kay. 1994. *How to Study Your Bible.* Eugene, Oreg.: Harvest House.

Atran, Scott. 2002. *In Gods We Trust: The Evolutionary Landscape of Religion.* Oxford: Oxford University Press.

Barr, James. 1978. *Fundamentalism.* Philadelphia: Westminster Press.

Barrett, Justin L. 2004. *Why Would Anyone Believe in God?* Walnut Creek, Calif.: AltaMira Press.

Bartkowski, John. 1996. "Beyond Biblical Literalism and Inerrancy: Conservative Protestants and the Hermeneutic Interpretation of Scripture." *Sociology of Religion* 57 (3): 259–272.

Bateson, Gregory. 1972. *Steps to an Ecology of Mind.* New York: Ballantine.

Bebbington, D. W. 1989. *Evangelicalism in Modern Britain: A History from the 1730s to the 1980s.* London: Unwin Hyman.

Blackmore, Susan J. 2000. "The Power of Memes." *Scientific American* (October): 64–73.

Boone, Kathleen C. 1989. *The Bible Tells Them So: The Discourse of Protestant Fundamentalism.* Albany: State University of New York Press.

Bottigheimer, Ruth B. 1996. *The Bible for Children: From the Age of Gutenberg to the Present.* New Haven: Yale University Press.

Boyer, Pascal. 1994. *The Naturalness of Religious Ideas: A Cognitive Theory of Religion.* Berkeley: University of California Press.

———. 2001. *Religion Explained: The Evolutionary Origins of Religious Thought.* New York: Basic Books.

Browne, Lewis. 1946. *The World's Great Scriptures: An Anthology of the Sacred Books of the Ten Principal Religions.* New York: Macmillan.

Bruce, F. F., and E. G. Rupp, eds. 1968. *Holy Book and Holy Tradition.* Manchester: Manchester University Press.

Burdi, Patrizia. 1993. "The Powerful and Perilous Text: The Symbolism of the 'Book' in a Southern Italian Village." In *Sociology of Sacred Texts,* eds. J. Davies and I. Wollaston, 63–71. Sheffield, England: Sheffield Academic Press.

Burgon, John W. 1990. *Unholy Hands on the Bible.* 2 vols. Lafayette, Ind.: Sovereign Grace Trust Fund.

Carpenter, Joel A. 1999. *Revive Us Again: The Reawakening of American Fundamentalism.* Oxford: Oxford University Press.

Carson, D. A. 1998. *The Inclusive-Language Debate: A Plea for Realism.* Grand Rapids, Mich.: Baker Books.

Carson, Donald A. 1979. *The King James Version Debate: A Plea for Realism.* Grand Rapids, Mich.: Baker Book House.

Charnock, Stephen. 2002 [1853]. *The Existence and Attributes of God.* Bellingham, Wash.: Logos Research Systems.

Chomsky, Noam. 1957. *Syntactic Structures.* The Hague: Mouton.

Collins, James. 1995. "Literacy and Literacies." *Annual Review of Anthropology* 24: 75–93.

Colwell, Ernest Cadman. 1952. *What Is the Best New Testament?* Chicago: University of Chicago Press.

Comfort, Philip Wesley. 1990. *Early Manuscripts and Modern Translations of the New Testament.* Wheaton, Ill.: Tyndale House.

Coward, Noel. 1988. *Sacred Word and Sacred Text: Scripture in World Religions.* Maryknoll, N.Y.: Orbis Books.

Crapanzano, Vincent. 2000. *Serving the Word: Literalism in America from the Pulpit to the Bench.* New York: The New Press.

Dawkins, Richard. 1976. *The Selfish Gene.* New York: Oxford University Press.

———. 1993. "Viruses of the Mind." *Free Inquiry* (Summer): 34–41.

———. 1997. The Selfish Meme: A Talk (videotape). Stanford University: Into the Classroom Media.

Dawkins, Richard, and Michael Krasny. 1997. "Religion Is a Virus." *Mother Jones* 22 (6): 60.

Denny, Frederick M., and Rodney L. Taylor, eds. 1985a. *The Holy Book in Comparative Perspective.* Columbia: University of South Carolina Press.

———. 1985b. "Introduction." In *The Holy Book in Comparative Perspective*, eds. F. M. Denny and R. L. Taylor. Columbia: University of South Carolina Press.

Dixon, R. D., L. P. Jones, and R. C. Lowery. 1992. "Biblical Authority Questions: Two Choices in Identifying Conservative Christian Subcultures." *Sociological Analysis* 53: 63–72.

Douglas, J. D., ed. 1978. *The New International Dictionary of the Christian Church.* Grand Rapids, Mich.: Zondervan.

Durkheim, Emile. 1995 [1912]. *The Elementary Forms of Religious Life.* Translated by K. E. Fields. New York: The Free Press.

Erasmus, Desiderius, and Johann Froben. 1516. *Novvm instrument*u omne, diligenter ab Erasmo Roterodamo recognitum & omendatum, no solum ad graecam ueritatem, uerumetiam ad multorum utriusq[ue]linguae codicum, eorumq[ue] ueterum simul & emendatorum fidem, postremo ad probatissimorum autorum citationem, emendationem & interpretationem, praecipue Origenis, Chrysostomi, Cyrilli, Vulgarij, Hieronymi, Cypriani, Ambrosij, Hilarij, Augustini, una c*u annotationibus, quae lectorem doceant, quid qua ratione mutatum sit.* Colophon: Basiliae in aedibus Ioannis Frobenij Hammelburgensis mense februario.

Fee, Gordon D. 1978. "Modern Textual Criticism and the Revival of the Textus Receptus." *Journal of the Evangelical Theological Society* 21: 19–33.

Fieser, James, and John Powers. 1998. *Scriptures of the World's Religions.* Boston: McGraw Hill.

Fuller, C. J. 1984. *Servants of the Goddess: The Priests of a South Indian Temple.* Cambridge: Cambridge University Press.

Fuller, David Otis. 1975. *Which Bible?* Grand Rapids, Mich.: Grand Rapids International Publications.

Gadamer, Hans Georg. 1999 [1975]. *Truth and Method.* New York: Seabury Press.

Geertz, Clifford. 1973. *The Interpretation of Cultures.* New York: Basic Books.

Geisler, Norman L., ed. 1980. *Inerrancy.* Grand Rapids, Mich.: Zondervan.

Goody, Jack. 2000. *The Power of the Written Tradition.* Washington, D.C.: Smithsonian Institution Press.

Graham, William A. 1987. *Beyond the Written Word: Oral Aspects of Scripture in the History of Religion.* New York: Cambridge University Press.

Gray, James M. 1993 [1917]. "The Inspiration of the Bible—Definition, Extent and Proof." In *The Fundamentals: A Testimony to the Truth*, eds. R. A. Torrey and A. C. Dixon, 9–43, vol. 2. Grand Rapids, Mich.: Baker Books.

Grice, H. P. 1989. *Studies in the Way of Words*. Cambridge, Mass.: Harvard University Press.

Harding, Susan Friend. 2000. *The Book of Jerry Falwell: Fundamentalist Language and Politics*. Princeton, N. J.: Princeton University Press.

Hills, Edward F. 1984 [1956]. *The King James Version Defended*. N.p.: Christian Research Press.

Hirschfeld, Lawrence A. 1996. *Race in the Making: Cognition, Culture, and the Child's Construction of Human Kinds*. Cambridge, Mass.: MIT Press.

Hodges, Z. C. 1968. "The Greek Text of the King James Version." *Bibliotheca Sacra* 125: 334–345.

Hodges, Zane, and Arthur Farstad, eds. 1985. *The Greek New Testament According to the Majority Text*. Nashville, Tenn.: Thomas Nelson.

Hunter, James Davison. 1981. "Operationalizing Evangelicalism: A Review, Critique, and Proposal." *Sociological Analysis* 42 (4): 363–372.

Jelen, T. G. 1989. "Biblical Literalism and Inerrancy: Does the Difference Make a Difference?" *Sociological Analysis* 49: 421–429.

Jobes, Karen H., and Moisés Silva. 2000. *Invitation to the Septuagint*. Grand Rapids, Mich.: Baker Academic.

Jodock, Darrell. 1989. *The Church's Bible: Its Contemporary Authority*. Minneapolis, Minn.: Fortress Press.

LaHaye, Tim. 1998. *How to Study the Bible for Yourself*. Eugene, Oreg.: Harvest House.

Levering, Miriam. 1989. "Rethinking Scripture." In *Rethinking Scripture: Essays from a Comparative Perspective*, ed. M. Levering. Albany: State University of New York.

Lindsell, Harold. 1976. *The Battle for the Bible*. Grand Rapids, Mich.: Zondervan.

MacArthur, John, ed. 1997. *The MacArthur Study Bible*. Nashville, Tenn.: Word Publishing.

Malley, Brian. 1995. Explaining Order in Religious Systems. *Method & Theory in the Study of Religion* 7 (1): 5–22.

Marsden, George M. 1980. *Fundamentalism and American Culture: The Shaping of Twentieth Century Evangelicalism, 1870–1925*. New York: Oxford University Press.

———. 1991. *Understanding Fundamentalism and Evangelicalism*. Grand Rapids, Mich.: Eerdmans.

McArthur, John. 1997. *How to Get the Most from God's Word*. Nashville, Tenn.: Word Publishing.

McDowell, Josh. 1982. *Josh McDowell's Guide to Understanding the Bible*. San Bernadino, Calif.: Here's Life Publishers.

McKim, Donald K. 1985. *What Christians Believe about the Bible*. Nashville, Tenn.: Thomas Nelson.

Metzger, Bruce Manning. 1987. *The Canon of the New Testament: Its Origin, Development, and Significance*. Oxford: Clarendon Press.

———. 1988. "Greek Manuscripts of John's Gospel with 'Hermeneiai.'" In *Text and Testimony, Essays on New Testament and Apocryphal Literature in Honour of A. F. J. Klijn*, ed. T. Baarda, 162–169. Kampen: Uitgeversmaatschappij J. H. Kok.

————. 1992. *The Text of the New Testament: Its Transmission, Corruption, and Restoration.* Oxford: Clarendon Press.

————. 1994. *Textual Commentary on the Greek New Testament.* New York: United Bible Societies.

Montgomery, John Warwick. 1985. "Inspiration and Inerrancy: A New Departure." In *Evangelicals and Inerrancy,* ed. R. Youngblood, 59–90. Nashville, Tenn.: Thomas Nelson.

Nagata, Judith. 2001. "Beyond Theology: Toward an Anthropology of 'Fundamentalism.'" *American Anthropologist* 103 (2): 481–498.

Nestle, Eberhard, Erwin Nestle, Kurt Aland, and Barbara Aland. 1985. *Novum Testamentum Graece.* Stuttgart: Deutsche Bibelstiftung.

Nielsen, B. E. 2000. "A Catalog of Duplicate Papyri." *Zeitschrift Fur Papyrologie Und Epigraphik* 129: 187–214.

Noll, Mark A. 2001. *American Evangelical Christianity: An Introduction.* Malden, Mass.: Blackwell.

North American Baptist Seminary. 2003. *Statement of Beliefs.* Volume 2003. Lawrence & Schiller Design and Programming. http://www.nabs.edu/About/StatementBeliefs.cfm.

Olasky, Susan. 1997. "Femme fatale." *World* 12 (2). Online at http://www.worldmag.com/world/issue/03-29-97/cover_1.asp.

Olson, David R. 1994. *The World on Paper: The Conceptual and Cognitive Implications of Writing and Reading.* Cambridge: Cambridge University Press.

Palmer, Edward Henry, and F. Max Müller. 1879. *The Sacred Books of the East.* Oxford: Clarendon Press.

Peterson, Eugene H., ed. 1995. *The Message: New Testament with Psalms and Proverbs.* Colorado Springs, Colo.: Navpress.

Pickering, Wilbur. 1981. *The Identity of the New Testament Text.* Nashville, Tenn.: Thomas Nelson.

Ramm, Bernard L. 1970. *Protestant Biblical Interpretation: A Textbook of Hermeneutics.* Grand Rapids, Mich.: Baker Books.

Rappaport, Roy A. 1979. *Ecology, Meaning, and Religion.* Berkeley, Calif.: North Atlantic Press.

————. 1984 [1968]. *Pigs for the Ancestors: Ritual in the Ecology of a New Guinea People.* New Haven, Conn.: Yale University Press.

————. 1999. *Ritual and Religion in the Making of Humanity.* Cambridge: Cambridge University Press.

Reid, Daniel G., Robert Dean Linder, Bruce L. Shelley, and Harry S. Stout. 1990. *Dictionary of Christianity in America.* Downers Grove, Ill.: InterVarsity Press.

Richardson, Alan. 1963. "The Rise of Modern Biblical Scholarship and Recent Discussion of the Authority of the Bible." In *The Cambridge History of the Bible: The West From the Reformation to the Present Day,* ed S. L. Greenslade, 294–338, vol. 3. Cambridge: Cambridge University Press.

Ricoeur, Paul. 1971. "The Model of the Text: Meaningful Action Considered as a Text." *Social Research* 38: 529–562.

————. 1979. "The 'Sacred' Text and the Community." In *The Critical Study of Sacred Texts,* ed. W. Doniger O'Flaherty. Berkeley Religious Studies Series. Berkeley, Calif.: Graduate Theological Union.

———. 1991 [1971]. "What Is a Text?" In *From Text to Action. Essays in Hermeneutics*, vol. 2. Translated by Kathleen Blamey and John B. Thompson. Evanston, Ill.: Northwestern University Press.

Riesebrodt, Martin. 1993. *Pious Passion: The Emergence of Modern Fundamentalism in the United States and Iran*. Berkeley: University of California Press.

Riplinger, Gail A. 1993. *New Age Bible Versions*. Munroe Falls, Ohio: A.V. Publications.

———. 1994. *Which Bible Is God's Word?* Oklahoma City, Okla.: Hearthstone Publishing.

Rogers, Jack B., and Donald K. McKim. 1979. *The Authority and Interpretation of the Bible: An Historical Approach*. San Francisco: Harper & Row.

Ruckman, Peter. 1964. *The Bible "Babel."* Pensacola, Fla.: Bible Baptist Bookstore.

———. 1983. *About the "New" King James Bible*. Pensacola, Fla.: Bible Baptist Bookstore.

———. 1988. *Why I Believe the King James Version Is the Word of God*. Pensacola, Fla.: Bible Baptist Bookstore.

Ruckman, Peter J. 1990. *The Christian's Handbook of Manuscript Evidence*. Pensacola, Fla.: Bible Press.

Ruel, Malcolm. 1982. "Christians as Believers." In *Religious Organization and Religious Experience*, ed. J. Davis, ix, 215. London: Academic Press.

Ryrie, Charles Caldwell. 1981. *What You Should Know about Inerrancy*. Chicago: Moody Press.

Sheeley, Steven M., and Robert N. Nash. 1999. *Choosing a Bible: A Guide to Modern English Translations and Editions*. Nashville, Tenn.: Abingdon Press.

Silverstein, Michael, and Greg Urban, eds. 1996a. *Natural Histories of Discourse*. Chicago: University of Chicago Press.

———. 1996b. "The Natural History of Discourse." In *Natural Histories of Discourse*, eds. M. Silverstein and G. Urban. Chicago: University of Chicago Press.

Smart, Ninian, and Richard Hecht, eds. 1982. *Sacred Texts of the World: A Universal Anthology*. New York: Crossroad.

Smith, Christian, and Michael Emerson. 1998. *American Evangelicalism: Embattled and Thriving*. Chicago, Ill.: University of Chicago Press.

Smith, Wilfred Cantwell. 1993. *What Is Scripture? A Comparative Approach*. Minneapolis, Minn.: Fortress Press.

Sperber, Dan. 1985. *On Anthropological Knowledge: Three Essays*. Cambridge: Cambridge University Press.

———. 1996. *Explaining Culture: A Naturalistic Approach*. Oxford: Blackwell.

Sperber, Dan, and Deirdre Wilson. 1995. *Relevance: Communication and Cognition*. Oxford: Blackwell.

Strauss, Claudia, and Naomi Quinn. 1997. *A Cognitive Theory of Cultural Meaning*. Cambridge: Cambridge University Press.

Taylor, Kenneth N., ed. 1971. *The Living Bible*. Wheaton, Ill.: Tyndale House.

Thuesen, Peter J. 1999. *In Discordance with the Scriptures: American Protestant Battles over Translating the Bible*. New York: Oxford University Press.

Torrey, R. A., and A. C. Dixon. 1993 [1909–1917]. *The Fundamentals: A Testimony to the Truth*. Grand Rapids, Mich.: Baker Books.

Trobisch, David. 2000. *The First Edition of the New Testament*. Oxford: Oxford University Press.

von Neumann, John. 1958. *The Computer and the Brain*. New Haven, Conn.: Yale University Press.

Wallace, Daniel. 1994. "The Majority-Text Theory: History, Methods, and Critique." *Journal of the Evangelical Theological Society* 37 (2): 185–215.

Waterworth, J., ed. 1848. *The Canons and Decrees of the Sacred and Oecumenical Council of Trent*. London: Dolman.

Westcott, Brooke Fost, Fenton John Anthony Hort, and Philip Schaff. 1881. *The New Testament in the Original Greek*. Cambridge: Macmillan.

White, James R. 1995. *The King James Only Controversy: Can You Trust the Modern Translations?* Minneapolis, Minn.: Bethany House.

Whitehouse, Harvey. 1995. *Inside the Cult: Religious Innovation and Transmission in Papua New Guinea*. Oxford: Clarendon Press.

———. 2000. *Arguments and Icons: Divergent Modes of Religiosity*. Oxford: Oxford University Press.

Wilson, Andrew. 1991. *World Scripture: A Comparative Anthology of Sacred Texts*. New York: Paragon House.

Woodbridge, John D. 1982. *Biblical Authority: A Critique of the Rogers/McKim Proposal*. Grand Rapids, Mich.: Zondervan.

———. 1986. "Some Misconceptions of the Impact of the 'Enlightenment' on the Doctrine of Scripture." In *Hermeneutics, Authority, and Canon*, ed. D. A. Carson and J. D. Woodbridge, 237–270. Grand Rapids, Mich.: Zondervan.

Youngblood, Ronald F. 1984. *Evangelicals and Inerrancy*. Nashville, Tenn.: Thomas Nelson.

Youtie, Herbert Chayyim. 1973. *Scriptiunculae*. Amsterdam: A. M. Hakkert.

Zuck, Roy B. 1996. "Preface." In *Rightly Divided: Readings in Biblical Hermeneutics*, ed. R. B. Zuck. Grand Rapids, Mich.: Kregel.

Index

About the Author

Brian Malley studied comparative religion at Western Michigan University (MA, 1994) and anthropology at the University of Michigan (PhD, 2002). His 1995 article "Explaining Order in Religious Systems" garnered the Distinguished Article Award from the Society for the Scientific Study of Religion. Dr. Malley currently lectures in psychology at the University of Michigan, and continues to pursue his research interests in religion and the intersection of culture and cognition.